BOOK 4 – CORPORATE FINANCE, PORTFOLIO MANAGEMENT, AND ANALYSIS OF EQUITY INVESTMENTS

READINGS AND LEARNING OUTCOME STATEMENTS

READINGS

The following material is a review of the Corporate Finance, Portfolio Management, and Analysis of Equity Investments principles designed to address the learning outcome statements set forth by CFA Institute.

STUDY SESSION 11

Reading Assignments

STUDY SESSION 12

Reading Assignments

STUDY SESSION 13

Reading Assignments

STUDY SESSION 14

Reading Assignments

LEARNING OUTCOME STATEMENTS (LOS)

STUDY SESSION 11

The topical coverage corresponds with the following CFA Institute assigned reading:

47. **Capital Budgeting**

The candidate should be able to:

a. define the capital budgeting process, explain the administrative steps of the process, and categorize the capital projects which can be evaluated. (page 10)

b. summarize and explain the principles of capital budgeting, including the choice of the proper cash flows and the identification of the proper discount rate. (page 11)

c. explain how the following project interactions affect the evaluation of a capital project: (1) independent versus mutually exclusive projects, (2) project sequencing, and (3) unlimited funds versus capital rationing. (page 12)

d. calculate and interpret the results produced from each of the following methods when evaluating a single capital project: net present value (NPV), internal rate of return (IRR), payback period, discounted payback period, average accounting rate of return (AAR), and profitability index (PI). (page 13)

e. explain the NPV profile, compare and contrast the NPV and IRR methods when evaluating more than one capital project, and describe the multiple IRR and no-IRR problems that can arise when calculating an IRR. (page 20)

f. describe the relative popularity of the various capital budgeting methods and explain the importance of the NPV in estimating the value of a stock price. (page 22)

The topical coverage corresponds with the following CFA Institute assigned reading:

48. **Cost of Capital**

The candidate should be able to:

a. determine and interpret the weighted average cost of capital (WACC) of a company, and explain the adjustments to it that an analyst should make in developing a cost of capital for a specific project. (page 30)

b. describe the role of taxes in the cost of capital from the different capital sources. (page 30)

c. describe alternative methods of calculating the weights used in the weighted average cost of capital, including the use of the company's target capital structure. (page 32)

    d.   explain the analyst's concern with the marginal cost of capital in evaluating investment projects, and explain the use of the marginal cost of capital and the investment opportunity schedule in determining the optimal capital budget for a company. (page 32)

    e.   explain the marginal cost of capital's role in determining the net present value of a project. (page 33)

    f.   calculate and analyze the cost of fixed rate debt capital using the yield-to-maturity approach and the debt-rating approach. (page 34)

    g.   calculate the cost of noncallable, nonconvertible preferred stock. (page 34)

    h.   calculate and analyze the cost of equity capital using the capital asset pricing model approach, the dividend discount approach, and the bond yield plus risk premium approach. (page 35)

The topical coverage corresponds with the following CFA Institute assigned reading:

49.   Capital Structure and Leverage

The candidate should be able to:

    a.   define and explain leverage, business risk, sales risk, operating risk, and financial risk (page 42)

    b.   calculate and interpret the degree of operating leverage, the degree of financial leverage, and the degree of total leverage. (page 42)

    c.   characterize the operating leverage, financial leverage, and total leverage of a company given a description of it. (page 45)

    d.   calculate the breakeven quantity of sales and determine the company's net income at various sales levels. (page 46)

    e.   describe the effect of financial leverage on a company's net income and return on equity. (page 48)

    f.   compare and contrast the risks of creditors and owners. (page 50)

The topical coverage corresponds with the following CFA Institute assigned reading:

50.   Dividends and Dividend Policy

The candidate should be able to:

    a.   review cash dividends, stock dividends, stocks splits, and reverse stock splits and calculate and discuss their impact on a shareholder. (page 55)

    b.   compare the impact on shareholder wealth of a share repurchase and a cash dividend of equal amount. (page 58)

    c.   calculate the earnings per share effect of a share repurchase when the repurchase is made with borrowed funds and the company's after-tax cost of debt is greater (less) than its earnings yield. (page 59)

    d.   calculate the book value effect of a share repurchase when the market value of a share is greater (less) than book value per share. (page 60)

    e.   compare and contrast share repurchase methods. (page 61)

    f.   review dividend payment chronology including declaration, holder-of-record, ex-dividend, and payment dates and indicate when the share price will most likely reflect the dividend. (page 57)

    g.   summarize the factors affecting dividend payout policy. (page 61)

    h.   calculate the effective tax rate on a dollar of corporate earnings distributed as a dividend using the double-taxation, split-rate, and tax imputation systems. (page 62)

    i.   discuss the types of information that dividend initiations, increases, decreases, and omissions may convey, and cross-country differences in the signalling content of dividends. (page 64)

The topical coverage corresponds with the following CFA Institute assigned reading:

51.   The Corporate Governance of Listed Companies: A Manual for Investors

The candidate should be able to:

    a.   define corporate governance. (page 71)

    b. discuss and critique characteristics and practices related to board and committee independence, experience, compensation, external consultants and frequency of elections and determine whether they are supportive of shareowner protection. (page 71)

    c. define board independence and explain the importance of independent board members in corporate governance. (page 72)

    d. identify factors that indicate a board and its members possess the experience required to govern the company for the benefit of its shareowners. (page 72)

    e. explain the provisions that should be included in a strong corporate code of ethics and the implications of a weak code of ethics with regard to related-party transactions and personal use of company assets. (page 73)

    f. state the key areas of responsibility for which board committees are typically created and explain the criteria for assessing whether each committee is able to adequately represent shareowner interests. (page 74)

    g. evaluate, from a shareowner's perspective, company policies related to voting rules, shareowner sponsored proposals, common stock classes and takeover defenses. (page 75)

STUDY SESSION 12

The topical coverage corresponds with the following CFA Institute assigned reading:

52. **The Asset Allocation Decision**

The candidate should be able to:

    a. describe the steps in the portfolio management process and explain the reasons for a policy statement. (page 82)

    b. explain why investment objectives should be expressed in terms of both risk and return and list the factors that may affect an investor's risk tolerance. (page 82)

    c. describe the return objectives of capital preservation, capital appreciation, current income, and total return and describe the investment constraints of liquidity, time horizon, tax concerns, legal and regulatory factors, and unique needs and preferences. (page 83)

    d. describe the importance of asset allocation, in terms of the percentage of a portfolio's return that can be explained by the target asset allocation and list reasons for the differences in the average asset allocation among citizens of different countries. (page 84)

The topical coverage corresponds with the following CFA Institute assigned reading:

53. **An Introduction to Portfolio Management**

The candidate should be able to:

    a. define risk aversion and discuss evidence that suggests that individuals are generally risk averse. (page 88)

    b. list the basic assumptions behind the Markowitz Portfolio Theory. (page 89)

    c. compute the expected return for an individual investment and for a portfolio. (page 89)

    d. compute the variance and standard deviation for an individual investment. (page 91)

    e. compute the covariance of rates of return, and show how it is related to the correlation coefficient. (page 93)

    f. list the components of the portfolio standard deviation formula, and explain which component is most important to consider when adding an investment to a portfolio. (page 96)

    g. describe the efficient frontier and explain the implications for incremental returns as an investor assumes more risk. (page 99)

    h. define optimal portfolio and show how each investor may have a different optimal portfolio. (page 100)

The topical coverage corresponds with the following CFA Institute assigned reading:

54. **An Introduction to Asset Pricing Models**
The candidate should be able to:
    a. list the assumptions of the capital market theory. (page 106)
    b. explain what happens to the expected return, the standard deviation of returns, and possible risk-return combinations when a risk-free asset is combined with a portfolio of risky assets. (page 106)
    c. identify the market portfolio, and describe the role of the market portfolio in the formation of the capital market line (CML). (page 108)
    d. define systematic and unsystematic risk and explain why an investor should not expect to receive additional return for assuming unsystematic risk. (page 109)
    e. describe the capital asset pricing model, diagram the security market line (SML), and define beta. (page 111)
    f. calculate and interpret using the SML, the expected return on a security, and evaluate whether the security is undervalued, overvalued, or properly valued. (page 113)
    g. describe the effect on the SML of relaxing each of its main underlying assumptions line. (page 115)

STUDY SESSION 13

The topical coverage corresponds with the following CFA Institute assigned reading:

55. **Organization and Functioning of Securities Markets**
The candidate should be able to:
    a. describe the characteristics of a well-functioning securities market. (page 123)
    b. distinguish between competitive bids, negotiated sales, and private placements for issuing bonds. (page 123)
    c. distinguish between primary and secondary capital markets, and explain how secondary markets support primary markets. (page 124)
    d. distinguish between call and continuous markets. (page 124)
    e. compare and contrast the structural differences among national stock exchanges, regional stock exchanges, and the over-the-counter (OTC) markets. (page 124)
    f. compare and contrast major characteristics of exchange markets, including exchange membership, types of orders, and market makers. (page 125)
    g. describe the process of selling a stock short and discuss an investor's likely motivation for selling short. (page 126)
    h. describe the process of buying a stock on margin, compute the rate of return on a margin transaction, define maintenance margin and determine the stock price at which the investor would receive a margin call. (page 127)
    i. discuss major effects of the institutionalization of securities markets. (page 128)

The topical coverage corresponds with the following CFA Institute assigned reading:

56. **Security-Market Indexes**
The candidate should be able to:
    a. discuss the source and direction of bias exhibited by each of the three predominant weighting schemes, and compute a price-weighted, a market-weighted, and an unweighted index series for three stocks. (page 135)
    b. compare and contrast major structural features of domestic and global stock indexes, bond indexes, and composite stock-bond indexes. (page 140)

The topical coverage corresponds with the following CFA Institute assigned reading:
57. **Efficient Capital Markets**
The candidate should be able to:
   a. define an efficient capital market, discuss arguments supporting the concept of efficient capital markets, describe and contrast the forms of the efficient market hypothesis (EMH): weak, semistrong, and strong, and describe the tests used to examine the weak form, the semistrong form, and the strong form of the EMH. (page 145)
   b. identify various market anomalies and explain their implications for the EMH, and explain the overall conclusions about each form of the EMH. (page 148)
   c. explain the implications of stock market efficiency for technical analysis and fundamental analysis, discuss the implications of efficient markets for the portfolio management process and the role of the portfolio manager, and explain the rationale for investing in index funds. (page 148)

The topical coverage corresponds with the following CFA Institute assigned reading:
58. **Market Efficiency and Anomalies**
The candidate should be able to:
   a. explain limitations to fully efficient markets. (page 155)
   b. describe the limits of arbitrage to correct anomalies. (page 155)
   c. illustrate why investors should be skeptical of anomalies. (page 156)

STUDY SESSION 14

The topical coverage corresponds with the following CFA Institute assigned reading:
59. **An Introduction to Security Valuation**
The candidate should be able to:
   a. explain the top-down approach, and its underlying logic, to the security valuation process. (page 160)
   b. explain the various forms of investment returns. (page 161)
   c. calculate and interpret the value of a preferred stock, or of a common stock, using the dividend discount model (DDM). (page 161)
   d. show how to use the DDM to develop an earnings multiplier model, and explain the factors in the DDM that affect a stock's price-to-earnings (P/E) ratio. (page 167)
   e. explain the components of an investor's required rate of return (i.e., the real risk-free rate, the expected rate of inflation, and a risk premium) and discuss the risk factors to be assessed in determining a country risk premium for use in estimating the required return for foreign securities. (page 168)
   f. estimate the implied dividend growth rate, given the components of the required return on equity and incorporating the earnings retention rate and current stock price. (page 169)
   g. describe a process for developing estimated inputs to be used in the DDM, including the required rate of return and expected growth rate of dividends. (page 170)

The topical coverage corresponds with the following CFA Institute assigned reading:
60. **Industry Analysis**
The candidate should be able to describe how structural economic changes (e.g., demographics, technology, politics, and regulation) may affect industries. (page 171)

The topical coverage corresponds with the following CFA Institute assigned reading:

61. **Equity: Concepts and Techniques**

The candidate should be able to:

a. classify business cycle stages and identify, for each stage, attractive investment opportunities. (page 180)

b. discuss, with respect to global industry analysis, the key elements related to return expectations. (page 180)

c. describe the industry life cycle and identify an industry's stage in its life cycle. (page 181)

d. interpret and explain the significance of a concentration ratio and a Herfindahl index. (page 181)

e. discuss, with respect to global industry analysis, the elements related to risk, and describe the basic forces that determine industry competition. (page 182)

The topical coverage corresponds with the following CFA Institute assigned reading:

62. **Company Analysis and Stock Valuation**

The candidate should be able to:

a. differentiate between 1) a growth company and a growth stock, 2) a defensive company and a defensive stock, 3) a cyclical company and a cyclical stock, 4) a speculative company and a speculative stock and 5) a value stock and a growth stock. (page 186)

b. describe and estimate the expected earnings per share (EPS) and earnings multiplier for a company. (page 187)

c. calculate and compare the expected rate of return (based on the estimate of intrinsic value) to the required rate of return. (page 188)

The topical coverage corresponds with the following CFA Institute assigned reading:

63. **Technical Analysis**

The candidate should be able to:

a. explain the underlying assumptions of technical analysis and explain how technical analysis differs from fundamental analysis. (page 192)

b. discuss the advantages and challenges of technical analysis. (page 193)

c. identify examples of each of the major categories of technical indicators. (page 194)

The topical coverage corresponds with the following CFA Institute assigned reading:

64. **Introduction to Price Multiples**

The candidate should be able to:

a. discuss the rationales for the use of price to earnings (P/E), price to book value (P/BV), price to sales (P/S), and price to cash flow (P/CF) in equity valuation and discuss the possible drawbacks to the use of each price multiple. (page 203)

b. calculate and interpret P/E, P/BV, P/S, and P/CF. (page 203)

The following is a review of the Corporate Finance principles designed to address the learning outcome statements set forth by CFA Institute®. This topic is also covered in:

CAPITAL BUDGETING

EXAM FOCUS

If you recollect little from your basic financial management course in college (or if you didn't take one) you will need to spend some time on this review and go through the examples quite carefully. To be prepared for the exam you need to know how to calculate all of the measures used to evaluate capital projects and the decision rules associated with them.

Be sure you can interpret an NPV profile; one could be given as part of a question. Finally, know the reasoning behind the facts that (1) IRR and NPV give the same accept/reject decision for a single project and (2) IRR and NPV can give conflicting rankings for mutually exclusive projects.

LOS 47.a: Define the capital budgeting process, explain the administrative steps of the process, and categorize the capital projects which can be evaluated.

The **capital budgeting process** is the process of identifying and evaluating capital projects, that is, projects where the cash flow to the firm will be received over a period longer than a year. Any corporate decisions with an impact on future earnings can be examined using this framework. Decisions about whether to buy a new machine, expand business in another geographic area, move the corporate headquarters to Cleveland, or replace a delivery truck, to name a few, can be examined using a capital budgeting analysis.

For a number of good reasons, capital budgeting may be the most important responsibility that a financial manager has. First, since a capital budgeting decision often involves the purchase of costly long-term assets with lives of many years, the decisions made may determine the future success of the firm. Second, the principles underlying the capital budgeting process also apply to other corporate decisions, such as working capital management and making strategic mergers and acquisitions. Finally, making good capital budgeting decisions is consistent with management's primary goal of maximizing shareholder value.

The capital budgeting process has four administrative steps:

Step 1:   *Idea generation.* The most important step in the capital budgeting process is generating good project ideas. Ideas can come from a number of sources including senior management, functional divisions, employees, or outside the company.

Step 2:   *Analyzing project proposals.* Since the decision to accept or reject a capital project is based on the project's expected future cash flows, a cash flow forecast must be made for each project to determine its expected profitability.

Step 3:   *Create the firm-wide capital budget.* Firms must prioritize profitable projects according to the timing of the project's cash flows, available company resources, and the company's overall strategic plan. Many projects that are attractive individually may not make sense strategically.

Step 4:   *Monitoring decisions and conducting a post-audit.* It is important to follow up on all capital budgeting decisions. An analyst should compare the actual results to the projected results, and project managers should explain why projections did or did not match actual performance. Since the capital budgeting process is only as good as the estimates of the inputs into the model used to forecast cash flows, a post-audit should be used to identify systematic errors in the forecasting process and improve company operations.

Categories of Capital Budgeting Projects

Capital budgeting projects may be divided into the following categories:

- *Replacement projects to maintain the business* are normally made without detailed analysis. The only issues are whether the existing operations should continue and, if so, whether existing procedures or processes should be maintained.
- *Replacement projects for cost reduction* determine whether equipment that is obsolete, but still usable, should be replaced. A fairly detailed analysis is necessary in this case.
- *Expansion projects* are taken on to grow the business and involve a complex decision making process since they require an explicit forecast of future demand. A very detailed analysis is required.
- *New product or market* development also entails a complex decision making process that will require a detailed analysis due to the large amount of uncertainty involved.
- *Mandatory projects* may be required by a governmental agency or insurance company and typically involve safety-related or environmental concerns. These projects typically generate little to no revenue, but they accompany new revenue-producing projects undertaken by the company.
- *Other projects.* Some projects are not easily analyzed through the capital budgeting process. Such projects may include a pet project of senior management (e.g., corporate perks), or a high-risk endeavor that is difficult to analyze with typical capital budgeting assessment methods (e.g., research and development projects).

LOS 47.b: Summarize and explain the principles of capital budgeting, including the choice of the proper cash flows and the identification of the proper discount rate.

The capital budgeting process involves five key principles:

1. *Decisions are based on cash flows, not accounting income.* The relevant cash flows to consider as part of the capital budgeting process are **incremental cash flows**, the changes in cash flows that will occur if the project is undertaken.

   Sunk costs are costs that cannot be avoided, even if the project is not undertaken. Since these costs are not affected by the accept/reject decision, they should not be included in the analysis. An example of a sunk cost is a consulting fee paid to a marketing research firm to estimate demand for a new product prior to a decision on the project.

   Externalities are the effects the acceptance of a project may have on other firm cash flows. The primary one is a negative externality called **cannibalization**, which occurs when a new project takes sales from an existing product. When considering externalities, the full implication of the new project (loss in sales of existing products) should be taken into account. An example of cannibalization is when a soft drink company introduces a diet version of an existing beverage. The analyst should subtract the lost sales of the existing beverage from the expected new sales of the diet version when estimated incremental project cash flows. A positive externality exists when doing the project would have a positive effect on sales of a firm's other project lines.

2. *Cash flows are based on opportunity costs.* **Opportunity costs** are cash flows that a firm will lose by undertaking the project under analysis. These are cash flows generated by an asset the firm already owns, that would be forgone if the project under consideration is undertaken. Opportunity costs should be included in project costs. For example, when building a plant, even if the firm already owns the land, the cost of the land should be charged to the project since it could be sold if not used.

3. *The timing of cash flows is important.* Capital budgeting decisions account for the time value of money, which means that cash flows received earlier are worth more than cash flows to be received later.

4. *Cash flows are analyzed on an after-tax basis.* The impact of taxes must be considered when analyzing all capital budgeting projects. Firm value is based on cash flows they get to keep, not those they send to the government.

5. *Financing costs are reflected in the project's required rate of return.* Do not consider financing costs specific to the project when estimating incremental cash flows. The discount rate used in the capital budgeting analysis takes account of the firm's cost of capital. Only projects that are expected to return more than the cost of the capital needed to fund them will increase the value of the firm.

LOS 47.c: Explain how the following project interactions affect the evaluation of a capital project: (1) independent versus mutually exclusive projects, (2) project sequencing, and (3) unlimited funds versus capital rationing.

Independent Versus Mutually Exclusive Projects

Independent projects are projects that are unrelated to each other, and allow for each project to be evaluated based on its own profitability. For example, if projects A and B are independent, and both projects are profitable, then the firm could accept both projects. **Mutually exclusive** means that only one project in a set of possible projects can be accepted and that the projects compete with each other. If projects A and B were mutually exclusive, the firm could accept either Project A or Project B, but not both. A capital budgeting decision between two different stamping machines with different costs and output would be an example of choosing between two mutually exclusive projects.

Project Sequencing

Some projects must be undertaken in a certain order, or sequence, so that investing in a project today creates the opportunity to invest in other projects in the future. For example, if a project undertaken today is profitable, that may create the opportunity to invest in a second project a year from now. However, if the project undertaken today turns out to be unprofitable, the firm will not invest in the second project.

Unlimited Funds Versus Capital Rationing

If a firm has unlimited access to capital, the firm can undertake all projects with expected returns that exceed the cost of capital. Many firms have constraints on the amount of capital they can raise, and must use *capital rationing.* If a firm's profitable project opportunities exceed the amount of funds available, the firm must ration, or prioritize, its capital expenditures with the goal of achieving the maximum increase in value for shareholders given its available capital.

LOS 47.d: Calculate and interpret the results produced from each of the following methods when evaluating a single capital project: net present value (NPV), internal rate of return (IRR), payback period, discounted payback period, average accounting rate of return (AAR), and profitability index (PI).

Net Present Value (NPV)

We first examined the calculation of net present value (NPV) in Quantitative Methods. The NPV is the sum of the present values of all the expected incremental cash flows if a project is undertaken. The discount rate used is the firm's cost of capital, adjusted for the risk level of the project. For a normal project, with an initial cash outflow followed by a series of expected after-tax cash inflows, the NPV is the present value of the expected inflows minus the initial cost of the project.

$$NPV = CF_0 + \frac{CF_1}{(1+k)^1} + \frac{CF_2}{(1+k)^2} + ... + \frac{CF_n}{(1+k)^n} = \sum_{t=0}^{n} \frac{CF_t}{(1+k)^t}$$

where:
CF_0 = the initial investment outlay (a negative cash flow)
CF_t = after tax cash flow at time t
k = required rate of return for project

A positive NPV project is expected to increase shareholder wealth, a negative NPV project is expected to decrease shareholder wealth, and a zero NPV project has no expected effect on shareholder wealth.

For *independent* projects, the *NPV decision rule* is simply to accept any project with a positive NPV and to reject any project with a negative NPV.

Example: NPV analysis

Using the project cash flows presented in Figure 1, compute the NPV of each project's cash flows and determine for each project whether it should be accepted or rejected. Assume that the cost of capital is 10%.

Figure 1: Expected Net After-Tax Cash Flows

Year (t)	Project A	Project B
0	–$2,000	–$2,000
1	1,000	200
2	800	600
3	600	800
4	200	1,200

Answer:

$$NPV_A = -2,000 + \frac{1,000}{(1.1)^1} + \frac{800}{(1.1)^2} + \frac{600}{(1.1)^3} + \frac{200}{(1.1)^4} = \$157.64$$

$$NPV_B = -2,000 + \frac{200}{(1.1)^1} + \frac{600}{(1.1)^2} + \frac{800}{(1.1)^3} + \frac{1,200}{(1.1)^4} = \$98.36$$

You may calculate the NPV directly by using the cash flow (CF) keys on your calculator. The process is illustrated in Figures 2 and 3 for project A.

Figure 2: Calculating NPV$_A$ With the TI Business Analyst II Plus

Key Strokes	Explanation	Display
[CF] [2nd] [CLR WORK]	Clear memory registers	CF0 = 0.00000
2,000 [+/−] [ENTER]	Initial cash outlay	CF0 = −2,000.00000
[↓] 1,000 [ENTER]	Period 1 cash flow	C01 = 1,000.00000
[↓]	Frequency of cash flow 1	F01 = 1.00000
[↓] 800 [ENTER]	Period 2 cash flow	C02 = 800.00000
[↓]	Frequency of cash flow 2	F02 = 1.00000
[↓] 600 [ENTER]	Period 3 cash flow	C03 = 600.00000
[↓]	Frequency of cash flow 3	F03 = 1.00000
[↓] 200 [ENTER]	Period 4 cash flow	C04 = 200.00000
[↓]	Frequency of cash flow 4	F04 = 1.00000
[NPV] 10 [ENTER]	10% discount rate	I = 10.00000
[↓] [CPT]	Calculate NPV	NPV = 157.63951

Figure 3: Calculating NPV$_A$ With the HP12C

Key Strokes	Explanation	Display
[f]→[FIN] → [f] → [REG]	Clear memory registers	0.00000
[f] [5]	Display 5 decimals. You only need to do this once.	0.00000
2,000 [CHS] [g] [CF0]	Initial cash outlay	−2,000.00000
1,000 [g] [CFj]	Period 1 cash flow	1,000.00000
800 [g] [CFj]	Period 2 cash flow	800.00000
600 [g] [CFj]	Period 3 cash flow	600.00000
200 [g] [CFj]	Period 4 cash flow	200.00000
10 [i]	10% discount rate	10.00000
[f] [NPV]	Calculate NPV	157.63951

Both Project A and Project B have positive NPVs, so both should be accepted.

Internal Rate of Return (IRR)

For a normal project, the **internal rate of return** (IRR) is the discount rate that makes the present value of the expected incremental after-tax cash inflows just equal to the initial cost of the project. More generally, the IRR is the discount rate that makes the present values of a project's estimated cash inflows equal to the present value of the project's estimated cash outflows. That is, IRR is the discount rate that makes the following relationship hold:

PV (inflows) = PV (outflows)

The IRR is also the discount rate for which the NPV of a project is equal to zero.

$$NPV = 0 = CF_0 + \frac{CF_1}{(1+IRR)^1} + \frac{CF_2}{(1+IRR)^2} + ... + \frac{CF_n}{(1+IRR)^n} = \sum_{t=0}^{n} \frac{CF_t}{(1+IRR)^t}$$

To calculate the IRR, you may use the trial-and-error method. That is, just keep guessing IRRs until you get the right one, or you may use a financial calculator.

IRR decision rule: First, determine the required rate of return for a given project. This is usually the firm's cost of capital. Note that the required rate of return may be higher or lower than the firm's cost of capital to adjust for differences between project risk and the firm's average project risk.

If IRR > the required rate of return, accept the project.

If IRR < the required rate of return, reject the project.

Example: IRR

Continuing with the cash flows presented in Figure 1 for projects A and B, compute the IRR for each project and determine whether to accept or reject each project under the assumptions that the projects are independent and that the required rate of return is 10%.

Answer:

$$\text{Project A: } 0 = -2,000 + \frac{1,000}{(1+IRR_A)^1} + \frac{800}{(1+IRR_A)^2} + \frac{600}{(1+IRR_A)^3} + \frac{200}{(1+IRR_A)^4}$$

$$\text{Project B: } 0 = -2,000 + \frac{200}{(1+IRR_B)^1} + \frac{600}{(1+IRR_B)^2} + \frac{800}{(1+IRR_B)^3} + \frac{1,200}{(1+IRR_B)^4}$$

With the cash flows entered as in Figures 2 or 3, (if you haven't changed them, they are still there from the calculation of NPV)

With the TI calculator the IRR can be calculated with:

[IRR] [CPT] to get 14.4888(%) for Project A and 11.7906(%) for Project B.

With the HP12C, the IRR can be calculated with:

[f] [IRR]

Both projects should be accepted because their IRRs are greater than the 10% required rate of return.

Payback Period

The **payback period** (PBP) is the number of years it takes to recover the initial cost of an investment.

Example: Payback period

Calculate the payback periods for the two projects that have the cash flows presented in Figure 1. Note the Year 0 cash flow represents the initial cost of each project.

Answer:

Note that the cumulative net cash flow (NCF) is just the running total of the cash flows at the end of each time period. Payback will occur when the cumulative NCF equals zero. To find the payback periods, construct the following table:

Figure 4: Cumulative Net Cash Flows

	Year (t)	0	1	2	3	4
Project A	Net cash flow	−2,000	1,000	800	600	200
	Cumulative NCF	−2,000	−1,000	−200	400	600
Project B	Net cash flow	−2,000	200	600	800	1,200
	Cumulative NCF	−2,000	−1,800	−1,200	−400	800

The payback period is determined from the cumulative net cash flow table as follows:

$$\text{payback period} = \text{full years until recovery} + \frac{\text{unrecovered cost at the beginning of last year}}{\text{cash flow during the last year}}$$

$$\text{payback period A} = 2 + \frac{200}{600} = 2.33 \text{ years}$$

$$\text{payback period B} = 3 + \frac{400}{1200} = 3.33 \text{ years}$$

Since the payback period is a measure of liquidity, for a firm with liquidity concerns, the shorter a project's payback period, the better. However, project decisions should not be made on the basis of their payback periods because of its drawbacks.

The main drawbacks of the payback period are that it does not take into account either the time value of money or cash flows beyond the payback period, which means terminal or salvage value wouldn't be considered. These drawbacks mean that the payback period is useless as a measure of profitability.

The main benefit of the payback period is that it is a good measure of project liquidity. Firms with limited access to additional liquidity often impose a maximum payback period, and then use a measure of profitability, such as NPV or IRR, to evaluate projects that satisfy this maximum payback period constraint.

Professor's Note: If you have the Professional model of the TI calculator, you can easily calculate the payback period and the discounted payback period (which follows). Once NPV is displayed, use the down arrow to scroll through NFV (net future value), to PB (payback), and DPB (discounted payback). You must use the compute key when "PB=" is

©2007 Schweser

displayed. If the annual net cash flows are equal, the payback period is simply project cost divided by the annual cash flow.

Discounted Payback Period

The **discounted payback method** uses the present values of the project's estimated cash flows. It is the number of years it takes a project to recover its initial investment in present value terms, and therefore must be greater than the payback period without discounting.

Example: Discounted payback method

Compute the discounted payback period for projects A and B described in Figure 5. Assume that the firm's cost of capital is 10% and the firm's maximum discounted payback period is four years.

Figure 5: Cash Flows for Projects A and B

	Year (t)	0	1	2	3	4
Project A	Net Cash Flow	−2,000	1,000	800	600	200
	Discounted NCF	−2,000	910	661	451	137
	Cumulative DNCF	−2,000	−1,090	−429	22	159
Project B	Net Cash Flow	−2,000	200	600	800	1,200
	Discounted NCF	−2,000	182	496	601	820
	Cumulative DNCF	−2,000	−1,818	−1,322	−721	99

Answer:

$$\text{discounted payback A} = 2 + \frac{429}{451} = 2.95 \text{ years}$$

$$\text{discounted payback B} = 3 + \frac{721}{820} = 3.88 \text{ years}$$

The discounted payback period addresses one of the drawbacks of the payback period by discounting cash flows at the project's required rate of return. However, the discounted payback period still does not consider any cash flows beyond the payback period, which means that it is a poor measure of profitability. Again, its use is primarily as a measure of liquidity.

Average Accounting Rate of Return (AAR)

The **average accounting rate of return** (AAR) is defined as the ratio of a project's average net income to its average book value. In equation form, this is expressed as:

$$AAR = \frac{\text{average net income}}{\text{average book value}}$$

Example: Average accounting rate of return

Presstech Printing Company invests $400,000 in a project that is depreciated on a straight-line basis over four years to a zero salvage value. Sales revenues, operating expenses, and net income for each year are shown in Figure 6. Calculate the AAR of the project.

Figure 6: Net Income for Calculating AAR

	Year 1	Year 2	Year 3	Year 4
Sales	$320,000	$360,000	$420,000	$280,000
Cash expenses	150,000	140,000	200,000	160,000
Depreciation	100,000	100,000	100,000	100,000
Earnings before taxes	70,000	120,000	120,000	20,000
Taxes (at 30%)	21,000	36,000	36,000	6,000
Net income	49,000	84,000	84,000	14,000

Answer:

For the 4-year period, the average net income is:

($49,000 + $84,000 + $84,000 + $14,000) / 4 = $57,750

The initial book value is $400,000, declining by $100,000 per year until the final book value is $0. The average book value for this asset is:

($400,000 − $0) / 2 = $200,000

The average accounting rate of return is:

$$AAR = \frac{\text{average net income}}{\text{average book value}} = \frac{\$57,750}{\$200,000} = 0.28875 = 28.9\%$$

The primary advantage of the AAR is that it is relatively easy to calculate. However, the AAR has some important disadvantages. The AAR is based on accounting income, and not on cash flows, which violates one of the basic principles of capital budgeting. In addition, the AAR does not account for the time value of money, making it a poor measure of profitability.

Professor's Note: In the accounting material, we usually calculated depreciation with an estimate of the actual salvage value of the asset. In capital budgeting, we usually assume a zero salvage value because, for tax reporting, the firm benefits from taking the most rapid depreciation allowed. For financial reporting, the goal should be to give users of financial statements the most accurate information on the true economic depreciation of the asset.

Profitability Index (PI)

The **profitability index** (PI) is the present value of a project's future cash flows divided by the initial cash outlay.

$$PI = \frac{\text{PV of future cash flows}}{CF_0} = 1 + \frac{NPV}{CF_0}$$

As you can see, the profitability index is closely related to the NPV. The PI is the ratio of the present value of future cash flows to the initial cash outlay, while the NPV is the difference between the present value of future cash flows and the initial cash outlay.

If the NPV of a project is positive, the PI will be greater than one. If the NPV is negative, the PI will be less than one. It follows that the *decision rule* for the PI is:

If PI > 1.0, accept the project.

If PI < 1.0, reject the project.

Example: Profitability index

Going back to our original example, calculate the PI for Projects A and B. Note that Figure 1 has been reproduced as Figure 7.

Figure 7: Expected Net After-Tax Cash Flows

Year (t)	Project A	Project B
0	–$2,000	–$2,000
1	1,000	200
2	800	600
3	600	800
4	200	1,200

Answer:

$$\text{PV future cash flows}_A = \frac{1{,}000}{(1.1)^1} + \frac{800}{(1.1)^2} + \frac{600}{(1.1)^3} + \frac{200}{(1.1)^4} = \$2{,}157.64$$

$$PI_A = \frac{\$2{,}157.64}{\$2{,}000} = 1.079$$

$$\text{PV future cash flows}_B = \frac{200}{(1.1)^1} + \frac{600}{(1.1)^2} + \frac{800}{(1.1)^3} + \frac{1{,}200}{(1.1)^4} = \$2{,}098.36$$

$$PI_B = \frac{\$2{,}098.36}{\$2{,}000} = 1.049$$

Decision: If projects A and B are independent, accept both projects A and B since PI > 1 for both projects.

Professor's Note: The accept/reject decision rule here is exactly equivalent to both the NPV and IRR decision rules. That is, if PI > 1, then the NPV must be positive, and the IRR must be greater than the discount rate. Note also that once you have the NPV, you can just add back the initial outlay to get the PV of the cash inflows used here. Recall that the NPV of Project B is $98.36 with an initial cost of $2,000. PI is simply (2,000 + 98.36) / 2000.

LOS 47.e: Explain the NPV profile, compare and contrast the NPV and IRR methods when evaluating more than one capital project, and describe the multiple IRR and no-IRR problems that can arise when calculating an IRR.

A project's **NPV profile** is a graph that shows a project's NPV for different discount rates. The NPV profiles for the two projects described in Figure 1 are presented in Figure 8. The discount rates are on the x-axis of the NPV profile, and the corresponding NPVs are plotted on the y-axis.

Note that the projects' IRRs are the discount rates where the NPV profiles intersect the x-axis, since these are the discount rates for which NPV equals zero. Recall that the IRR is the discount rate that results in an NPV of zero.

Figure 8: NPV Profiles

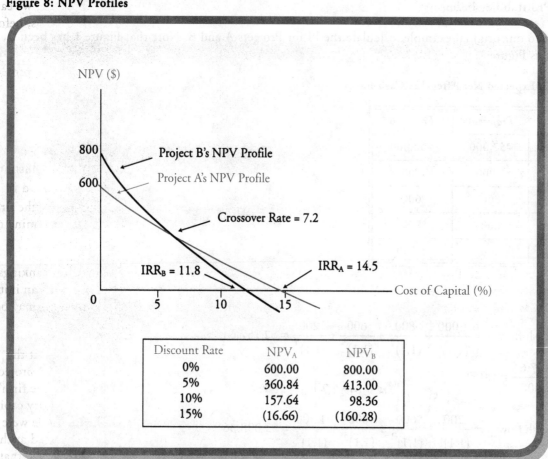

Discount Rate	NPV$_A$	NPV$_B$
0%	600.00	800.00
5%	360.84	413.00
10%	157.64	98.36
15%	(16.66)	(160.28)

Also notice in Figure 8 that the NPV profiles intersect. They intersect at the discount rate for which NPVs of the projects are equal. At discount rates below 7.2% (to the left of the intersection), Project B has the greater NPV, and at discount rates above 7.2%, Project A has a greater NPV. Clearly, the discount rate used in the analysis can determine which one of two mutually exclusive projects will be accepted.

The NPV profiles for Projects A and B intersect because of a difference in the timing of the cash flows. Examining the cash flows for the projects (Figure 2), we can see that the total cash inflows for Project B are greater ($2,800) than those of Project A ($2,600). Since they both have the same initial cost ($2,000), at a discount rate of zero, Project B has a greater NPV (2,800 – 2,000 = $800) than Project A (2,600 – 2000 = $600).

We can also see that the cash flows for Project B come later in the project's life. That's why the NPV of Project B falls faster than the NPV of Project A as the discount rate increases, and the NPVs are eventually equal at a discount rate of 7.2%. At discount rates above 7.2%, the fact that the total cash flows of Project B are greater in nominal dollars is overridden by the fact that Project B's cash flows come later in the project's life than those of Project A.

The Relative Advantages and Disadvantages of the NPV and IRR Methods

A **key advantage of NPV** is that it is a direct measure of the expected increase in the value of the firm. NPV is the theoretically best method. Its main weakness is that it does not include any consideration of the size of the project. For example, an NPV of $100 is great for a project costing $100 but not so great for a project costing $1 million.

A **key advantage of IRR** is that it measures profitability as a percentage, showing the return on each dollar invested. The IRR provides information on the margin of safety that the NPV does not. From the IRR, we can tell how much below the IRR (estimated return) the actual project return could fall, in percentage terms, before the project becomes uneconomic (has a negative NPV).

The *disadvantages* of the IRR method are (1) the possibility of producing rankings of mutually exclusive projects different from those from NPV analysis, and (2) the possibility that there are multiple IRRs or no IRR for a project.

Conflicting Project Rankings

For Projects A and B from our examples we noted that IRR$_A$ > IRR$_B$, 14.5% > 11.8%. In Figure 8 we illustrated that for discount rates less than 7.2%, the NPV$_B$ > NPV$_A$. When such a conflict occurs, the NPV method is preferred because it identifies the project that is expected to produce the greater increase in the value of the firm. Recall that the reason for different NPV rankings at different discount rates was the difference in the timing of the cash flows between the two projects.

Another reason, besides cash flow timing differences, that NPV and IRR may give conflicting project rankings is differences in project size. Consider two projects, one with an initial outlay of $100,000, and one with an initial outlay of $1 million. The smaller project may have a higher IRR, but the increase in firm value (NPV) may be small compared to the increase in firm value (NPV) of the larger project, even though its IRR is lower.

It is sometimes said that the NPV method implicitly assumes that project cash flows can be reinvested at the discount rate used to calculate NPV. This is a realistic assumption, since it is reasonable to assume that project cash flows could be used to reduce the firm's capital requirements. Any funds that are used to reduce the firm's capital requirements allow the firm to avoid the cost of capital on those funds. Just by reducing its equity capital and debt, the firm could "earn" its cost of capital on funds used to reduce its capital requirements. If we were to rank projects by their IRRs, we would be implicitly assuming that project cash flows could be reinvested at the project's IRR. This is unrealistic and, strictly speaking, if the firm could earn that rate on invested funds, that rate should be the one used to discount project cash flows.

The "Multiple IRR" and "No IRR" Problems

If a project has cash outflows during its life or at the end of its life in addition to its initial cash outflow, the project is said to have a *non-normal* cash-flow pattern. Projects with such cash flows may have more than one IRR (there may be more than one discount rate that will produce an NPV equal to zero).

It is also possible to have a project where there is no discount rate that results in a zero NPV, that is, the project does not have an IRR. A project with no IRR may actually be a profitable project. The lack of an IRR results from the project having non-normal cash flows, where mathematically, no IRR exists. NPV does not have this problem and produces theoretically correct decisions for projects with non-normal cash flow patterns.

Neither of these problems can arise with the NPV method. If a project has non-normal cash flows, the NPV method will give the appropriate accept/reject decision.

LOS 47.f: Describe the relative popularity of the various capital budgeting methods and explain the importance of the NPV in estimating the value of a stock price.

Despite the superiority of NPV and IRR methods for evaluating projects, surveys of corporate financial managers show that a variety of methods are used. The surveys show that the capital budgeting method used by a company varied according to four general criteria:

- **Location.** European countries tended to use the payback period method as much or more than the IRR and NPV methods.
- **Size of the company.** The larger the company, the more likely it was to use discounted cash flow techniques such as the NPV and IRR methods.
- **Public vs. private.** Private companies used the payback period more often than public companies. Public companies tended to prefer discounted cash flow methods.
- **Management education.** The higher the level of education (i.e., MBA), the more likely the company was to use discounted cash flow techniques such as the NPV and IRR methods.

The Relationship Between NPV and Stock Price

Since the NPV method is a direct measure of the expected change in firm value from undertaking a capital project, it is also the criterion most related to stock prices. In theory, a positive NPV project should cause a proportionate increase in a company's stock price.

Example: Relationship Between NPV and Stock Price

Presstech is investing $500 million in new printing equipment. The present value of the future after-tax cash flows resulting from the equipment is $750 million. Presstech currently has 100 million shares outstanding, with a current market price of $45 per share. Assuming that this project is new information and is independent of other expectations about the company, calculate the effect of the new equipment on the value of the company, and the effect on Presstech's stock price.

Answer:

NPV of the new printing equipment project = $750 million – $500 million = $250 million.

Value of company prior to new equipment project = 100 million shares × $45 per share = $4.5 billion.

Value of company after new equipment project = $4.5 billion + $250 million = $4.75 billion.

Price per share after new equipment project = $4.75 billion / 100 million shares = $47.50

The stock price should increase from $45.00 per share to $47.50 per share as a result of the project.

In reality, the impact of a project on the company's stock price is more complicated than the example above. A company's stock price is a function of the present value of its expected future earnings stream. As a result, changes in the stock price will result more from changes in *expectations* about a project's profitability. If a company announces a project for which managers expect a positive NPV, but analysts expect a lower level of profitability from the project than the company does, the stock price may actually drop on the announcement. In another example, a project announcement may be taken as a signal about other future capital projects, resulting in a stock price increase that is much greater than what the NPV of the announced project would justify.

KEY CONCEPTS

1. Capital budgeting is the process of evaluating expenditures on assets whose cash flows are expected to extend beyond one year.
2. There are four administrative steps to the capital budgeting process:
   - Generating investment ideas.
   - Analyzing project ideas.
   - Creating the firm-wide capital budget.
   - Monitoring decisions and conducting a post-audit.
3. Categories of capital projects include:
   - Replacement projects for maintaining the business.
   - Replacement projects for cost reduction purposes.
   - Expansion projects.
   - New product/market development.
   - Mandatory environmental/regulatory projects.
   - Other projects, such as pet projects of the CEO.
4. The capital budgeting process is based on five key principles:
   - Decisions are based on after-tax cash flows, not accounting income.
   - Cash flow estimates include cash opportunity costs.
   - Timing of cash flows is important.
   - Financing costs and the project's risk are reflected in the required rate of return used to evaluate the project.
5. Mutually exclusive means that only one of a set of projects can be selected. Independent projects are unrelated to one another, so each can be evaluated on its own.
6. Project sequencing refers to projects that follow a certain sequence so that investing in a project today creates opportunities to invest in other projects in the future.
7. If a firm has unlimited funds, it can undertake all profitable projects. If additional capital is limited, the firm must ration its capital to fund that group of projects that are expected to produce the greatest increase in firm value.
8. The NPV of a project is the present value of future cash flows discounted at the firm's cost of capital, less the project's initial cost, and can be interpreted as the expected change in shareholder wealth from undertaking the project.
9. The IRR is the rate of return that equates the PVs of the project's expected cash inflows and outflows, and is also the discount rate that will produce an NPV of zero.
10. The payback period is the number of years required to recover the original cost of the investment, and the discounted payback period is the time it takes to recover the investment using the present values of future cash flows.
11. The AAR is the ratio of a project's average net income to its average book value.
12. The PI is the ratio of the present value of a project's future cash flows to its initial cash outlay.
13. The NPV profile shows a project's NPV as a function of the discount rate used.
14. The IRR is easily interpreted because it's a rate of return, can provide information on a project's margin of safety, and gives identical accept/reject decisions to the NPV method for independent projects. However, it can give project rankings that conflict with the NPV method when project size or cash flow patterns differ, and non-normal projects can have no IRR or multiple IRRs.
15. NPV analysis is theoretically preferred in all applications.
16. Despite the theoretical superiority of discounted cash flow techniques such as NPV, studies show that companies use a variety of methods to evaluate capital projects, with small companies, private companies, and companies outside the U.S. more likely to use simpler techniques such as payback period.
17. The NPV method is a direct measure of the expected change in firm value, and as a result, is also the criterion most closely related to stock price changes.

CONCEPT CHECKERS: CAPITAL BUDGETING

1. Which of the following statements concerning the principles underlying the capital budgeting process is **TRUE**?
    A. Cash flows are analyzed on a pre-tax basis.
    B. Financing costs should be added to the required rate of return on the project.
    C. Cash flows should be based on opportunity costs.
    D. The net income for a project is essential for making a correct capital budgeting decision.

2. Which of the following statements about the payback period method is **FALSE**? The:
    A. payback period provides a rough measure of a project's liquidity.
    B. payback method considers all cash flows throughout the entire life of a project.
    C. cumulative net cash flow is the running total through time of a project's cash flows.
    D. payback period is the number of years it takes to recover the original cost of the investment.

3. Which of the following statements about NPV and IRR is **FALSE**?
    A. The discount rate that gives an NPV of zero is the project's IRR.
    B. The IRR is the discount rate that equates the present value of the cash inflows with the present value of outflows.
    C. For mutually exclusive projects, if the NPV method and the IRR method give conflicting rankings, you should use the IRRs to select the project.
    D. The NPV method assumes that cash flows will be reinvested at the cost of capital, while IRR rankings implicitly assume that cash flows are reinvested at the IRR.

4. Which of the following statements is **FALSE**? The discounted payback:
    A. method frequently ignores terminal values.
    B. method can give results that conflict with the NPV method.
    C. period is generally shorter than the regular payback.
    D. period is the time it takes for the present value of the project's cash inflows to equal the initial cost of the investment.

5. Which of the following statements about NPV and IRR is **FALSE**?
    A. The IRR can be positive even if the NPV is negative.
    B. The NPV method is not affected by the multiple IRR problem.
    C. When the IRR is equal to the cost of capital, the NPV will be zero.
    D. The NPV will be positive if the IRR is less than the cost of capital.

Use the following data to answer Questions 6 through 10.

A company is considering the purchase of a copier that costs $5,000. Assume a required rate of return of 10% and the following cash flow schedule:

*   Year 1: $3,000.
*   Year 2: $2,000.
*   Year 3: $2,000.

6. What is the project's payback period?
    A. 1.5 years.
    B. 2.0 years.
    C. 2.5 years.
    D. 3.0 years.

7. What is the project's discounted payback period?
    A. 1.4 years.
    B. 2.0 years.
    C. 2.4 years.
    D. 2.6 years.

8. What is the project's NPV?
    A. –$309.
    B. +$243.
    C. +$883.
    D. +$1,523.

9. What is the project's IRR (approximately)?
    A. 5%.
    B. 10%.
    C. 15%.
    D. 20%.

10. What is the project's profitability index (PI)?
    A. 0.18.
    B. 0.72.
    C. 1.18.
    D. 1.72.

11. An analyst has gathered the following information about a company:
    • Cost $10,000.
    • Annual cash inflow $4,000.
    • Life   4 years.
    • Cost of capital   12%.

    Which of the following statements about the project is **FALSE**? The:
    A. payback period is 2.5 years.
    B. IRR of the project is 21.9%; accept the project.
    C. discounted payback period is 3.5 years.
    D. NPV of the project is +$2,149; accept the project.

Use the following data for Questions 12 and 13.

An analyst has gathered the following data about two projects, each with a 12% required rate of return.

	Project A	Project B
Initial cost	$15,000	$20,000
Life	5 years	4 years
Cash inflows	$5,000/year	$7,500/year

12. If the projects are independent, the company should:
    A. reject both projects.
    B. accept Project A and reject Project B.
    C. reject Project A and accept Project B.
    D. accept both projects.

13. If the projects are mutually exclusive, the company should:
    A. reject both projects.
    B. accept A and reject B.
    C. reject A and accept B.
    D. accept both projects.

14. The NPV profiles of two projects will intersect if the projects have different:
    A. sizes and different lives.
    B. IRRs and different lives.
    C. IRRs and different costs of capital.
    D. sizes and different costs of capital.

15. The post-audit is used to:
    A. improve cash flow forecasts and stimulate management to improve operations and bring results into line with forecasts.
    B. improve cash flow forecasts and eliminate potentially profitable but risky projects.
    C. stimulate management to improve operations and bring results into line with forecasts and eliminate potentially profitable but risky projects.
    D. improve cash flow forecasts, stimulate management to improve operations and bring results into line with forecasts, and eliminate potentially profitable but risky projects.

16. Columbus Sign Company invests $270,000 in a project that is depreciated on a straight-line basis over three years to a zero salvage value. The relevant details for the project over its 3-year life are shown below:

	Year 1	Year 2	Year 3
Sales	$220,000	$190,000	$200,000
Cash expenses	50,000	40,000	60,000
Depreciation	90,000	90,000	90,000
Earnings before taxes	80,000	60,000	50,000
Taxes (at 30%)	24,000	18,000	15,000
Net income	56,000	42,000	35,000

    The AAR for the project is *closest* to:
    A. 8.9%.
    B. 16.4%.
    C. 32.8%.
    D. 49.3%.

17. Based on surveys of comparable firms, which of the following firms would be *most likely* to use NPV as its preferred method for evaluating capital projects?
    A. A small public industrial company located in France.
    B. A private company located in the United States.
    C. A small public retailing firm located in the United States.
    D. A large public company located in the United States.

18. Fullen Machinery is investing $400 million in new industrial equipment. The present value of the future after-tax cash flows resulting from the equipment is $700 million. Fullen currently has 200 million shares of common stock outstanding, with a current market price of $36 per share. Assuming that this project is new information and is independent of other expectations about the company, what is the theoretical effect of the new equipment on Fullen's stock price?
    A. The stock price will remain unchanged.
    B. The stock price will increase to $37.50.
    C. The stock price will decrease to $33.50.
    D. The stock price will increase to $39.50.

ANSWERS – CONCEPT CHECKERS: CAPITAL BUDGETING

1. **C** Cash flows are based on opportunity costs. The cost of capital is implicit in the project's required rate of return; adding the cost of capital to the required return would be double counting. Cash flows are analyzed on an after-tax basis. Accounting net income, which includes non-cash expenses, is irrelevant; incremental cash flows are essential for making correct capital budgeting decisions.

2. **B** The payback period ignores cash flows that go beyond the payback period.

3. **C** NPV should always be used if NPV and IRR give conflicting decisions.

4. **C** The discounted payback is longer than the regular payback because cash flows are discounted to their present value.

5. **D** If IRR is less than the cost of capital, the result will be a negative NPV.

6. **B** Cash flow (CF) after year 2 = −5,000 + 3,000 + 2,000 = 0. Cost of copier is paid back in the first two years.

7. **C** Year 1 discounted cash flow = 3,000 / 1.10 = 2,727; year 2 DCF = 2,000 / 1.10^2 = 1,653; year 3 DCF = 2,000 / 1.10^3 = 1,503. CF required after year 2 = −5,000 + 2,727 +1,653 = -\$620. 620 / year 3 DCF = 620 / 1,503 = 0.41, for a discounted payback of 2.4 years.

    Using a financial calculator:
    Year 1: I = 10%; FV = 3,000; N = 1; PMT = 0; CPT $\rightarrow$ PV = −2,727

    Year 2: N = 2; FV = 2,000; CPT $\rightarrow$ PV = −1,653

    Year 3: N = 3; CPT $\rightarrow$ PV = −1,503
    [5,000 − (2,727 + 1,653) = 620]. 620 / 1,503 = 0.413, so discounted payback = 2 + 0.4 = 2.4.

8. **C** NPV = CF_0 + (discounted cash flows years 0 to 3 calculated in Question 7) = −5,000 + (2,727 + 1,653 + 1,503) = −5,000 + 5,833 = \$883

9. **D** Intuition: You know the NPV is positive, so the IRR must be greater than 10%. You only have two choices, 15% and 20%. Pick one and solve the NPV; if it's not close to zero, you guessed wrong—pick the other one. Alternatively, you can solve directly for the IRR as CF_0 = −5,000, CF_1 = 3,000, CF_2 = 2,000, CF_3 = 2,000.
    IRR = 20.64%.

10. **C** PI = PV of future cash flows / CF_0 (discounted cash flows years 0 to 3 calculated in Question 7).
    PI = (2,727 + 1,653 + 1,503) / 5,000 = 1.177.

11. **C** The discounted payback period of 3.15 is calculated as follows:

$$CF_0 = -10,000; \quad PVCF_1 = \frac{4,000}{1.12} = 3,571; \quad PVCF_2 = \frac{4,000}{1.12^2} = 3,189; \quad PVCF_3 = \frac{4,000}{1.12^3} = 2,847;$$

$$\text{and } PVCF_4 = \frac{4,000}{1.12^4} = 2,542. \quad \text{CF after year 3} = -10,000 + 3,571 + 3,189 + 2,847 = -393$$

$$\frac{393}{\text{year 4 DCF}} = \frac{393}{2,542} = 0.15, \text{ for a discounted payback period of 3.15 years.}$$

12. **D** Independent projects accept all with positive NPVs or IRRs greater than cost of capital. NPV computation is easy—treat cash flows as an annuity.

NPV_A: N = 5; I = 12; PMT = 5,000; FV = 0; CPT $\rightarrow$ PV = –18,024
NPV_A = 18,024 – 15,000 = $3,024
NPV_B: N = 4; I = 12; PMT = 7,500; FV = 0; CPT $\rightarrow$ PV = –22,780
NPV_B = 22,780 – 20,000 = $2,780

13. **B** Accept the project with the highest NPV.

14. **A** NPV profiles will intersect due to different sizes and lives.

15. **A** A post-audit identifies what went right and what went wrong. It is used to improve forecasting and operations.

16. **C** For the three year period, the average net income is (56,000 + 42,000 + 35,000) / 3 = $44,333. The initial book value is $270,000, declining by $90,000 per year until the final book value is $0. The average book value for this asset is ($270,000 – $0) / 2 = $135,000. The average accounting rate of return is ($44,333 / $135,000) = 0.328, or 32.8%.

17. **D** According to survey results, large companies, public companies, U.S. companies, and companies managed by a corporate manager with an advanced degree, are more likely to use discounted cash flow techniques like NPV to evaluate capital projects.

18. **B** The NPV of the new equipment is $700 million – $400 million = $300 million. The value of this project is added to Fullen's current market value. On a per-share basis, the addition is worth $300 million / 200 million shares, for a net addition to the share price of $1.50. $36.00 + $1.50 = $37.50.

The following is a review of the Corporate Finance principles designed to address the learning outcome statements set forth by CFA Institute®. This topic is also covered in:

COST OF CAPITAL

EXAM FOCUS

The firm must decide how to raise the capital to fund its business or finance its growth, dividing it among common equity, debt, and preferred stock. The mix that produces the minimum overall cost of capital will maximize the value of the firm (share price). From this topic review, you must get an understanding of weighted average cost of capital and its calculation, and be ready to calculate the costs of retained earnings, new common stock, preferred stock, and the after-tax cost of debt. Don't worry about choosing among the methods for calculating the cost of retained earnings; the information given in the question will make it clear which one to use. This is very testable material and you must know all these formulas and understand why the marginal cost of capital increases as greater amounts of capital are raised over a given period (usually taken to be a year).

LOS 48.a: Determine and interpret the weighted average cost of capital (WACC) of a company, and explain the adjustments to it that an analyst should make in developing a cost of capital for a specific project.

LOS 48.b: Describe the role of taxes in the cost of capital from the different capital sources.

The capital budgeting process involves discounted cash flow analysis. To conduct such analysis, you must know the firm's proper discount rate. This topic review discusses how, as an analyst, you can determine the proper rate at which to discount the cash flows associated with a capital budgeting project. This discount rate is the firm's **weighted average cost of capital** (WACC) and is also referred to as the **marginal cost of capital** (MCC).

Basic definitions. On the right (liability) side of a firm's balance sheet, we have debt, preferred stock, and common equity. These are normally referred to as the *capital components* of the firm. Any increase in a firm's total assets will have to be financed through an increase in at least one of these capital accounts. The cost of each of these components is called the *component cost* of capital.

Throughout this review we focus on the following capital components and their component costs:

k_d The rate at which the firm can issue new debt. This is the yield to maturity on existing debt. This is also called the before-tax component cost of debt.

$k_d(1-t)$ The after-tax cost of debt. Here, t is the firm's marginal tax rate. The after-tax component cost of debt, $k_d(1-t)$, is used to calculate the WACC.

k_{ps} The cost of preferred stock.

k_{ce} The cost of common equity. It is the required rate of return on common stock and is generally difficult to estimate.

In many countries, the interest paid on corporate debt is tax deductible. Since we are interested in the after-tax cost of capital, we adjust the cost of debt, k_d, for the firm's marginal tax rate, t. Since there is typically no tax deduction allowed for payments to common or preferred stockholders, there is no equivalent deduction to k_{ps} or k_{ce}.

How a company raises capital and how they budget or invest it are considered independently. Most companies have separate departments for the two tasks. The financing department is responsible for keeping costs low and using a balance of funding sources: common equity, preferred stock, and debt. Generally, it is necessary to raise each type of capital in large sums. The large sums may temporarily overweight the most recently issued capital, but in the long run, the firm will adhere to target weights. Because of these and other financing considerations, each investment decision must be made assuming a WACC which includes each of the different sources of capital and is based on the long-run target weights. A company creates value by producing a return on assets that is higher than the required rate return on the capital needed to fund those assets.

The WACC as we have described it is the cost of financing firm assets. We can view this cost as an opportunity cost. Consider how a company could reduce its costs if it found a way to produce its output using fewer assets, say less working capital. If we need less working capital, we can use the funds freed up to buy back our debt and equity securities in a mix that just matches our target capital structure. Our after-tax savings would be the WACC based on our target capital structure, times the total value of the securities that are no longer outstanding.

For these reasons, any time we are considering a project that requires expenditures, comparing the return on those expenditures to the WACC is the appropriate way to determine whether undertaking that project will increase the value of the firm. This is the essence of the capital budgeting decision. Since a firm's WACC reflects the average risk of the projects that make up the firm, it is not appropriate for evaluating all new projects. It should be adjusted upward for projects with greater-than-average risk and downward for projects with less-than-average risk.

The weights in the calculation of a firm's WACC are the proportions of each source of capital in a firm's capital structure.

Calculating a Company's Weighted-Average Cost of Capital

The WACC is given by:

$$\text{WACC} = (w_d)[k_d(1-t)] + (w_{ps})(k_{ps}) + (w_{ce})(k_{ce})$$

where:
w_d = the percentage of debt in the capital structure
w_{ps} = the percentage of preferred stock in the capital structure
w_{ce} = the percentage of common stock in the capital structure

Example: Computing WACC

Suppose Dexter's target capital structure is as follows:

$$w_d = 0.45, \ w_{ps} = 0.05, \text{ and } w_{ce} = 0.50$$

Its before-tax cost of debt is 8%, its cost of equity is 12%, its cost of preferred stock is 8.4%, and its marginal tax rate is 40%. Calculate Dexter's WACC.

Answer:

Dexter's WACC will be:

$$WACC = (w_d)(k_d)(1-t) + (w_{ps})(k_{ps}) + (w_{ce})(k_{ce})$$
$$WACC = (0.45)(0.08)(0.6) + (0.05)(0.084) + (0.50)(0.12) = 0.0858 \cong 8.6\%$$

LOS 48.c: Describe alternative methods of calculating the weights used in the weighted average cost of capital, including the use of the company's target capital structure.

The weights in the calculation of WACC should be based on the firm's target capital structure, that is, the proportions (based on market values) of debt, preferred stock, and equity that the firm expects to achieve over time. In the absence of any explicit information about a firm's target capital structure from the firm itself, an analyst may simply use the firm's current capital structure (based on market values) as the best indication of its target capital structure. If there has been a noticeable trend in the firm's capital structure, the analyst may want to incorporate this trend into his estimate of the firm's target capital structure. For example, if a firm has been reducing its proportion of debt financing each year for two or three years, the analyst may wish to use a weight on debt that is lower than the firm's current weight on debt in constructing the firm's target capital structure.

Alternatively, an analyst may wish to use the industry average capital structure as the target capital structure for a firm under analysis.

Example: Determining target capital structure weights

The market values of a firm's capital are as follows:

- Debt outstanding: $8 million
- Preferred stock outstanding: $2 million
- Common stock outstanding: $10 million
- Total capital: $20 million

What is the firm's target capital structure based on its existing capital structure?

Answer:

debt 40%, $w_d = 0.40$

preferred stock 10%, $w_{ps} = 0.10$

common stock 50%, $w_{ce} = 0.50$

For the industry average approach, we would simply use the arithmetic average of the current market weights (for each capital source) from a sample of industry firms.

LOS 48.d: Explain the analyst's concern with the marginal cost of capital in evaluating investment projects, and explain the use of the marginal cost of capital and the investment opportunity schedule in determining the optimal capital budget for a company.

A company increases its value and creates wealth for its shareholders by earning more on its investment in assets than is required by those who provide the capital for the firm. A firm's WACC may increase as larger amounts of capital are raised. Thus, its marginal cost of capital, the cost of raising additional capital, can increase as larger amounts are invested in new projects. This is illustrated by the upward sloping **marginal cost of capital curve** in Figure 1. Given the expected returns (IRRs) on potential projects, we can order the expenditures on additional projects from highest to lowest IRR. This will allow us to construct a downward sloping **investment opportunity schedule** such as that shown in Figure 1.

Figure 1: The Optimal Capital Budget

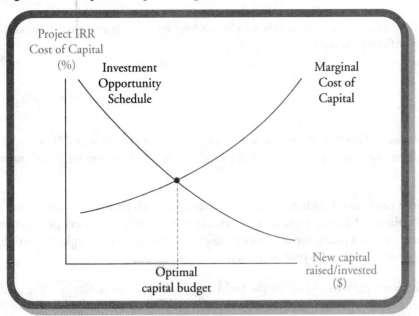

The intersection of the investment opportunity schedule with the marginal cost of capital curve identifies the amount of the optimal capital budget. The intuition here is that the firm should undertake all those projects with IRRs greater than the cost of funds, the same criterion developed in the capital budgeting topic review. This will maximize the value created. At the same time, no projects with IRRs less than the marginal cost of the additional capital required to fund them should be undertaken, as they will erode the value created by the firm.

LOS 48.e: Explain the marginal cost of capital's role in determining the net present value of a project.

One cautionary note regarding the simple logic behind Figure 1 is in order. All projects do not have the same risk. The WACC is the appropriate discount rate for projects that have approximately the same level of risk as the firm's existing projects. This is because the component costs of capital used to calculate the firm's WACC are based on the existing level of firm risk. To evaluate a project with greater than (the firm's) average risk, a discount rate greater than the firm's existing WACC should be used. Projects with below-average risk should be evaluated using a discount rate less than the firm's WACC.

An additional issue to consider when using a firm's WACC (marginal cost of capital) to evaluate a specific project is that there is an implicit assumption that the capital structure of the firm will remain at the target capital structure over the life of the project.

These complexities aside, we can still conclude that the NPVs of potential projects of firm-average risk should be calculated using the marginal cost of capital for the firm. Projects for which the present value of the after-tax cash inflows is greater than the present value of the after-tax cash outflows, should be undertaken by the firm.

LOS 48.f: Calculate and analyze the cost of fixed rate debt capital using the yield-to-maturity approach and the debt-rating approach.

The **after-tax cost of debt**, $k_d(1 - t)$, is used in computing the WACC. It is the interest rate at which firms can issue new debt (k_d) net of the tax savings from the tax-deductibility of interest, $k_d(t)$.

after-tax cost of debt = interest rate – tax savings = $k_d - k_d(t) = k_d(1 - t)$

after-tax cost of debt = $k_d (1 - t)$

Example: Cost of debt

Dexter, Inc., is planning to issue new debt at an interest rate of 8%. Dexter has a 40% marginal federal-plus-state tax rate. What is Dexter's cost of debt capital?

Answer:

$$k_d (1 - t) = 8\% (1 - 0.4) = 4.8\%$$

Professor's Note: It is important that you realize that the cost of debt is the market interest rate (YTM) on new (marginal) debt, not the coupon rate on the firm's existing debt. CFA Institute may provide you with both rates, and you need to select the current market rate.

If a market YTM is not available because the firm's debt is not publicly traded, the analyst may use the rating and maturity of the firm's existing debt to estimate the before-tax cost of debt. If, for example the firm's debt carries a single-A rating and has an average maturity of 15 years, the analyst can use the yield curve for single-A rated debt to determine the current market rate for debt with a 15-year maturity.

If any characteristics of the firm's anticipated debt would affect the yield (e.g. covenants or seniority), the analyst should make the appropriate adjustment to his estimated before-tax cost of debt. For firms that primarily employ floating-rate debt, the analyst should estimate the longer-term cost of the firm's debt using the current yield curve (term structure) for debt of the appropriate rating category.

LOS 48.g: Calculate the cost of noncallable, nonconvertible preferred stock.

The **cost of preferred stock** (k_{ps}) is:

$$k_{ps} = D_{ps} / P$$

where:
D_{ps} = preferred dividends
P = market price of preferred

Example: Cost of preferred stock

Suppose Dexter has preferred stock that pays an $8 dividend per share and sells for $100 per share. What is Dexter's cost of preferred stock?

Answer:

$$k_{ps} = D_{ps} / P$$
$$k_{ps} = \$8 / \$100 = 0.08 = 8\%$$

Note that the equation $k_{ps} = D_{ps} / P$ is just a rearrangement of the preferred stock valuation model $P = D_{ps} / k_{ps}$, where P is the market price.

LOS 48.h: Calculate and analyze the cost of equity capital using the capital asset pricing model approach, the dividend discount approach, and the bond yield plus risk premium approach.

The opportunity **cost of equity capital** (k_{ce}) is the required rate of return on the firm's common stock. The rationale here is that the firm could avoid part of the cost of common stock outstanding by using retained earnings to buy back shares of its own stock. The cost of (i.e., the required return) on common equity can be estimated using one of the following three approaches:

1. **The capital asset pricing model approach.**

   Step 1:   Estimate the risk-free rate, RFR. The short-term Treasury bill (T-bill) rate is usually used, but some analysts feel the long-term Treasury rate should be used.

   Step 2:   Estimate the stock's beta, β. This is the stock's risk measure.

   Step 3:   Estimate the expected rate of return on the market $E(R_{mkt})$.

   Step 4:   Use the capital asset pricing model (CAPM) equation to estimate the required rate of return:

   $$k_{ce} = RFR + \beta[E(R_m) - RFR]$$

   Example: Using CAPM to estimate k_{ce}

   Suppose RFR = 6%, R_{mkt} = 11%, and Dexter has a beta of 1.1.

   Answer:

   Then the required rate of return for Dexter's stock is:

   $$k_{ce} = 6\% + 1.1(11\% - 6\%) = 11.5\%$$

2. **The dividend discount model approach.** If dividends are expected to grow at a constant rate, g, then the current price of the stock is given by the dividend growth model:

   $$P_0 = \frac{D_1}{k_{ce} - g}$$

   where:
   D_1 = next year's dividend
   k_{ce} = the required rate of return on common equity
   g = the firm's expected constant growth rate

   Rearranging the terms, you can solve for k_{ce}:

   $$k_{ce} = \frac{D_1}{P_0} + g$$

   In order to use $k_{ce} = \dfrac{D_1}{P_0} + g$, you have to estimate the expected growth rate, g. This can be done by:

   - Using the growth rate as projected by security analysts.
   - Using the following equation to estimate a firm's sustainable growth rate:

     $$g = (\text{retention rate})(\text{return on equity}) = (1 - \text{payout rate})(ROE)$$

   The difficulty with this model is estimating the firm's future growth rate.

Example: Estimating k_{ce} using the dividend discount model

Suppose Dexter's stock sells for $21.00, next year's dividend is expected to be $1.00, Dexter's expected ROE is 12%, and Dexter is expected to pay out 40% of its earnings. What is Dexter's cost of equity?

Answer:

$$
\begin{aligned}
g &= (ROE)(\text{retention rate}) \\
g &= (0.12)(1 - 0.4) = 0.072 = 7.2\% \\
k_{ce} &= (1 / 21) + 0.072 = 0.12 \text{ or } 12\%
\end{aligned}
$$

3. **Bond yield plus risk premium approach.** Analysts often use an ad hoc approach to estimate the required rate of return. They add a risk premium (3 to 5 percentage points) to the market yield on the firm's long-term debt.

    $$k_{ce} = \text{bond yield} + \text{risk premium}$$

Example: Estimating k_{ce} with bond yields plus a risk premium

Dexter's interest rate on long-term debt is 8%. Suppose the risk premium is estimated to be 5%. Estimate Dexter's cost of equity.

Answer:

Dexter's estimated cost of equity is:

$$k_{ce} = 8\% + 5\% = 13\%$$

Note that the three models gave us three different estimates of k_{ce}. The CAPM estimate was 11.5%, the dividend discount model estimate was 12%, and the bond yield plus risk premium estimate was 13%. Analysts must use their judgment to decide which is most appropriate.

KEY CONCEPTS

1. The WACC is given by $WACC = (w_d)(k_d)(1 - t) + (w_{ps})(k_{ps}) + (w_{ce})(k_{ce})$.

2. The pre-tax cost of debt must be reduced by the firm's tax rate to get an after-tax cost of debt capital.

3. Target weights can be simply the firm's current proportions of capital based on market values, current proportions adjusted for trends in the firm's capital structure, or based on average industry weights for capital sources.

4. The intersection of the investment opportunity schedule with the marginal cost of capital curve illustrates the optimal capital budget with which a firm can finance all positive NPV projects.

5. The marginal cost of capital (MCC) is the cost of additional capital.

6. The WACC for additional capital (the MCC) should be used as the discount rate when calculating project NPVs for capital budgeting decisions. Adjustments are appropriate for projects that differ in risk from the average risk of a firm's existing projects.

7. After-tax cost of debt = interest rate – tax savings = $k_d - k_d t = k_d (1 - t)$.

8. Cost of preferred stock = $k_{ps} = \dfrac{D_{ps}}{P}$.

9. Cost of retained earnings—three approaches:
   - Bond yield plus risk premium approach: k_{ce} = market yield on the firm's long-term debt + RP.
   - CAPM approach: $k_{ce} = RFR + \beta[E(R_{mkt}) - RFR]$.
   - Discounted cash flow approach: $k_{ce} = \dfrac{D_1}{P_0} + g$.

CONCEPT CHECKERS: THE COST OF CAPITAL

1. A company has $5 million in debt outstanding with a coupon rate of 12%. Currently the yield to maturity (YTM) on these bonds is 14%. If the firm's tax rate is 40%, what is the company's after-tax cost of debt?
    A. 8.4%.
    B. 5.6%.
    C. 12.0%.
    D. 14.0%.

2. The cost of preferred stock is equal to:
    A. the preferred stock dividend divided by its par value.
    B. the preferred stock dividend multiplied by the market price.
    C. [(1 – tax rate) times the preferred stock dividend] divided by price.
    D. the preferred stock dividend divided by the market price.

3. A company's $100, 8% preferred is currently selling for $85. What is the company's cost of preferred equity?
    A. 8.0%.
    B. 8.5%.
    C. 9.4%.
    D. 10.8%.

4. The expected dividend is $2.50 for a share of stock priced at $25. What is the cost of equity if the long-term growth in dividends is projected to be 8%?
    A. 15%.
    B. 16%.
    C. 18%.
    D. 19%.

5. An analyst gathered the following data about a company:

Capital Structure	Required Rate of Return
30% debt	10% for debt
20% preferred stock	11% for preferred stock
50% common stock	18% for common stock

    Assuming a 40% tax rate, what after-tax rate of return must the company earn on its investments?
    A. 10.0%.
    B. 13.0%.
    C. 14.2%.
    D. 18.0%.

6. A company is planning a $50 million expansion. The expansion is to be financed by selling $20 million in new debt and $30 million in new common stock. The before-tax required return on debt is 9% and 14% for equity. If the company is in the 40% tax bracket, what is the company's marginal cost of capital?
    A. 9.0%.
    B. 10.0%.
    C. 10.6%.
    D. 11.5%.

©2007 Schweser

Use the following data to answer Questions 7 through 10.

- The company has a target capital structure of 40% debt and 60% equity.
- Bonds with face value of $1,000 pay a 10% coupon (semiannual), mature in 20 years, and sell for $849.54 with a yield to maturity of 12%.
- The company stock beta is 1.2.
- Risk-free rate is 10%, and market risk premium is 5%.
- The company is a constant-growth firm that just paid a dividend of $2.00, sells for $27.00 per share, and has a growth rate of 8%.
- The company's marginal tax rate is 40%.

7. The company's after-tax cost of debt is:
    A. 7.2%.
    B. 8.0%.
    C. 9.1%.
    D. 10.0%.

8. The company's cost of equity using the capital asset pricing model (CAPM) approach is:
    A. 13.6%.
    B. 16.0%.
    C. 16.6%.
    D. 16.9%.

9. The company's cost of equity using the dividend discount model is:
    A. 13.6%.
    B. 16.0%.
    C. 16.6%.
    D. 16.9%.

10. The company's weighted average cost of capital (using the cost of equity from CAPM) is:
    A. 12.5%.
    B. 13.0%.
    C. 13.5%.
    D. 14.0%.

11. What happens to a company's weighted average cost of capital (WACC) if the firm's corporate tax rate increases and if the Federal Reserve causes an increase in the risk-free rate, respectively? (Consider the events independently, and assume a beta of less than 1.) WACC will:

Tax rate increase	Increase in risk-free rate
A. Decrease	Increase
B. Decrease	Decrease
C. Increase	Increase
D. Remain the same	Increase

12.   Given the following information on a company's capital structure, what is the company's weighted average cost of capital? The marginal tax rate is 40%.

Type of capital	Percent of capital structure	Before-tax component cost
Bonds	40%	7.5%
Preferred stock	5%	11%
Common stock	55%	15%

   A. 7.1%.
   B. 10.0%.
   C. 10.6%.
   D. 13.3%.

ANSWERS – CONCEPT CHECKERS: THE COST OF CAPITAL

1. **A** $k_d(1 - t) = (0.14)(1 - 0.4) = 8.4\%$

2. **D**   Cost of preferred stock $= k_{ps} = D_{ps} / P$

3. **C** $k_{ps} = D_{ps} / P_{ps}$, $D_{ps} = \$100 \times 8\% = \$8$, $k_{ps} = 8 / 85 = 9.4\%$

4. **C**   Using the dividend yield plus growth rate approach: $k_{ce} = (D_1 / P_0) + g = (2.50 / 25.00) + 8\% = 18\%$.

5. **B** $WACC = (w_d)(k_d)(1 - t) + (w_{ps})(k_{ps}) + (w_{ce})(k_{ce}) = (0.3)(0.1)(1 - 0.4) + (0.2)(0.11) + (0.5)(0.18) = 13\%$

6. **C** $w_d = 20 / (20 + 30) = 0.4$, $w_{ce} = 30 / (20 + 30) = 0.6$

    $WACC = (w_d)(k_d)(1 - t) + (w_{ce})(k_{ce}) = (0.4)(9)(1 - 0.4) + (0.6)(14) = 10.56\% = MCC$

7. **A** $k_d(1 - t) = 12(1 - 0.4) = 7.2\%$

8. **B**   Using the CAPM formula, $k_{ce} = RFR + [E(R_{mkt}) - RFR]Beta = 10 + (5)(1.2) = 16\%$.

9. **B** $D_1 = D_0 (1 + g) = 2(1.08) = 2.16$; $k_{ce} = (D_1 / P_0) + g = (2.16 / 27) + 0.08 = 16\%$

10. **A** $WACC = (w_d)(k_d)(1 - t) + (w_{ce})(k_{ce}) = (0.4)(7.2) + (0.6)(16) = 12.48\%$

11. **A**   An increase in the corporate tax rate will reduce the after-tax cost of debt, causing the WACC to fall. More specifically, since the after-tax cost of debt $= (k_d)(1 - t)$, the term $(1 - t)$ decreases, decreasing the after-tax cost of debt. If the risk-free rate were to increase, the costs of debt and equity would both increase, thus causing the firm's cost of capital to increase.

12. **C** $WACC = (w_d)(k_d)(1 - t) + (w_{ps})(k_{ps}) + (w_{ce})(k_{ce}) = (0.4)(7.5)(1 - 0.4) + (0.05)(11) + (0.55)(15) = 10.6\%$

CAPITAL STRUCTURE AND LEVERAGE

EXAM FOCUS

The focus of this topic review is how a firm's fixed operating costs and the proportion of debt in its capital structure affect its risk and expected earnings per share. You should be able to calculate and interpret the degree of operating leverage, degree of financial leverage, and degree of total leverage. You should also be able to discuss the impact of leverage on a firm's risk, return on equity, and share price.

LOS 49.a: Define and explain leverage, business risk, sales risk, operating risk, and financial risk.

Leverage, in the sense we use it here, refers to the amount of fixed costs a firm has. These fixed costs may be fixed operating expenses, such as building or equipment leases, or fixed financing costs, such as interest payments on debt. Greater leverage leads to greater variability of the firm's after-tax operating earnings and net income. A given change in sales will lead to a greater change in operating earnings when the firm employs operating leverage; a given change in operating earnings will lead to a greater change in net income when the firm employs financial leverage.

Professor's Note: The British refer to leverage as "gearing," which to me is actually more descriptive.

Business risk refers to the risk associated with a firm's operating income and is the result of uncertainty about a firm's revenues and the expenditures necessary to produce those revenues. Business risk is the combination of sales risk and operating risk.

- **Sales risk** is the uncertainty about the firm's sales.
- **Operating risk** refers to the additional uncertainty about operating earnings caused by fixed operating costs. The greater the proportion of fixed costs to variable costs, the greater a firm's operating risk.

Financial risk refers to the additional risk that the firm's common stockholders must bear when a firm uses fixed cost (debt) financing. When a company finances its operations with debt, it takes on fixed expenses in the form of interest payments. The greater the proportion of debt in a firm's capital structure, the greater the firm's financial risk.

LOS 49.b: Calculate and interpret the degree of operating leverage, the degree of financial leverage, and the degree of total leverage.

The **degree of operating leverage** (DOL) is defined as the percentage change in operating income (EBIT) that results from a given percentage change in sales:

$$
DOL = \frac{\text{percentage change in EBIT}}{\text{percentage change in sales}} = \frac{\dfrac{\Delta EBIT}{EBIT}}{\dfrac{\Delta Q}{Q}}
$$

To calculate a firm's DOL for a particular level of unit sales, Q, DOL is:

$$DOL = \frac{Q(P-V)}{Q(P-V)-F}$$

where:
Q = quantity of units sold
P = price per unit
V = variable cost per unit
F = fixed costs

Multiplying we have:

$$DOL = \frac{S-TVC}{S-TVC-F}$$

where:
S = sales
TVC = total variable costs
F = fixed costs

Note that in this form, the denominator is operating earnings (EBIT).

Example: Degree of operating leverage

Consider the costs for the projects presented in Figure 1. Assuming that 100,000 units are produced for each firm, calculate the DOL for Atom Company and Beta Company.

Figure 1: Operating Costs for Atom Company and Beta Company

	Atom Company	*Beta Company*
Price	$4.00	$4.00
Variable costs	$3.00	$2.00
Fixed costs	$40,000	$120,000
Revenue	$400,000	$400,000

Answer:

For Atom Company:

$$DOL(Atom) = \frac{Q(P-V)}{\left[Q(P-V)-F\right]} = \frac{100,000(4-3)}{\left[100,000(4-3)-40,000\right]}$$

$$DOL(Atom) = \frac{100,000}{60,000} = 1.67$$

For Beta Company:

$$DOL(Beta) = \frac{Q(P-V)}{[Q(P-V)-F]} = \frac{100,000(4-2)}{[100,000(4-2)-120,000]}$$

$$DOL(Beta) = \frac{200,000}{80,000} = 2.50$$

The results indicate that if Beta Company has a 10% increase in sales, its EBIT will increase by 2.50 × 10% = 25%, while for Atom Company, the increase in EBIT will be 1.67 × 10% = 16.7%.

It is important to note that the degree of operating leverage for a company depends on the level of sales. For example, if Atom Company sells 300,000 units, the DOL is decreased:

$$DOL(Atom) = \frac{Q(P-V)}{[Q(P-V)-F]} = \frac{300,000(4-3)}{[300,000(4-3)-40,000]} = \frac{300,000}{260,000} = 1.15$$

DOL is highest at low levels of sales and declines at higher levels of sales.

The **degree of financial leverage** (DFL) is interpreted as the ratio of the percentage change in net income (or EPS) to the percentage change in EBIT.

$$DFL = \frac{\text{percentage change in EPS}}{\text{percentage change in EBIT}}$$

For a particular level of operating earnings, DFL is calculated as:

$$DFL = \frac{EBIT}{EBIT - \text{interest}}$$

Professor's Note: The terms "earnings per share" (EPS) and "net income" are used interchangeably in this topic review.

Example: Degree of financial leverage

From the previous example, Atom Company's operating income for selling 100,000 units is $60,000. Assume that Atom Company has annual interest expense of $18,000. If Atom's EBIT increases by 10%, by how much will its earnings per share increase?

Answer:

$$DFL = \frac{EBIT}{EBIT - I} = \frac{\$60,000}{\$60,000 - \$18,000} = 1.43$$

$$\%\Delta EPS = DFL \times \%\Delta EBIT = 1.43 \times 10\% = 14.3\%$$

Hence, earnings per share will increase by 14.3%.

Professor's Note: Look back at the formulas for DOL and DFL and convince yourself that if there are no fixed costs, DOL is equal to one, and that if there are no interest costs, DFL is equal to one. Values of one mean no leverage. No fixed costs, no operating leverage. No interest costs, no financial leverage. This should help tie these formulas to the concepts and help you know when you have the formulas right (or wrong). If you plug in zero for fixed costs, DOL should be one, and if you plug in zero for interest, DFL should be one.

The **degree of total leverage** (DTL) combines the degree of operating leverage and financial leverage. DTL measures the sensitivity of EPS to change in sales. DTL is computed as:

$$DTL = DOL \times DFL$$

$$DTL = \frac{\%\Delta EBIT}{\%\Delta sales} \times \frac{\%\Delta EPS}{\%\Delta EBIT} = \frac{\%\Delta EPS}{\%\Delta sales}$$

$$DTL = \frac{Q(P-V)}{Q(P-V)-F-I}$$

$$DTL = \frac{S-TVC}{S-TVC-F-I}$$

Example: Degree of total leverage

Continuing with our previous example, how much will Atom's EPS increase if Atom increases its sales by 10%?

Answer:

From the previous examples:

$$DOL_{Atom} = 1.67$$

$$DFL_{Atom} = 1.43$$

$$DTL = DOL \times DFL = 1.67 \times 1.43 = 2.39$$

Professor's Note: There is some rounding here. If we use 1.6666 for DOL and 1.42857 for DFL, we obtain the DTL of 2.38.

Note that we also could have calculated the DTL the long way. From the previous example, the current value of Atom's dollar sales is $4 \times 100,000 = \$400,000$.

$$DTL = \frac{S-TVC}{S-TVC-F-I} = \frac{\$400,000-\$300,000}{\$400,000-\$300,000-\$40,000-\$18,000} = 2.38$$

$$\%\Delta EPS = DTL \times \%\Delta sales = 2.38 \times 10\% = 23.8\%$$

EPS will increase by 23.8%.

LOS 49.c: Characterize the operating leverage, financial leverage, and total leverage of a company given a description of it.

Operating leverage is the result of a greater proportion of fixed costs compared to variable costs in a firm's capital structure. A firm with high operating leverage will have EBIT that is highly sensitive to changes in revenues and, as a result, has high operating risk. A given percentage change in sales leads to a greater percentage change in EBIT. However, higher operating risk also means a greater opportunity for reward as the firm can earn larger profits as the number of units sold increases. A firm with low operating leverage will have EBIT that is less sensitive to the number of units sold.

Software and pharmaceutical companies (e.g., Microsoft, Pfizer) typically have high operating leverage. These firms typically spend a large amount producing and bringing a new product to market, which results in high fixed costs, but the variable costs to distribute the product are usually quite small. Retailers (e.g., Target, Wal-Mart) tend to have a variable cost structure, meaning their operating leverage is low.

Financial leverage refers to the use of fixed cost financing, such as debt or preferred stock. Financial leverage magnifies the variability of earnings per share compared to the variability of operating earnings (EBIT). Firms with a high degree of financial leverage will experience large changes in EPS for a given change in EBIT. A firm without debt financing (and a constant tax rate) will have equal changes in operating earnings and EPS (in the absence of non-operating income and losses).

Industrial firms that have higher percentage of tangible assets, such as land and equipment, tend to have higher amounts of financial leverage. Debt financing is relatively more attractive for these firms because the fixed assets provide a measure of security that the debt will be repaid. Technology and pharmaceutical companies, which tend to have fewer fixed assets, tend to use less debt and have less financial leverage.

Total leverage, the combination of operating and financial leverage, measures the sensitivity of EPS to changes in sales. If a firm has operating leverage of 3 and financial leverage of 2, its total leverage is 6. If a firm has high total leverage, a small change in sales will produce a large change in EPS. The key is that the combination of fixed operating costs and fixed financing costs magnifies the volatility of earnings for the owners of a business.

LOS 49.d: Calculate the breakeven quantity of sales and determine the company's net income at various sales levels.

The level of sales that a firm must generate to cover all of its fixed and variable costs is called the breakeven point. The **breakeven quantity of sales** is the quantity where sales revenues equal operating costs. The important point to understand here is that we can calculate breakeven quantity by simply determining how many units must be sold to just cover fixed costs.

For each unit sold, P – V (the difference between price and variable cost per unit) is available to help cover fixed costs. At F / (P – V) units, fixed costs are just covered, and the firm will break even.

$$Q_{BE} = \frac{\text{fixed costs}}{\text{price} - \text{variable cost per unit}}$$

Example: Breakeven quantity

Consider the prices and costs for Atom Company and Beta Company shown in Figure 2. Compute and illustrate the breakeven point for each company.

Figure 2: Operating Costs for Atom Company and Beta Company

	Atom Company	*Beta Company*
Price	$4.00	$4.00
Variable costs	$3.00	$2.00
Fixed costs	$40,000	$120,000

Study Session 11

Cross-Reference to CFA Institute Assigned Reading #49 – Aggarwal et al.

Answer:

For Atom Company, the breakeven quantity is:

$$Q_{BE}(Atom) = \frac{\$40,000}{\$4.00 - \$3.00} = 40,000 \text{ units}$$

Similarly for Beta Company, the breakeven quantity is:

$$Q_{BE}(Beta) = \frac{\$120,000}{\$4.00 - \$2.00} = 60,000 \text{ units}$$

The breakeven quantity and the relationship between sales revenue, total operating cost, operating profit, and operating loss are illustrated in Figures 3 and 4.

Figure 3: Breakeven Analysis for Atom Company

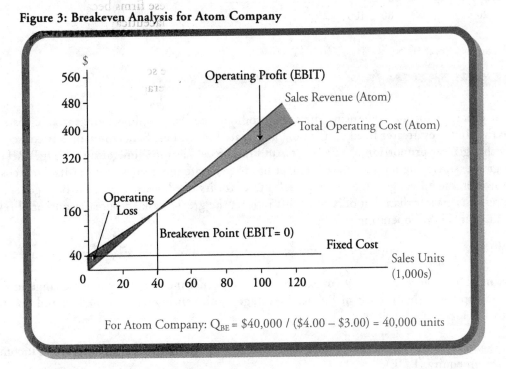

For Atom Company: $Q_{BE} = \$40,000 / (\$4.00 - \$3.00) = 40,000$ units

Figure 4: Breakeven Analysis for Beta Company

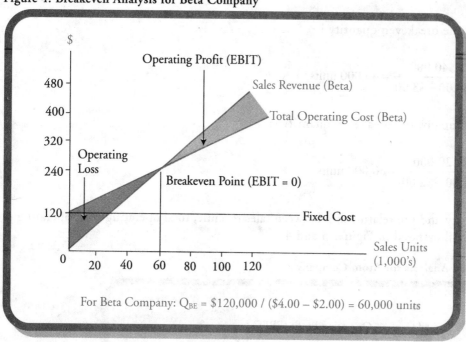

For Beta Company: $Q_{BE} = \$120,000 / (\$4.00 - \$2.00) = 60,000$ units

There may be different processes for manufacturing the same product, one that employs more variable costs (more labor) and one that involves greater fixed costs (a big automated machine). Beta company has chosen an operating structure with a greater proportion of fixed costs, and therefore, has more operating leverage. Beta Company's choice of greater operating leverage means that it has to generate more sales to cover its fixed costs and make a profit. However, once Beta generates enough sales to cover its fixed costs, the profit Beta generates beyond its breakeven point is greater than that of Atom. This reflects the greater risk and greater potential reward that Beta has as a result of its higher operating leverage.

LOS 49.e: Describe the effect of financial leverage on a company's net income and return on equity.

Earlier we defined financial leverage as the change in earnings per share (net income) for a given change in EBIT (operating income), and explained that the use of financial leverage significantly increases the risk and potential reward to common stockholders.

Let's look at a pair of examples involving Beta Company to quantify how financial leverage affects net income and shareholders' return on equity (ROE).

Example 1: Beta Company financed with 100% equity

Assume that the Beta Company has $500,000 in assets that are financed with 100% equity. Beta is expected to sell 100,000 units, resulting in operating income of [100,000 ($4 – $2)] – $120,000= $80,000. Calculate Beta's net income and return on equity if its EBIT increases or decreases by 10%. Beta's tax rate is 40%.

Answer:

Figure 5: Beta's Return on Equity with 100% Equity Financing

	EBIT Less 10%	Expected EBIT	EBIT Plus 10%
EBIT	$72,000	$80,000	$88,000
Interest expense	0	0	0
Income before taxes	$72,000	$80,000	$88,000
Taxes	28,800	32,000	35,200
Net income	$43,200	$48,000	$52,800
Shareholders' equity	$500,000	$500,000	$500,000
Return on equity (ROE)	8.64%	9.60%	10.56%

Example 2: Beta Company financed with 50% equity and 50% debt

Assume that Beta Company has $500,000 in assets that are financed with 50% equity and 50% debt. The interest rate on the debt is 6%. Beta is expected to sell 100,000 units, resulting in operating income of [100,000 ($4 – $2)] – $120,000 = $80,000. Calculate Beta's net income and return on equity if its EBIT increases or decreases by 10%. Beta's tax rate is 40%.

Answer:

Figure 6: Beta's Return on Equity with 50% Equity Financing

	EBIT Less 10%	Expected EBIT	EBIT Plus 10%
EBIT	$72,000	$80,000	$88,000
Interest expense (at 6%)	15,000	15,000	15,000
Income before taxes	$57,000	$65,000	$73,000
Taxes	22,800	26,000	29,200
Net income	$34,200	$39,000	$43,800
Shareholders' equity	$250,000	$250,000	$250,000
Return on equity (ROE)	13.68%	15.60%	17.52%

Comparing Figures 5 and 6, the interest expense associated with using debt represents a fixed cost that reduces net income. However, the lower net income value is spread over a smaller base of shareholders' equity, serving to magnify the ROE. In all three of the scenarios shown, ROE is higher using leverage than it is without leverage.

Further analyzing the differences between Figures 5 and 6, we can see that the use of financial leverage not only increases the *level* of ROE, it also increases the *rate of change* for ROE. In the unleveraged scenario, ROE varies directly with the change in EBIT. For an increase in EBIT of 10%, the ROE increases from 9.60% to 10.56%, for a rate of change of 10%. In the leveraged scenario, ROE is more volatile. For an increase in EBIT of 10%, the ROE increases from 15.60% to 17.52%, for a rate of change of 12.3%.

Bottom line: The use of financial leverage increases the risk of default, but also increases the potential return for equity holders.

Professor's Note: Note the relationship between this LOS and the DuPont formula used to analyze ROE. One of the components of the DuPont formula is the equity multiplier (assets/equity), which captures the effect of financial leverage on ROE.

LOS 49.f: Compare and contrast the risks of creditors and owners.

Creditors. In exchange for loaning money to a business, creditors receive interest and principal payments that must be made regardless of the business's profitability. If the business defaults on its debt payments, it can lead to bankruptcy. If bankruptcy occurs, creditors have a priority claim on the assets of the business, which gives them a higher level of safety compared to owners. Creditors have less risk than owners, but they also have less potential for return. Even if the business is extremely profitable, debt holders will not receive more than the interest and principal payments they have been promised.

Owners. The equity holders of a business have a claim to what is left over after all expenses, including scheduled principal and interest payments on debt, have been paid. In the event of bankruptcy, all creditors must be paid in full before equity holders are paid anything (strictly speaking). In many cases, the value of the equity stake in the business is reduced to zero as a result of bankruptcy. In exchange for this risk, equity holders make the business decisions, including the hiring or firing of managers and dividend payouts.

Professor's Note: Because decisions by equity owners can affect the risk of bondholders, bond covenants place restrictions on those actions of management that could significantly increase the risk of debt after the debt has been issued. This is covered in more detail in the study sessions on debt.

KEY CONCEPTS

1. Leverage increases the risk and potential return of a firm's earnings and cash flows.
2. Operating leverage results from fixed operating costs, while financial leverage results from the use of debt financing and its associated fixed costs.
3. Business risk is reflected in the variability of EBIT and results from a combination of sales risk and operating risk.
4. Financial risk is reflected in the greater variability of EPS compared to the variability of operating earnings (EBIT) as a result of using debt in the firm's capital structure.
5. The degree of operating leverage (DOL) is calculated as $\dfrac{Q(P-V)}{Q(P-V)-F}$ and is interpreted as $\dfrac{\%\Delta EBIT}{\%\Delta sales}$.
6. The degree of financial leverage (DFL) is calculated as $\dfrac{EBIT}{EBIT-I}$ and is interpreted as $\dfrac{\%\Delta EPS}{\%\Delta EBIT}$.
7. The degree of total leverage (DTL) is the combination of operating and financial leverage and is calculated as $DOL \times DFL$ and interpreted as $\dfrac{\%\Delta EPS}{\%\Delta sales}$.
8. The breakeven point is the number of units produced and sold where a company's fixed costs are just covered: $Q_{BE} = \dfrac{F}{P-V}$.
9. The use of debt in a company's capital structure reduces net income due to the added interest expense, but can increase equity owners' ROE.
10. A creditor of a firm has priority claim on the assets of the business in the event of bankruptcy, but the creditor's potential reward is limited to the promised interest and principal payments on the firm's debt.
11. A firm's owners have a residual claim on the firm's assets and earnings (they receive what is left after all expenses, including debt service, have been paid) and bear greater risk, but also have greater potential upside returns than creditors.

Study Session 11

Cross-Reference to CFA Institute Assigned Reading #49 – Aggarwal et al.

CONCEPT CHECKERS: CAPITAL STRUCTURE AND LEVERAGE

1. Business risk is the combination of:
    A. operating risk and financial risk.
    B. sales risk and financial risk.
    C. sales risk and liquidity risk.
    D. operating risk and sales risk.

2. Which of the following choices is a key determinant of operating leverage?
    A. The firm's beta.
    B. Level and cost of debt.
    C. The competitive nature of the business.
    D. The trade-off between fixed and variable costs.

3. Which of the following statements about capital structure and leverage is **TRUE**?
    A. Financial leverage is directly related to operating leverage.
    B. Increasing the corporate tax rate will not affect capital structure decisions.
    C. A firm with low operating leverage has a small proportion of its total costs in fixed costs.
    D. A firm with high business risk is more likely to increase its use of financial leverage than a firm with low business risk.

4. Jayco, Inc. sells blue ink for $4.00 a bottle. The ink's variable cost per bottle is $2.00. Ink has fixed cost of $10,000. What is Jayco's breakeven point, in units?
    A. 2,500.
    B. 5,000.
    C. 6,000.
    D. 7,500.

5. Jayco, Inc. has a division that makes red ink for the accounting industry. The unit has fixed costs of $10,000 per month and is expected to sell 40,000 bottles of ink per month. If the variable cost per bottle is $2.00, what price must the division charge in order to break even?
    A. $2.25.
    B. $2.50.
    C. $2.75.
    D. $3.25.

Use the following data to answer Questions 6 and 7.

If Jayco's sales increase by 10%, Jayco's EBIT increases by 15%. If Jayco's EBIT increases by 10%, Jayco's EPS increases by 12%.

6. Jayco's degree of operating leverage (DOL) and degree of financial leverage (DFL) are *closest* to:

DOL	DFL
A. 1.8	1.2
B. 1.5	1.2
C. 1.8	1.4
D. 1.5	1.4

7. Jayco's degree of total leverage (DTL) is *closest* to:
    A. 1.2.
    B. 1.7.
    C. 1.8.
    D. 2.7.

Use the following data to answer Questions 8 and 9.

Jayco, Inc. sells 10,000 units at a price of $5 per unit. Jayco's fixed costs are $8,000, interest expense is $2,000, variable costs are $3 per unit, and EBIT is $12,000.

8. Jayco's degree of operating leverage (DOL) and degree of financial leverage (DFL) are *closest* to:

	DOL	DFL
A.	1.40	1.56
B.	1.40	1.20
C.	1.67	1.20
D.	1.67	1.56

9. Jayco's degree of total leverage (DTL) is *closest* to:
    A. 1.25.
    B. 1.50.
    C. 1.75.
    D. 2.00.

10. Vischer Concrete has $1.2 million in assets that are currently financed with 100% equity. Vischer's EBIT is $300,000 and its tax rate is 30%. If Vischer changes its capital structure (recapitalizes) to include 40% debt, what is Vischer's ROE before and after the change? Assume that the interest rate on debt is 5%.

	ROE at 100% equity	ROE at 60% equity
A.	17.5%	37.5%
B.	17.5%	26.8%
C.	25.0%	26.8%
D.	25.0%	37.5%

11. Which of the following statements regarding the risks and potential rewards for owners and creditors of a business is **TRUE**?
    A. The potential reward for creditors is virtually unlimited assuming the business is profitable.
    B. In the event of bankruptcy, creditors have a claim to the assets of the firm that must be met before equity owners receive anything.
    C. Owners have less risk than creditors.
    D. In exchange for the risk they bear, creditors have the authority to make decisions regarding how the business is run.

ANSWERS – CONCEPT CHECKERS: CAPITAL STRUCTURE AND LEVERAGE

1. **D** Business risk refers to the risk associated with a firm's operating income and is the result of uncertainty about a firm's revenues and the expenditures necessary to produce those revenues. Business risk is the combination of sales risk (the uncertainty associated with the price and quantity of goods and services sold) and operating risk (the leverage created by the use of fixed costs in the firm's operations).

2. **D** The extent to which costs are fixed determines operating leverage.

3. **C** Operating leverage is separate from financial leverage; increasing the tax rate would make the after-tax cost of debt cheaper; a firm that already has high operating risk will be less likely to take on more financial risk as the relationship is multiplicative.

4. **B** $Q_{BE} = \dfrac{F}{P-V} = \dfrac{10,000}{4-2} = 5,000$

5. **A** We can rearrange the formula $Q_{BE} = \dfrac{F}{P-V}$ as $P = \dfrac{F}{Q} + V$, or $P = \dfrac{10,000}{40,000} + 2 = \$2.25$

6. **B** $DOL = \dfrac{\text{increase in EBIT}}{\text{increase in sales}} = \dfrac{0.15}{0.10} = 1.5$; $DOL = \dfrac{\text{increase in EPS}}{\text{increase in EBIT}} = \dfrac{0.12}{0.10} = 1.2$

7. **C** $DTL = DOL \times DFL = 1.2 \times 1.5 = 1.8$

8. **C** $DOL = \dfrac{Q(P-V)}{\left[Q(P-V)-F\right]} = \dfrac{10,000(5-3)}{\left[10,000(5-3)-8,000\right]} = 1.67$

   $DFL = \dfrac{EBIT}{EBIT-I} = \dfrac{12,000}{12,000-2,000} = 1.2$

9. **D** $DTL = \dfrac{Q(P-V)}{\left[Q(P-V)-F-I\right]} = \dfrac{10,000(5-3)}{\left[10,000(5-3)-8,000-2,000\right]} = 2$

   or since we calculated the components in Question 8, $DTL = DOL \times DFL = 1.67 \times 1.2 = 2.0$

10. **B** With 100% equity:

EBIT	$300,000
Interest expense	0
Income before taxes	$300,000
Taxes at 30%	90,000
Net income	$210,000
Shareholder's equity	$1,200,000
ROE = NI/Equity	17.5%

With 60% equity:

EBIT	$300,000
Interest expense ($480,000 at 5%)	24,000
Income before taxes	$276,000
Taxes at 30%	82,800
Net income	$193,200
Shareholders' equity	$720,000
ROE = NI/Equity	26.8%

11. **B** In the event of bankruptcy, owners do not have a claim to corporate assets until creditors have been paid in full. Creditors have a less risky position since they are first in line to receive assets in the event of bankruptcy, but their potential reward is limited to the promised interest and principal payments on the debt.

DIVIDENDS AND DIVIDEND POLICY

EXAM FOCUS

Besides the basics of dividend distribution and stock splits, the important topic here is share repurchases as an alternative to cash dividends. In recent years, firms have announced plans to repurchase record numbers of shares, making this an important and timely topic. Beyond this, make sure you can do the calculations indicated by the three LOS that begin with the word *calculate*. A basic understanding of the factors that affect a firm's payout policy, and of the signals investors may get from dividend changes, should be sufficient for any Level 1 questions.

LOS 50.a: Review cash dividends, stock dividends, stock splits, and reverse stock splits and calculate and discuss their impact on a shareholder.

Cash dividends, as the name implies, are payments made to shareholders in cash. They come in three forms:

- **Regular dividends** occur when a company pays out a portion of profits on a consistent schedule (e.g., quarterly). A long-term record of stable or increasing dividends is widely viewed by investors as a sign of a company's financial stability.
- **Special dividends** are used when the company does not have a regular dividend schedule or if favorable circumstances allow the firm to make a one-time cash payment to shareholders. Many cyclical firms (e.g., automakers) will use a special dividend to share profits with shareholders when times are good, but maintain the flexibility to conserve cash when profits are down. Other names for special dividends include "extra dividends" and "irregular dividends."
- **Liquidating dividends** occur when a company goes out of business and distributes the proceeds to shareholders. For tax purposes, a liquidating dividend is treated as a return of capital and amounts over the investor's tax basis are taxed as capital gains.

No matter which form cash dividends take, their net effect is to transfer cash from the company to its shareholders. The payment of a cash dividend reduces a company's assets and the market value of its equity. This means that immediately after a dividend is paid, the price of the stock should drop by the amount of the dividend. For example, if a company's stock price is $25 per share and the company pays $1 per share as a dividend, the price of the stock should immediately drop to $24 per share to account for the lower asset and equity values of the firm.

Stock dividends are dividends paid out in new shares of stock rather than cash. In this case, there will be more shares outstanding, but each one will be worth less. Stock dividends are commonly expressed as a percentage. A 20% stock dividend means every shareholder gets 20% more stock.

Example: Stock dividend

Dwight Craver owns 100 shares of Carson Construction Company at a current price of $30 per share. Carson has 1,000,000 shares of stock outstanding, and its earnings per share (EPS) for the last year were $1.50. Carson declares a 20% stock dividend to all shareholders of record as of June 30.

What is the effect of the stock dividend on the market price of the stock, and what is the impact of the dividend on Craver's ownership position in the company?

Answer:

Figure 1: Impact of 20% Stock Dividend on Shareholders

	Before Stock Dividend	After Stock Dividend
Shares outstanding	1,000,000	1,000,000 × 1.20 = 1,200,000
Earnings per share	$1.50	$1.50 / 1.20 = $1.25
Stock price	$30.00	$30.00 / 1.20 = $25.00
Total market value	1,000,000 × $30 = $30,000,000	1,200,000 × $25 = $30,000,000
Shares owned	100	100 × 1.20 = 120
Ownership value	100 × $30 = $3,000	120 × $25 = $3,000
Ownership stake	100 / 1,000,000 = 0.01%	120 / 1,200,000 = 0.01%

The effect of the stock dividend is to increase the number of shares outstanding by 20%. However, since company earnings stay the same, EPS decline and the price of the firm's stock drops from $30 to $25. Craver's receipt of more shares is exactly offset by the drop in stock price, and his wealth and ownership position in the company are unchanged.

Stock splits divide each existing share into multiple shares, thus creating more shares. There are now more shares, but the price of each share will drop correspondingly to the number of shares created, so there is no change in the owner's wealth. Splits are expressed as a ratio. In a 3-for-1 stock split, each old share is split into three new shares. Stock splits are more common today than stock dividends.

Example: Stock split

Carson Construction Company declares a 3-for-2 stock split. The current stock price is $30, earnings for last year were $1.50, dividends were $0.60 per share, and there are 1 million shares outstanding. What is the impact on Carson's shares outstanding, stock price, EPS, dividends per share, dividend yield, P/E, and market value?

Answer:

Figure 2: Impact of a 3-for-2 Stock Split on Shareholders

	Before Stock Split	After Stock Split
Shares outstanding	1,000,000	1,000,000 × (3/2) = 1,500,000
Stock price	$30.00	$30.00 / (3/2) = $20.00
Earnings per share	$1.50	$1.50 / (3/2) = $1.00
Dividends per share	$0.60	$0.60 / (3/2) = $0.40
Dividend yield	$0.60 / $30.00 = 2.0%	$0.40 / $20.00 = 2.0%
P/E ratio	$30.00 / $1.50 = 20	$20.00 / $1.00 = 20
Total market value	1,000,000 × $30 = $30,000,000	1,500,000 × $20 = $30,000,000

The number of shares outstanding increases, but the stock price, EPS, and dividends per share decrease by a proportional amount. The dividend yield, P/E ratio, and total market value of the firm remain the same.

The bottom line for stock splits and stock dividends is that they increase the total number of shares outstanding, but because the stock price and earnings per share are adjusted proportionally, a shareholder's total wealth is unchanged.

Some firms use stock splits and stock dividends to keep stock prices within a perceived optimal trading range of $20 to $80 per share. What does academic research have to say about this?

- Stock prices tend to rise after a split or stock dividend.
- Price increases appear to be because stock splits are taken as a positive signal from management about future earnings.
- If a report of good earnings does not follow a stock split, prices tend to revert to their original (split-adjusted) levels.
- Stock splits and dividends tend to reduce liquidity due to higher percentage brokerage fees on lower-priced stocks.

The conclusion is that stock splits and stock dividends just create more shares but don't increase shareholder value.

Reverse stock splits are the opposite of stock splits. After a reverse split there are fewer shares outstanding but higher stock prices. Since these factors offset one another, shareholder wealth is unchanged. The logic behind a reverse stock split is that the perceived optimal stock price range is $20 to $80 per share, and most investors consider a stock with a price less than $5 per share less than investment grade. A company in financial distress whose stock has fallen dramatically may declare a reverse stock split to increase the stock price.

LOS 50.f: Review dividend payment chronology including declaration, holder-of-record, ex-dividend, and payment dates and indicate when the share price will most likely reflect the dividend.

Professor's Note: This LOS has been taken out of order because some of the terms introduced here (e.g., ex-dividend) will be used in our discussion going forward.

An example of a typical dividend payment schedule is shown in Figure 3.

Figure 3: Dividend Payment Chronology

| Declaration date | Ex-dividend date | Holder-of-record date | Payment date |
| August 25 | September 15 | September 17 | September 30 |

- **Declaration date**. The date the board of directors approves payment of the dividend.
- **Ex-dividend date**. The first day a share of stock trades without the dividend. The ex-dividend date is also the cut-off date for receiving the dividend and occurs two business days before the holder-of-record date. If you buy the share on or after the ex-dividend date, you will not receive the dividend.

- **Holder-of-record date.** The date on which the shareholders of record are designated to receive the dividend.
- **Payment date.** The date the dividend checks are mailed out, or when the payment is electronically transferred to shareholder accounts.

Stocks are traded ex-dividend on and after the ex-dividend date, so stock prices should fall by the amount of the dividend on the ex-dividend date. Because of taxes, however, the drop in price may be closer to the after-tax value of dividends.

Professor's Note: The reason that the holder-of-record date is two days after the ex-dividend date has to with the fact that the settlement date for stocks is three days after the trade date (t + 3). If an investor buys a stock the day before the ex-dividend date, the trade will settle three days later on the holder-of-record date, and the investor will receive the dividend.

LOS 50.b: Compare the impact on shareholder wealth of a share repurchase and a cash dividend of equal amount.

A **share repurchase** is a transaction in which a company buys back shares of its own common stock. Since shares are bought using a company's own cash, a share repurchase can be considered an alternative to a cash dividend.

Example: Impact of share repurchase and cash dividend of equal amounts

Spencer Pharmaceuticals Inc. (SPI) has 20,000,000 shares outstanding with a current market value of $50 per share. SPI made $100 million in profits for the recent quarter, and since only 70% of these profits will be reinvested back into the company, SPI's Board of Directors is considering two alternatives for distributing the remaining 30% to shareholders:

- Pay a cash dividend of $30,000,000 / 20,000,000 shares = $1.50 per share.
- Repurchase $30,000,000 worth of common stock.

Assume that dividends are received when the shares go ex-dividend, the stock can be repurchased at the market price of $50 per share, and there are no differences in tax treatment between the two alternatives. How would the wealth of an SPI shareholder be affected by the board's decision on the method of distribution?

Answer:

(1) Cash dividend

After the shares go ex-dividend, a shareholder of a single share would have $1.50 in cash and a share worth $50 − $1.50 = $48.50.

The ex-dividend value of $48.50 can also be calculated as the market value of equity after the distribution of the $30 million, divided by the number of shares outstanding after the dividend payment.

$$\frac{(20,000,000)(\$50) - \$30,000,000}{20,000,000} = \$48.50$$

Total wealth from the ownership of one share = $48.50 + $1.50 = $50

(2) Share repurchase

With $30,000,000, SPI could repurchase $30,000,000 / $50 = 600,000 shares of common stock. The share price after the repurchase is calculated as the market value of equity after the $30,000,000 repurchase divided by the shares outstanding after the repurchase:

$$\frac{(20,000,000)(\$50) - \$30,000,000}{20,000,000 - 600,000} = \frac{\$970,000,000}{19,400,000} = \$50$$

Total wealth from the ownership of one share = $50

Assuming the tax treatment of the two alternatives is the same, a share repurchase has the same impact on shareholder wealth as a cash dividend payment of an equal amount.

LOS 50.c: Calculate the earnings per share effect of a share repurchase when the repurchase is made with borrowed funds and the company's after-tax cost of debt is greater (less) than its earnings yield.

In our previous example, we assumed that the company used cash to repurchase its stock. What if the company borrows funds to buy back the stock?

Example: Share repurchase when the after-tax cost of debt is less than the earnings yield

Spencer Pharmaceuticals, Inc. (SPI) plans to borrow $30 million that it will use to repurchase shares. SPI's Chief Financial Officer has compiled the following information:

- Share price at the time of buyback = $50.
- Shares outstanding before buyback = 20,600,000.
- EPS before buyback = $5.00.
- Earnings yield = $5.00 / $50 = 10%.
- After-tax cost of borrowing = 8%.
- Planned buyback = 600,000 shares.

Calculate the EPS after the buyback.

Answer:

total earnings = $5.00 × 20,600,000 = $103,000,000

$$\text{EPS after buyback} = \frac{\text{total earnings} - \text{after-tax cost of funds}}{\text{shares outstanding after buyback}}$$

$$= \frac{\$103,000,000 - (600,000 \text{ shares} \times \$50 \times 0.08)}{(20,600,000 - 600,000) \text{ shares}}$$

$$= \frac{\$103,000,000 - \$2,400,000}{20,000,000 \text{ shares}}$$

$$= \frac{\$100,600,000}{20,000,000 \text{ shares}}$$

$$= \$5.03$$

Since the after-tax cost of borrowing of 8% is less than the 10% earnings yield (E/P) of the shares, the share repurchase will increase the company's EPS.

Example: Share repurchase with borrowed funds where after-tax cost of debt exceeds the earnings yield

Spencer Pharmaceuticals, Inc. (SPI) plans to borrow $30 million that it will use to repurchase shares; however, creditors perceive the company to be a significant credit risk, and the after-tax cost of borrowing has jumped to 15%. Using the other information from the previous example, calculate the EPS after the buyback.

Answer:

$$\text{EPS after buyback} = \frac{\text{total earnings} - \text{after-tax cost of funds}}{\text{shares outstanding after buyback}}$$

$$= \frac{\$103,000,000 - (600,000 \text{ shares} \times \$50 \times 0.15)}{(20,600,000 - 600,000) \text{ shares}}$$

$$= \frac{\$103,000,000 - \$4,500,000}{20,000,000 \text{ shares}}$$

$$= \frac{\$98,500,000}{20,000,000 \text{ shares}}$$

$$= \$4.93$$

Since the after-tax cost of borrowing of 15% exceeds the earnings yield of 10%, the added interest paid reduces earnings, and the EPS after the buyback is less than the original $5.00.

The conclusion is that a share repurchase using borrowed funds will increase EPS if the after-tax cost of debt used to buy back shares is less than the earnings yield of the shares before the repurchase. It will decrease EPS if the cost of debt is greater than the earnings yield, and it will not change EPS if the two are equal.

LOS 50.d: Calculate the book value effect of a share repurchase when the market value of a share is greater (less) than book value per share.

Share repurchases may also have an impact on the book value of a share of stock.

Example: Effect of a share repurchase on book value per share

The share prices of Blue Inc. and Red Company are both $25 per share, and each company has 20 million shares outstanding. Both companies have announced a $10 million stock buyback. Blue Inc. has a book value of $300 million, while Red Company has a book value of $700 million.

Calculate the book value per share (BVPS) of each company after the share repurchase.

Answer:

Share buyback for both companies = $10 million / $25 per share = 400,000 shares.

Remaining shares for both companies = 20 million – 400,000 = 19.6 million.

Blue Inc.:

Blue Inc.'s current BVPS = $300 million / 20 million = $15.
The market price per share of $25 is greater than the BVPS of $15.

> Book value after repurchase: $300 million – $10 million = $290 million
> BVPS = $290 million / 19.6 million = $14.80
> BVPS decreased by $0.20.

Red Company:

Red Company's current BVPS = $700 million / 20 million = $35.
The market price per share of $25 is less than the BVPS of $35.

> Book value after repurchase: $700 million – $10 million = $690 million
> BVPS = $690 million / 19.6 million = $35.20
> BVPS increased by $0.20.

The conclusion is that BVPS will decrease if the share price is greater than the original BVPS and increase if the share price is less than the original BVPS.

LOS 50.e: Compare and contrast share repurchase methods.

Three repurchase methods:

1. **Buy in the open market.** Companies may repurchase stock in the open market at the prevailing market price. A share repurchase is authorized by the board of directors for a certain number of shares. Buying in the open market gives the company the flexibility to choose the timing of the transaction.

2. **Buy a fixed number of shares at a fixed price.** A company may repurchase stock by making a *tender offer* to repurchase a specific number of shares at a price that is usually at a premium to the current market price. Shareholders may tender their shares according to the terms of the offer. If shareholders try to tender more shares than the total repurchase, the company will typically buy back a pro rata amount from each shareholder.

3. **Repurchase by direct negotiation.** Companies may negotiate directly with a large shareholder to buy back a block of shares, usually at a premium to the market price. A company may engage in direct negotiation in order to keep a large block of shares from coming into the market and reducing the stock price, or to repurchase shares from a potential acquirer after an unsuccessful takeover attempt. If the firm pays more than market value for the shares, the result is an increase in wealth for the seller and an equal decrease in wealth for remaining firm shareholders.

LOS 50.g: Summarize the factors affecting dividend payout policy.

A company's dividend payout policy is the approach a company follows in determining the amount and timing of dividend payments to shareholders. Six primary factors affect a company's dividend payout policy:

Signaling effect. Unexpected changes in a company's dividend policy are often viewed by investors as a signal from management about projections of the firm's future performance. In other words, stockholders perceive changes in dividend policy as conveying important information about the firm.

Taxation of dividends. Investors are concerned about after-tax returns. Investment income is taxed by most countries; however, the ways that dividends are taxed vary widely from country to country. The method and amount of tax applied to a dividend payment can have a significant impact on a firm's dividend policy.

Clientele effect. This refers to the varying preferences for dividends of different groups of investors, such as individuals, institutions, and corporations. The dividend clientele effect states that different groups desire different levels of dividends. Rationales for the existence of the clientele effect include:

- *Tax considerations.* High-tax-bracket investors (like some individuals) prefer low dividend payouts, and low-tax-bracket investors (like corporations and pension funds) prefer high dividend payouts.
- *Requirements of institutional investors.* Some institutional investors will invest only in companies that pay a dividend or have a dividend yield above some target threshold. Examples are dividend-focused mutual funds and some trusts that are required hold dividend-paying stocks.
- *Individual investor preference.* Some investors prefer to buy stocks so they can spend the dividends while preserving the principal.

Restrictions on dividend payments. Companies may be restricted from paying dividends either by legal requirements or by implicit restrictions caused by cash needs of the business. Common restrictions on dividend payments include:

- *The impairment of capital rule.* A legal requirement in some countries mandates that dividends paid cannot be in excess of retained earnings.
- *Debt covenants.* These are designed to protect bondholders and dictate things a company must or must not do. Many covenants require a firm to meet or exceed a certain target for liquidity ratios (e.g., current ratio) and coverage ratios (e.g., interest coverage ratio) before they can pay a dividend.
- *Cash flow.* A company may pay a dividend in excess of earnings for a short period of time, but most companies will not pay a dividend in excess of their cash from operations (CFO) unless the company is going out of business.
- *Industry life cycle.* A firm early in its life will not typically pay a dividend because the firm would prefer to reinvest profits back into the company to facilitate growth.

Flotation costs on new issues vs. cost of retained earnings. When a company issues new shares of common stock, a *flotation cost* of 3% to 7% is taken from the amount of capital raised to pay for investment bankers and other costs associated with issuing the new stock. Since retained earnings have no such fee, the cost of new equity capital is always higher than the cost of retained earnings. A company that has a sufficient amount of positive net present value (NPV) projects would prefer to fund those projects using retained earnings rather than paying a dividend and issuing new shares. Note also that flotation costs make it unprofitable for a company to fund its dividend payments by issuing new shares of stock.

Shareholder preference for current income vs. capital gains. A lower tax rate for dividends compared to capital gains does not necessarily mean companies will raise their dividend payouts. Investors may not prefer a higher dividend, even if the tax rate on dividends is more favorable, for multiple reasons:

- Taxes on dividends are paid when the dividend is received, while capital gains taxes are paid only when shares are sold.
- The cost basis of shares may receive a step-up in valuation at the shareholder's death. This means that taxes on capital gains may not have to be paid at all.
- Tax-exempt institutions such as pension funds and endowments will be indifferent between dividends or capital gains.

LOS 50.h: Calculate the effective tax rate on a dollar of corporate earnings distributed as a dividend using the double-taxation, split-rate, and tax imputation systems.

Dividends paid in the United States are taxed according to what is called a **double-taxation** system. Earnings are taxed at the corporate level regardless of whether they are distributed as dividends, and dividends are taxed again at the shareholder level. In 2003, new tax legislation was passed in the U.S. that reduced the maximum tax rate on dividends at the individual shareholder level from 39.6% to 15%.

Since a dollar of earnings distributed as dividends is the first taxed at the corporate level, with the after-corporate-tax amount taxed at the individual level, we can calculate the total effective tax rate as:

corporate tax rate + (1 – corporate tax rate)(individual tax rate) = effective tax rate

Example: Effective tax rate under a double taxation system

A U.S. company's annual earnings are $300, and the corporate tax rate is 35%. Assume that the company pays out 100% of its earnings as dividends. Calculate the effective tax rate on a dollar of corporate earnings paid out as dividends under the 2003 U.S. tax laws.

Answer:

0.35 + (1 – 0.35)(0.15) = 0.4475 or 44.75%.

A **split-rate** corporate tax system taxes earnings distributed as dividends at a lower rate than retained earnings. The effect is to offset the higher tax rate applied to dividends at the individual level. Germany has a split-rate system. The calculation of the effective tax rate on a euro of corporate income distributed as dividends is based on the corporate tax rate for distributed income.

Example: Effective tax rate under a split-rate system

A German company's annual pretax earnings are €300. The corporate tax rate on retained earnings is 35%, and the corporate tax rate that applies to earnings paid out as dividends is 20%. Assuming that the company pays out 50% of its earnings as dividends and the individual tax rate that applies to dividends is 35%, calculate the effective tax rate on one euro of corporate earnings paid out as a dividend.

Answer:

effective tax rate on income distributed as dividends = 20% + [(1 – 20%) × 35%] = 48%

Under a split-rate tax system, shareholders in a low individual bracket would prefer a higher dividend payout since distributed income is taxed at a lower rate. However, shareholders in a high individual bracket would prefer a lower dividend payout since the tax rate on capital gains would be more favorable in their situation.

Under an **imputation tax system**, taxes are paid at the corporate level but are attributed to the shareholder, so that *all taxes are effectively paid at the shareholder rate*. Shareholders deduct their portion of the taxes paid by the corporation from their tax return. If the shareholder tax bracket is lower than the company rate, the shareholder would receive a tax credit equal to the difference between the two rates. If the shareholder tax bracket is higher than the company rate, the shareholder pays the difference between the two rates.

Example: Effective tax rate under an imputation system

Phil Cornelius and Ian Todd both own 100 shares of stock in a British corporation that makes £1.00 per share in net income. The corporation pays out all of its income as dividends. Cornelius is in the 20% individual tax bracket, while Todd is in the 40% individual tax bracket. The tax rate applicable to the corporation is 30%. Calculate the effective tax rate on the dividend for each shareholder.

Answer:

Figure 4: Effective Tax Rate Under an Imputation System

	Cornelius: 20% Rate	Todd: 40% Rate
Pretax income	£100	£100
Taxes at 30% corporate tax rate	£30	£30
Net income after tax	£70	£70
Dividend assuming 100% payout	£70	£70
Shareholder taxes	£20	£40
Less tax credit for corporate payment	£30	£30
Tax due from shareholder	(£10)	£10
Effective tax rate on dividend	20 / 100 = 20%	40 / 100 = 40%

Under an imputation system, the effective tax rate on the dividend is simply the shareholder's individual tax rate.

LOS 50.i: Discuss the types of information that dividend initiations, increases, decreases, and omissions may convey, and cross-country differences in the signalling content of dividends.

The information conveyed by **dividend initiation** is ambiguous. On one hand, a dividend initiation could mean that a company is sharing its wealth with shareholders—a positive signal. On the other hand, initiating a dividend could mean that a company has a lack of profitable reinvestment opportunities—a negative signal.

An **unexpected dividend increase** can signal to investors that a company's future business prospects are strong and that managers will share the success with shareholders. Studies have found that companies with a long history of dividend increases, such as GE and Exxon Mobil, are dominant in their industries and have high returns on assets and low debt ratios.

Unexpected dividend decreases or omissions are typically negative signals that the business is in trouble and that management does not think the current dividend payment can be maintained. In rare instances, however, management can attempt to send a positive signal by cutting the dividend. Management may believe profitable investment opportunities are available and that shareholders would ultimately receive a greater benefit by having earnings reinvested in the company rather than being paid out as dividends.

The information content in dividend policy changes is viewed differently across countries. In the United States, investors infer that even small changes in a dividend send a major signal about a company's prospects. However, in Japan and other Asian countries, investors are less likely to assume that even a large change in dividend policy signals anything about a company's future. As a result, Asian companies are freer to raise and lower their dividends as circumstances change without being concerned about how investor reactions may affect the stock price.

KEY CONCEPTS

1. Cash dividends are a payment from a company to a shareholder that reduces both the value of the company's assets and the market value of equity. They can come in the forms of regular, special, or liquidating dividends.

2. Stock dividends are new share distributions rather than cash dividends. Stock splits divide each existing share into multiple shares. Both create more shares, but there is a proportionate drop in the price per share, so there is no effect on shareholder wealth.

3. The chronology of a dividend payout is:
   • Declaration date.
   • Ex-dividend date.
   • Holder-of-record date.
   • Payment date.
   Stocks traded on or after the ex-dividend date will not receive the dividend.

4. A share repurchase is economically equivalent to a cash dividend of an equal amount, assuming the tax treatment of the two alternatives is the same.

5. The effect of share repurchases using borrowed funds on EPS is:
   • If the company's E/P is equal to the after-tax cost of borrowing, there will be no effect on EPS.
   • If the company's E/P is greater than (less than) the after-tax cost of borrowing, EPS will increase (decrease).

6. The effect of a share repurchase on BVPS is:
   • If the share price is greater than the original BVPS, the post-repurchase BVPS will decline.
   • If the share price is less than the original BVPS, the post-repurchase BVPS will increase.

7. Companies can repurchase shares of their own stock by buying shares in the open market, buying back a fixed number of shares at a fixed price through a tender offer, or directly negotiating to buy a large block of shares from a large shareholder.

8. Six main factors affect dividend payout policy:
   • Taxation of dividends.
   • Shareholder preference for current income vs. capital gains.
   • Flotation costs on new issues vs. cost of retained earnings.
   • Restrictions on dividend payments.
   • Clientele effect.
   • Signaling effect.

9. The effective tax rate on a dollar of corporate income distributed as dividends depends on the tax system.
   • Under a double-taxation or a split-tax rate system: effective rate = corporate rate + (1 – corporate rate)(individual rate). This helps offset the higher individual tax rate applied to dividends compared to capital gains.
   • Under a tax-imputation system, the effective tax rate on a dollar of income distributed as dividends is equal to the shareholder's rate.

10. Clientele effect refers to the varying preferences for dividends of different groups of investors, such as individuals, institutions, and corporations.

11. The signaling effect is based on the idea that dividends convey information about future earnings from management to investors. In general, unexpected increases are good news and unexpected decreases are bad news as seen by U.S. investors. In other countries such as Japan, changes in dividend policy do not have the same signaling impact.

CONCEPT CHECKERS: DIVIDENDS AND DIVIDEND POLICY

1. The Board of Directors of Sarkel Systems Corporation is considering approving an 8-for-5 stock split for the company's common stock. The company currently has 1.5 million shares outstanding, and EPS for the prior year were $0.60. The company intends to maintain a 50% payout ratio. The company's stock price is currently $40 per share. Sarkel's CFO provided a memo to the board to help them with their decision of whether to approve the dividend. The memo contained the following statements:
    (1) The stock price after the split will be $25 per share.
    (2) The company's dividend yield after the split will be 1.2%.
    (3) After the split, the company's price-to-earnings ratio will remain 41.7× earnings.

    Which of the following regarding statements in the memo is **TRUE**?

	Statement 1	Statement 2	Statement 3
A.	Incorrect	Incorrect	Correct
B.	Incorrect	Correct	Incorrect
C.	Correct	Incorrect	Incorrect
D.	Correct	Incorrect	Correct

2. Studdard Controls (STU) recently declared a quarterly dividend of $1.25 payable on Thursday, April 25 to holders of record on Friday, April 12. What is the last day an investor could purchase STU stock and still receive the quarterly dividend?
    A. April 9.
    B. April 10.
    C. April 12.
    D. April 25.

Use the following information to answer Questions 3 through 5.

Klaatu is a country that taxes dividends based on a double-taxation system. The corporate tax rate on company profits is 35%. Barada is a country that taxes dividends based on a split-rate tax system. The corporate tax rate applied to retained earnings is 36%, while the corporate tax rate applied to earnings paid out as dividends is 20%. Nikto is a country that taxes dividends based on an imputation tax system. The corporate tax rate on earnings is 38%.

3. An investor living in Klaatu holds 100 shares of stock in the Lucas Corporation. Lucas' pretax earnings for the current year are $2.00 per share, and the company has a payout ratio of 100%. The investor's individual tax rate on dividends is 30%. The effective tax rate on a dollar of funds to be paid out as dividends is *closest* to:
    A. 35.0%.
    B. 54.5%.
    C. 62.3%.
    D. 65.0%.

4. An investor living in Barada holds 100 shares of Prowse Inc. Prowse's pre-tax earnings in the current year are $1.00 per share, and Prowse pays dividends based on a target payout ratio of 40%. The individual tax rate that applies to dividends is 28%, and the individual tax rate that applies to capital gains is 15%. The effective tax rate on earnings distributed as dividends is:
    A. 20.0%.
    B. 38.8%.
    C. 42.4%.
    D. 53.9%.

5. Jenni White and Janet Langhals are each shareholders that live in Nikto, and each owns 100 shares of OCP Inc., which has €1.00 per share in net income. OCP pays out 100% of its earnings as dividends. White is in the 25% tax bracket, while Langhals is in the 42% tax bracket. The effective tax rate on earnings paid out as dividends is:
    A. 53.5%.
    B. 64.0%.
    C. 53.5% for White and 64.0% for Langhals.
    D. 25.0% for White and 42.0% for Langhals.

6. Nick Adams is recommending to the Board of Directors that they share the profits from an excellent year with shareholders by either declaring a special cash dividend of $20 million, or using the $20 million to repurchase shares of Volksberger common stock in the open market. Selected financial information about the firm is shown below.

Shares outstanding:	40 million
Current stock price:	$28.00
52-week trading range:	$20.00 to $36.00
Book value of equity:	$880 million
After-tax cost of borrowing:	5.5%

    Adams drafts a memo to the Board of Directors detailing the financial impact of declaring a special cash dividend versus repurchasing shares. His memo includes two statements:
    (1) The total shareholder wealth resulting from owning one share of stock with the special dividend option is $28.50, assuming the stock price doesn't change on the announcement of the special dividend.
    (2) Our company's P/E ratio after the share buyback will remain 20 times earnings.

    Which of the following regarding Adams' statements is **TRUE**?

	Statement 1	Statement 2
A.	Correct	Incorrect
B.	Incorrect	Correct
C.	Correct	Correct
D.	Incorrect	Incorrect

7. Which of the following would **NOT** be a good reason for a company to repurchase shares of its own stock? Management:
    A. believes a stable cash dividend is in the best interests of shareholders.
    B. believes its stock is overvalued.
    C. wants to send a signal to investors that its outlook for the future is positive.
    D. wants to increase the amount of leverage in its capital structure.

8. Arizona Seafood, Inc. plans $45 million in new borrowing to repurchase 3,600,000 shares at their market price of $12.50. The yield on the new debt will be 12%. The company has 36 million shares outstanding and EPS of $0.60 before the repurchase. The company's tax rate is 40%. The company's EPS after the share repurchase will be *closest* to:
    A. $0.43.
    B. $0.50.
    C. $0.57.
    D. $0.64.

9. Northern Financial Co. has a BVPS of $5.00. The company has announced a $15 million share buyback. The share price is $60 and the company has 40 million shares outstanding. After the share repurchase, the company's BVPS will be *closest* to:
    A. $4.65.
    B. $4.78.
    C. $4.90.
    D. $5.03.

10. Which of the following factors would encourage a company to maintain a high dividend payout ratio?
    A. The company is in the early stage of its life cycle.
    B. The double-taxation system is in place in the company's home country.
    C. Most of the shares in the company are held by income-oriented mutual funds.
    D. The company's debt covenants require an interest coverage ratio of at least 2.0x.

11. Two public companies, one based in the United States and one based in Japan, unexpectedly announce decreases in the regular quarterly dividends on their common shares. What is the *most likely* reaction of the two firms' share prices?

	Share price of U.S. firm	Share price of Japanese firm
A.	Decrease	Decrease
B.	Increase	No change
C.	No change	Decrease
D.	Decrease	No change

ANSWERS – CONCEPT CHECKERS: DIVIDEND POLICY

1. **C**   A stock split will increase the number of shares outstanding, but since the price of the stock drops proportionally, there is no change in shareholder value. Statement 1 is correct. After the 8-for-5 stock split, the price of the stock will drop from its current level of $40 to (40 / (8/5)) = $25. Statement 2 is incorrect. The stock's current dividend yield is $0.30 / $40 = 0.75%. After the stock split, dividends per share will be $0.30 / (8/5) = $0.1875, and the dividend yield will remain $0.1875 / $25 = 0.75%. Statement 3 is incorrect. The P/E ratio will remain unchanged at $40 / $0.60 = 66.67×. After the split, EPS will be $0.60 / (8/5) = $0.375, and the P/E ratio will be $25 / $0.375 = 66.67×.

2. **A**   If an investor purchases shares of stock on or after the ex-dividend date, she will NOT receive the dividend. Therefore, to receive the dividend, the investor must purchase stock the day before the ex-dividend date. The ex-dividend day is always two business days before the holder-of-record date. Two days before April 12 is April 10; therefore, the last day the investor can purchase shares and still receive the dividend is April 9.

3. **B**   The effective tax rate on earnings distributed as dividends is 0.35 + (1 − 0.35)(0.30) = 0.545 = 54.5%.

4. **C**   The effective tax rate on earnings distributed as dividends is 0.20 + (1 − 0.20)(0.28) = 0.424 = 42.4%.

5. **D**   Under an imputation tax system, the effective tax rate on earnings distributed as dividends is the tax rate of the shareholder receiving the dividends.

6. **B**   Adams is incorrect with respect to Statement 1. If the firm pays its special dividend of $20 million, both the assets and equity of the firm will drop by $20 million. The total wealth from owning one share will be [(40 million)($28) − $20 million] / 40 million = $27.50, plus $20 million / 40 million = $0.50 per share as a dividend, so the total shareholder wealth resulting from owning one share of stock is $28. Note that the total shareholder wealth of $28 is the same whether the cash dividend or share repurchase option is chosen. Adams is correct with respect to Statement 2. The current EPS is $56 million / 40 million = $1.40, so the current P/E ratio is $28 / $1.40 = 20 times earnings. A share buyback will result in fewer shares but a lower equity value, so the price per share will remain the same. Since the price is the same, and earnings are the same, the P/E ratio will remain 20 times earnings after the repurchase.

7. **B**   Management would repurchase shares of its own stock if it believed the shares were undervalued, not overvalued.

8. **C**   Total earnings are $0.60 × 36,000,000 = $21,600,000.

    After-tax cost of debt is 12% × (1 − 0.40) = 7.2%.

    $$\text{EPS after buyback} = \frac{\text{total earnings} - \text{after-tax cost of funds}}{\text{shares outstanding after buyback}}$$

    $$= \frac{\$21,600,000 - (3,600,000 \text{ shares} \times \$12.50 \times 0.072)}{36,000,000 \text{ shares} - 3,600,000 \text{ shares}}$$

    $$= \frac{\$21,600,000 - \$3,240,000}{32,400,000 \text{ shares}} = \frac{\$18,360,000}{32,400,000 \text{ shares}}$$

    EPS = $0.57

9. **A**   Shares to be repurchased are $15 million / $60 = 250,000 shares.
    Remaining shares after the repurchase will be 40,000,000 − 250,000 = 39,750,000 shares.
    Book value before the repurchase is 40,000,000 × $5.00 = $200,000,000.
    Book value after the repurchase will be $200,000,000 − $15,000,000 = $185,000,000.
    BVPS = $185,000,000 / 39,750,000 = $4.654 per share.

10. **C** Institutional investors such as income-oriented mutual funds would invest in companies that pay a high dividend. The clientele effect suggests a company should maintain its current dividend payout policy. A company in the early stage of its life cycle typically does not pay a dividend. Double taxation of dividends and debt covenants both encourage low dividend payout ratios.

11. **D** Unexpected dividend decreases or omissions are typically seen by U.S. investors as a signal that the business is in trouble and management does not believe it can maintain the current dividend. In Japan and other Asian countries, investors are less likely to assume a change in dividend policy signals anything about a company's prospects.

The following is a review of the Corporate Finance principles designed to address the learning outcome statements set forth by CFA Institute®. This topic is also covered in:

THE CORPORATE GOVERNANCE OF LISTED COMPANIES: A MANUAL FOR INVESTORS

EXAM FOCUS

Due to the collapses of some major corporations and associated investor losses, corporate governance has become a hot topic in the investment community. The prominence of the issue has likely been a factor in the decision to include this topic in the curriculum. Corporate governance encompasses the internal controls that outline how a firm is managed. The material here is not particularly challenging. You need to understand well the specific issues that are covered under the heading of "corporate governance" and which practices are considered good. You should know the characteristics of an independent and effective board of directors. Much of the rest of the material has to do with shareholder interests and whether a firm's actions and procedures promote the interests of shareholders.

LOS 51.a: Define corporate governance.

Corporate governance is the set of internal controls, processes, and procedures by which firms are managed. It defines the appropriate rights, roles, and responsibilities of management, the board of directors, and shareholders within an organization. It is the firm's checks and balances. Good corporate governance practices seek to ensure that:

- The board of directors protects shareholder interests.
- The firm acts lawfully and ethically in dealings with shareholders.
- The rights of shareholders are protected and shareholders have a voice in governance.
- The board acts independently from management.
- Proper procedures and controls cover management's day-to-day operations.
- The firm's financial, operating, and governance activities are reported to shareholders in a fair, accurate, and timely manner.

LOS 51.b: Discuss and critique characteristics and practices related to board and committee independence, experience, compensation, external consultants and frequency of elections and determine whether they are supportive of shareowner protection.

To properly protect their long-term interests as shareholders, investors should consider whether:

- A majority of the board of directors is comprised of independent members (not management).
- The board meets regularly outside the presence of management.
- The chairman of the board is also the CEO or a former CEO of the firm. This may impair the ability and willingness of independent board members to express opinions contrary to those of management.
- Independent board members have a primary or leading board member in cases where the chairman is *not* independent.
- Board members are closely aligned with a firm supplier, customer, share-option plan or pension adviser. Can board members recuse themselves on any potential areas of conflict?

A non-independent board is more likely to make decisions that unfairly or improperly benefit management and those who have influence over management. These also may harm shareholders' long-term interests.

There is often a need for specific, specialized, independent advice on various firm issues and risks, including compensation, mergers and acquisitions, legal, regulatory, and financial matters, and issues relating to the firm's reputation. A truly independent board will have the ability to hire external consultants without management approval. This enables the board to receive specialized advice on technical issues and provides the board with independent advice that is not influenced by management interests.

Frequency of Board Elections

Anything beyond a two- or three-year limit on board member tenure limits shareowners' ability to change the board's composition if board members fail to represent shareowners' interests fairly.

While reviewing firm policy regarding election of the board, investors should consider:

- Whether there are annual elections or staggered multiple-year terms (a **classified board**). A classified board may serve another purpose—to act as a takeover defense.
- Whether the board filled a vacant position for a remaining term without shareholder approval.
- Whether shareholders can remove a board member.
- Whether the board is the proper size for the specific facts and circumstances of the firm.

LOS 51.c: Define board independence and explain the importance of independent board members in corporate governance.

A board can be considered independent if its decisions are not controlled or biased by the management of the firm. To be independent, a board member must not have any material relationship with:

- The firm and its subsidiaries, including former employees, executives, and their families.
- Individuals or groups, such as a shareholder(s) with a controlling interest, which can influence the firm's management.
- Executive management and their families.
- The firm's advisers, auditors, and their families.
- Any entity which has a cross directorship with the firm.

An independent board member must work to protect shareholders' long-term interests. Board members need to have not only independence, but experience and resources. The board of directors must have autonomy to operate independently from management.

If board members are not independent, they may be more likely to make decisions that benefit either management or those who have influence over management, thus harming shareholders' long-term interests.

To make sure board members act independently, the firm should have policies in place to discourage board members from receiving consulting fees for work done on the firm's behalf or receiving finders' fees for bringing mergers, acquisitions, and sales to management's attention. Further, procedures should limit board members' and associates' ability to receive compensation beyond the scope of their board responsibilities.

The firm should disclose all material related party transactions or commercial relationships it has with board members or nominees. The same goes for any property that is leased, loaned, or otherwise provided to the firm by board members or executive officers. Receiving personal benefits from the firm can create conflicts of interest.

LOS 51.d: Identify factors that indicate a board and its members possess the experience required to govern the company for the benefit of its shareowners.

Board members without the requisite skills and experience are more likely to defer to management when making decisions. This can be a threat to shareholder interests.

When evaluating the qualifications of board members, consider whether board members:

- Can make informed decisions about the firm's future.
- Can act with care and competence as a result of their experience with:
  - Technologies, products, services which the firm offers.
  - Financial operations and accounting and auditing topics.
  - Legal issues.
  - Strategies and planning.
  - Business risks the firm faces.
- Have made any public statements indicating their ethical stances.
- Have had any legal or regulatory problems as a result of working for or serving on the firm's board or the board of another firm.
- Have other board experience.
- Regularly attend meetings.
- Are committed to shareholders. Do they have significant stock positions? Have they eliminated any conflicts of interest?
- Have necessary experience and qualifications.
- Have served on board for more than ten years. While this adds experience, these board members may be too closely allied with management.

Investors should also consider how many board and committee meetings are held, and the attendance record of the meetings; whether the board and its committees conduct self-assessments; and whether the board provides adequate training for its members.

LOS 51.e: Explain the provisions that should be included in a strong corporate code of ethics and the implications of a weak code of ethics with regard to related-party transactions and personal use of company assets.

A code of ethics for a firm sets the standard for basic principles of integrity, trust, and honesty. It gives the staff behavioral standards and addresses conflicts of interest. Ethical breaches can lead to big problems for firms, resulting in sanctions, fines, management turnover, and unwanted negative publicity. Having an ethical code can be a mitigating factor with regulators if a breach occurs.

When analyzing ethics codes, these are items to be considered:

- Make sure the board of directors receives relevant corporate information in a timely manner.
- Ethics codes should be in compliance with the corporate governance laws of the location country and with the governance requirements set forth by the local stock exchange. Firms should disclose whether they adhered to their own ethical code, including any reasons for failure.
- The ethical code should prohibit advantages to the firm's insiders that are not offered to shareowners.
- A person should be designated to be responsible for corporate governance.
- If selected management personnel receive waivers from the ethics code, reasons should be given.
- If any provisions of the ethics code were waived recently, the firm should explain why.
- The firm's ethics code should be audited and improved periodically.

In evaluating management, investors should:

- Verify that the firm has committed to an ethical framework and adopted a code of ethics.
- See if the firm permits board members or management to use firm assets for personal reasons.
- Analyze executive compensation to assess whether it is commensurate with responsibilities and performance.
- Look into the size, purpose, means of financing, and duration of any share-repurchase programs.

LOS 51.f: State the key areas of responsibility for which board committees are typically created and explain the criteria for assessing whether each committee is able to adequately represent shareowner interests.

Audit Committee

This committee ensures that the financial information provided to shareholders is complete, accurate, reliable, relevant, and timely. Investors must determine whether:

- Proper accounting and auditing procedures have been followed.
- The external auditor is free from management influence.
- Any conflicts between the external auditor and the firm are resolved in a manner that favors the shareholder.
- Independent auditors have authority over the audit of all the company's affiliates and divisions.
- All board members serving on the audit committee are independent.
- Committee members are financial experts.
- The shareholders vote on the approval of the board's selection of the external auditor.
- The audit committee has authority to approve or reject any proposed non-audit engagements with the external audit firm.
- The firm has provisions and procedures that specify to whom the internal auditor reports. Internal auditors must have no restrictions on their contact with the audit committee.
- There have been any discussions between the audit committee and the external auditor resulting in a change in financial reports due to questionable interpretation of accounting rules, fraud, etc.
- The audit committee controls the audit budget.

Remuneration/Compensation Committee

Investors should be sure a committee of independent board members sets executive compensation, commensurate with responsibilities and performance. The committee can further these goals by making sure all committee members are independent, and by linking compensation to long-term firm performance and profitability.

Investors, when analyzing this committee, should determine whether:

- Executive compensation is appropriate.
- The firm has provided loans or the use of company property to board members.
- Committee members attend regularly.
- Policies and procedures for this committee are in place.
- The firm has provided details to shareholders regarding compensation in public documents.
- Terms and conditions of options granted are reasonable.
- Any obligations regarding share-based compensation are met through issuance of new shares.
- The firm and the board are required to receive shareholder approval for any share-based remuneration plans, since these plans can create potential dilution issues.
- Senior executives from other firms have cross-directorship links with the firm or committee members. Watch for situations where individuals may benefit directly from reciprocal decisions on board compensation.

Nominations Committee

The nominations committee handles recruiting of new (independent) board members. It is responsible for:

- Recruiting qualified board members.
- Regularly reviewing performance, independence, skills, and experience of existing board members.
- Creating nomination procedures and policies.
- Preparing an executive management succession plan.

Candidates proposed by this committee will affect whether or not the board works for the benefit of shareholders. Performance assessment of board members should be fair and appropriate. Investors should review company reports over several years to see if this committee has properly recruited board members who have fairly protected shareholder interests. Investors should also review:

- Criteria for selecting new board members.
- Composition, background, and expertise of present board members. How do proposed new members complement the existing board?
- The process for finding new members (i.e., input from outside the firm versus management suggestions).
- Attendance records.
- Succession plans for executive management (if such plans exist).
- The committee's report, including any actions, decisions, and discussion.

Other Board Committees

Additional committees can provide more insight into goals and strategies of the firm. These committees are more likely to fall outside typical corporate governance codes, so they are more likely to be comprised of members of executive management. Be wary of this—independence is once again critical to maintain shareowners' best interests.

LOS 51.g: Evaluate, from a shareowner's perspective, company policies related to voting rules, shareowner sponsored proposals, common stock classes and takeover defenses.

The ability to vote proxies is a fundamental shareholder right. If the firm makes it difficult to vote proxies, it limits the ability of shareholders to express their views and affect the firm's future direction.

Investors should consider whether the firm:

- Limits the ability to vote shares by requiring attendance at annual meeting.
- Groups its meetings to be held the same day as other companies in the same region and also requires attendance to cast votes.
- Allows proxy voting by some remote mechanism.
- Is allowed under its governance code to use **share blocking**, a mechanism that prevents investors who wish to vote their shares from trading their shares during a period prior to the annual meeting.

Confidential Voting

Investors should determine if shareholders are able to cast confidential votes. This can encourage unbiased voting. In looking at this issue, investors should consider whether:

- The firm uses a third party to tabulate votes.
- The third party or the firm retains voting records.
- The tabulation is subject to audit.
- Shareholders are entitled to vote only if present.

Cumulative Voting

Shareholders may be able to cast the cumulative number of votes allotted to their shares for one or a limited number of board nominees. Be cautious in the event the firm has a considerable minority shareholder group, such as a founding family, that can serve its own interests through cumulative voting.

Information on possible cumulative voting rights will be contained in the articles of organization and by-laws, the prospectus, or Form 8-A, which must be filed with the Securities and Exchange Commission in the United States.

Voting for Other Corporate Changes

Changes to corporate structure or policies can change the relationship between shareholders and the firm. Watch for changes to:

- Articles of organization.
- By-laws.
- Governance structures.
- Voting rights and procedures.
- Poison pill provisions (these are impediments to an acquisition of the firm).
- Provisions for change-in-control.

Regarding issues requiring shareholder approval, consider whether shareholders:

- Must approve corporate change proposals with supermajority votes.
- Will be able to vote on the sale of the firm, or part of it, to a third-party buyer.
- Will be able to vote on major executive compensation issues.
- Will be able to approve any anti-takeover measures.
- Will be able to periodically reconsider and re-vote on rules that require supermajority voting to revise any governance documents.
- Have the ability to vote for changes in articles of organization, by-laws, governance structures, and voting rights and procedures.
- Have the ability to use their relatively small ownership interest to force a vote on a special interest issue.

Investors should also be able to review issues such as:

- Share buy-back programs that may be used to fund share-based compensation grants.
- Amendments or other changes to a firm's charter and by-laws.
- Issuance of new capital stock.

Shareowner-Sponsored Board Nominations

Investors need to determine whether the firm's shareholders have the power to put forth an independent board nominee. Having such flexibility is positive for investors as it allows them to address their concerns and protect their interests through direct board representation. Additional items to consider:

- Under what circumstances can a shareholder nominate a board member?
- Can shareowners vote to remove a board member?
- How does the firm handle contested board elections?

The proxy statement is a good source document for information about these issues in the United States. In many jurisdictions, articles of organization and corporate by-laws are other good sources of information on shareholder rights.

Shareowner-Sponsored Resolutions

The right to propose initiatives for consideration at the annual meeting is an important shareholder method to send a message to management.

Investors should look at whether:

- The firm requires a simple majority or a supermajority vote to pass a resolution.
- Shareholders can hold a special meeting to vote on a special initiative.
- Shareholder-proposed initiatives will benefit all shareholders, rather than just a small group.

Advisory or Binding Shareowner Proposals

Investors should find out if the board and management are required to actually implement any shareholder-approved proposals. Investors should determine whether:

- The firm has implemented or ignored such proposals in the past.
- The firm requires a supermajority of votes to approve changes to its by-laws and articles of organization.
- Any regulatory agencies have pressured firms to act on the terms of any approved shareholder initiatives.

Different Classes of Common Equity

Different classes of common equity within a firm may separate the voting rights of those shares from their economic value.

Firms with dual classes of common equity could encourage prospective acquirers to only deal directly with shareholders with the supermajority rights. Firms that separate voting rights from economic rights have historically had more trouble raising equity capital for fixed investment and product development than firms that combine those rights.

When looking at a firm's ownership structure, examine whether:

- Safeguards in the by-laws and articles of organization protect shareholders who have inferior voting rights.
- The firm was recently privatized by a government entity and the selling entity retained voting rights. This may prevent shareholders from receiving full value for their shares.
- Any super-voting rights kept by certain classes of shareholders impair the firm's ability to raise equity capital. If a firm has to turn to debt financing, the increase in leverage can harm the firm.

Information on these issues can be found in the proxy, web site, prospectus, or notes to the financial statements.

Shareowner Legal Rights

Examine whether the investor has the legal right under the corporate governance code and other legal statutes of the jurisdiction in which the firm is headquartered to seek legal redress or regulatory action to enforce and protect shareholder rights.

Investors should determine whether:

- Legal statutes allow shareholders to take legal actions to enforce ownership rights.
- The local market regulator, in similar situations, has taken action to enforce shareholder rights.
- Shareholders are allowed to take legal or regulatory action against the firm's management or board in the case of fraud.
- Shareholders have "dissenters' rights," which require the firm to repurchase their shares at fair market value in the event of a problem.

Takeover Defenses

Examples of takeover defenses include golden parachutes, poison pills, and greenmail (use of corporate funds to buy back the shares of a hostile acquirer at a premium to their market value). All of these defenses may be used to counter a hostile bid, and their probable effect is to decrease share value.

When reviewing the firm's takeover defenses, investors should:

- Ask whether the firm requires shareholder approval to implement such takeover measures.
- Ask whether the firm has received any acquisition interest in the past.

- Consider that the firm may use its cash to "pay off" a hostile bidder. Shareholders should take steps to discourage this activity.
- Consider whether any change of control issues would invoke the interest of a national or local government and, as a result, pressure the seller to change the terms of the acquisition or merger.

KEY CONCEPTS

1. Corporate governance is the set of internal controls, processes, and procedures by which firms are managed.

2. A non-independent board of directors is more likely to make decisions in the interests of management rather than shareholders. Investors should consider whether the board has a majority of independent members, meets outside management's presence, and is free from conflicts of interest.

3. A board can be considered independent if its decisions are not controlled or biased by the management of the firm. An independent board member must work to protect the long-term interests of shareholders.

4. Board members should have the skills and experience required to make informed decisions about the firm's future.

5. A firm's code of ethics sets the standard for basic principles of integrity, trust, and honesty. Having a code of ethics can be a mitigating factor with regulators if a breach occurs.

6. The audit, compensation, and nominations committees execute the key responsibilities of the board.

7. Company policies can make it difficult to vote proxies. Minority shareholder groups can serve their own interests through cumulative voting. Corporate structure changes can alter the relationship between shareholders and the firm. Different classes of equity may separate the voting rights of shares from their economic value.

CONCEPT CHECKERS: THE CORPORATE GOVERNANCE OF LISTED COMPANIES: A MANUAL FOR INVESTORS

1. Which of the following board characteristics would *least likely* be an indication of high quality corporate governance?
    A. Board members have staggered terms.
    B. The board can hire independent consultants.
    C. The board has a separate committee to set executive pay.
    D. Several members who are not involved with the day-to-day operations of the company.

2. Which of the following board members would *most likely* be considered to be well chosen based on the principles of good corporate governance?
    A. A board member of Company B who is also the CEO of Company B.
    B. A board member of Company B who is an ex-employee of Company B.
    C. A board member of Company B who is a partner in an accounting firm that competes with the firm's auditor.
    D. A board member of Company A who is president of Company B, when the CFO of company A sits on Company B's board.

3. Which of the following is likely to be the *least important* in enabling a corporate board to exercise its duty by acting in the long-term interest of shareholders?
    A. The board meets regularly outside the presence of management.
    B. A majority of the board members are independent of firm management.
    C. The board has representatives from key suppliers and important customers.
    D. When the board chairman is the CEO, there is a leading independent board member.

4. Which of the following would *most likely* be considered a negative factor in assessing the suitability of a board member? The board member:
    A. has served for ten years.
    B. has served on other boards.
    C. owns stock in the company.
    D. is a former CEO of another firm.

5. Which of the following would *least likely* be an indication of poor corporate governance?
    A. A board member leases office space in a building he owns to the company.
    B. There are board members who do not have previous experience in the industry the firm operates in.
    C. A board member has a consulting contract with the firm to provide strategic vision for the technology research and development effort.
    D. Board members can receive a finder's fee for bringing attractive acquisition targets to management and the board if they are subsequently acquired.

6. Which of the following would *most likely* be considered a poor corporate practice in terms of promoting shareholder interests?
    A. The firm can use "share blocking."
    B. The firm allows voting by some remote mechanism.
    C. The firm uses a third party to tabulate shareholder votes.
    D. Voting for board members does not allow cumulative voting by shareholders of all votes allotted to their shares.

7.   Two analysts are discussing shareholder defenses against hostile takeovers. Alice states, "It is positive for shareholders that the board has shown a willingness to buy back shares from holders who may be in a position to effect a hostile takeover of the firm at less than its long-term value to shareholders." Bradley states, "Firms that are likely takeover targets should offer valuable exit packages in the event of a hostile takeover because they are necessary to recruit highly talented top executives, such as the CEO." From the perspective of good corporate governance, should you agree or disagree with each of these statements?

	Alice	Bradley
A.	Agree	Agree
B.	Agree	Disagree
C.	Disagree	Agree
D.	Disagree	Disagree

ANSWERS – CONCEPT CHECKERS: THE CORPORATE GOVERNANCE OF LISTED COMPANIES: A MANUAL FOR INVESTORS

1. **A** Staggered terms make it more difficult for shareholders to change the board of directors. Annual elections of all members make the board more responsive to shareholder wishes.

2. **C** A board member who is a partner in an unrelated accounting firm would be considered independent, has no particular relation to firm management, and could be a valuable addition to the board.

3. **C** Board members should not be closely aligned with a firm's suppliers or customers since they may act in the interest of suppliers and customers rather than in the interest of shareholders.

4. **A** While experience may be a good thing, a board member with long tenure may be too closely aligned with management to be considered an independent member.

5. **B** Lack of previous experience in the firm's industry is not necessarily a negative and can be consistent with an independent board member who acts in shareholders' long-term interests. Examples might be board members with specialized knowledge of finance, marketing, management, accounting, or auditing. The other answers all indicate possible conflicts of interest.

6. **A** Share blocking prevents shareholders from trading their shares over a period prior to the annual meeting and is considered a restriction on the ability of shareholders to express their opinions and act in their own interests. Cumulative voting can allow a minority group, such as a founding family, to serve its own interests. The other answers are considered good corporate governance practices.

7. **D** Defenses against hostile takeovers such as greenmail (Alice) or golden parachutes (Bradley) tend to protect entrenched or poorly performing managements and typically decrease share values. Shareholders as a group always have the choice not to sell when a takeover offer is not in their long-term interests.

THE ASSET ALLOCATION DECISION

EXAM FOCUS

There is nothing difficult here, but the material is important because it is likely to be tested and it is the foundation for the portfolio construction material at Level 2 and especially Level 3. You should be ready to explain the what and why of an investment policy statement and know the objectives (risk and return) and the constraints: liquidity, legal, time horizon, tax treatment, and unique circumstances. Know the four common return objectives, why the objectives part of the investment policy statement should include risk objectives, and (in broad strokes) the factors that influence risk tolerance.

LOS 52.a: Describe the steps in the portfolio management process and explain the reasons for a policy statement.

There are four general steps in the **portfolio management process**:

1. *Write a policy statement* that specifies the investor's goals and constraints and itemize the risks the investor is willing to take to meet these goals.

2. *Develop an investment strategy* designed to satisfy the investor's policy statement based on an analysis of the current financial and economic conditions.

3. *Implement the plan* by constructing the portfolio and allocating the investor's assets across countries, asset classes, and securities based on current and future forecasts of economic conditions.

4. *Monitor and update* the investor's needs and market conditions. Rebalance the investor's portfolio as needed. Rebalancing refers to shifting assets when the account allocations to different asset classes deviate significantly from the strategic asset allocation specified.

The **policy statement** is the framework that provides structure to the investment process. It forces investors to understand their own needs and constraints and to articulate them within the construct of realistic goals. The policy statement helps investors understand the risks and costs of investing and guides the actions of the portfolio manager. In essence, the purpose of the policy statement is to impose investment discipline on the client and the portfolio manager.

Performance cannot be judged without an objective standard. The policy statement should state the standards by which the portfolio's performance will be judged and specify the benchmark that represents the investor's risk preferences. The portfolio performance should be measured relative to the stated benchmark and not simply by the portfolio's raw returns.

LOS 52.b: Explain why investment objectives should be expressed in terms of both risk and return and list the factors that may affect an investor's risk tolerance.

Investment objectives must be stated in terms of both risk and return.

Return objectives may be stated in absolute terms (dollar amounts) or percentages. Return considerations also cover capital preservation, capital appreciation, current income needs, and total returns.

Specifying investment goals in terms of just return may expose an investor to inappropriate, high-risk investment strategies. Also, return-only objectives can lead to unacceptable behavior on the part of investment managers, such as excessive trading to generate commissions (churning).

Risk tolerance is a function of the investor's psychological makeup and personal factors such as age, family situation, existing wealth, insurance coverage, current cash reserves, and income.

LOS 52.c: Describe the return objectives of capital preservation, capital appreciation, current income, and total return and describe the investment constraints of liquidity, time horizon, tax concerns, legal and regulatory factors, and unique needs and preferences.

Return Objectives

Capital preservation is the objective of earning a return on an investment that is at least equal to the inflation rate with little or no chance of loss. The concern here is the maintenance of purchasing power. To achieve this objective, the nominal rate of return must at least equal the inflation rate. This is an appropriate goal when the funds will be needed in the near future.

Capital appreciation is the objective of earning a nominal return that exceeds the rate of inflation over some period of time. Achieving this goal means that the purchasing power of the initial investment increases over time, usually through capital gains. This is an appropriate goal when the need for the funds is further in the future, such as for retirement.

Current income is the objective when the primary purpose of an account is to produce income as opposed to capital appreciation. The current income objective is usually appropriate when an investor wants or needs to supplement other sources of income to meet living expenses or some other planned spending need, as in retirement.

Total return is the objective of having a portfolio grow in value to meet a future need through both capital gains and the reinvestment of current income. The total return objective is riskier than the income objective but less risky than the capital appreciation objective. This would be an appropriate objective for an investor with a longer-term investment horizon but only moderate risk tolerance.

Investment Constraints

Liquidity refers to the ability to quickly convert investments into cash at a price close to their fair market value. Liquidity, from the investor's view, is the potential need for ready cash. This may necessitate selling assets at unfavorable terms if adequate liquidity is not provided in the portfolio.

Time horizon (investment horizon) refers to the time between making an investment and needing the funds. There is a relationship between an investor's time horizon, liquidity needs, and ability to handle risk. Since losses are harder to overcome in a short time frame, investors with shorter time horizons usually prefer lower-risk investments.

Tax concerns play an important role in investment planning because after-tax returns are what investors should be concerned with. The tax codes in the U.S., as in most other countries, are complex. For instance, in the U.S., interest and dividends were, until recently, taxed at the investor's marginal tax rate, while capital gains were taxed at another rate. Taxes on unrealized capital gains can be deferred indefinitely, and estate taxes must be considered. Other tax-related issues include the following:

- There is a trade-off between taxes and diversification needs. The decision to sell some stock to diversify one's portfolio by reinvesting the proceeds in other assets must be balanced against the resulting tax liability.
- Some sources of income are tax exempt at the federal and state levels. For example, high-income individuals are motivated to invest in municipal bonds because the interest income is tax free.

- The investor must also consider tax-deferred investment opportunities such as IRAs, 401(k) and 403(b) plans, and various life insurance contracts.
- Young investors will want to put as much as possible into tax-deferred plans. The only drawback is the loss of liquidity.
- For older retirees, the need for tax-deferred investments may decrease. Also, taxable income may now offer higher after-tax returns than tax-exempt income. If a retirement account contains a lot of an old employer's stock, diversification becomes more important than taxes.

Legal and regulatory factors are more of a concern to institutional investors than individuals, but the investment strategies of both may be restricted due to these constraints.

Unique needs and preferences are constraints that investors may have that address special needs or place special restrictions on investment strategies for personal or socially conscious reasons. This is a catch-all constraint category for those "special" circumstances that don't fit neatly into one of the other constraint areas.

LOS 52.d: Describe the importance of asset allocation, in terms of the percentage of a portfolio's return that can be explained by the target asset allocation and list reasons for the differences in the average asset allocation among citizens of different countries.

Several studies support the idea that approximately 90% of a portfolio's returns can be explained by its target asset allocations. The clear implication of this result is that differences in returns among asset classes are much more important than differences in security selection in determining overall portfolio returns. For actively managed funds, actual portfolio returns are slightly less than those that would have been achieved if the manager strictly maintained the target asset allocation. This illustrates the real difficulty of improving returns by varying from target allocations (market timing) or by selecting undervalued securities in very efficiently priced markets.

Average asset allocations across countries differ for reasons related to demographics, social factors, legal constraints, and taxation. Countries with younger populations tend to have greater average allocations to equities. Some countries have legal restrictions on the percentage of equities that various institutions can hold. The existence of a strong government pension program in Germany tends to decrease the equity holdings of workers and private pension plans since less growth is needed for retirement funding needs. The German society also has an historical aversion to financial risk, and equity ownership is not typical for its citizens. Differences in historical inflation rates are correlated with differences in equity allocations across countries as well. Countries with higher historical inflation rates tend to have greater allocations to equities.

KEY CONCEPTS

1. The four-step portfolio management (investment) process:
   - Write a policy statement.
   - Develop an investment strategy.
   - Implement the plan by constructing the portfolio and allocating the assets.
   - Monitor, update, and rebalance the portfolio.
2. An investment policy statement provides investment discipline by requiring investors to articulate their needs, goals, and risk tolerance, ensuring that goals are realistic, and providing an objective measure of portfolio performance.
3. Investment objectives should be expressed in terms of both risk and return so that meeting the return objective does not expose the investor to more risk than he is prepared to tolerate.
4. Risk tolerance depends on an investor's psychological profile and other personal factors, including family situation, wealth, income, age, and insurance coverage.
5. Common return objectives are:
   - Capital preservation—minimizing the risk of loss in real terms.
   - Capital appreciation—managing real growth in the portfolio to meet some future need.
   - Income—meeting specified spending needs.
   - Total return—growing a portfolio through capital appreciation and reinvested income.

6. Investment constraints include:
   - Liquidity—for cash spending needs (anticipated or unexpected).
   - Time horizon—when funds will be needed.
   - Tax—the tax treatments of various accounts, and the investor's marginal tax bracket.
   - Legal—restrictions on investments in retirement, personal, and trust accounts.
   - Unique needs—constraints because of investor preferences or other factors not already considered.
7. Target allocations to different asset classes can explain approximately 90% of the differences in portfolio returns over time.
8. Differences in average asset allocations across countries exist due to differences in social factors, demographics, legal constraints, tax laws, and historical inflation rates.

CONCEPT CHECKERS: THE ASSET ALLOCATION DECISION

1. Which of the following is **NOT** an example of a portfolio constraint?
   A. Tax concerns.
   B. Liquidity needs.
   C. Total return requirement of 15%.
   D. Legal and regulatory requirements.

2. Which of the following statements about investment policy statements is **TRUE**?
   A. For some investors, specifying an investment goal in terms of return alone is appropriate.
   B. An investment policy statement should have objectives and constraints.
   C. Risk is an important investment policy constraint.
   D. Taxes are the most important legal constraint.

3. The approximate percentage of a portfolio's returns that can be explained by differences in target portfolio asset allocations is:
   A. 10%.
   B. 50%.
   C. 90%.
   D. 100%.

4. The return objective of an investor who is relatively risk averse yet has a long time horizon and little need for liquidity would *most likely* be described as:
   A. capital preservation.
   B. capital appreciation.
   C. total return.
   D. long-term appreciation.

5. In determining the appropriate asset allocation for a client's investment account, the manager should:
   A. consider only the investor's risk tolerance.
   B. consider the investor's risk tolerance and future needs, but not market conditions.
   C. not consider market conditions but should consider the taxable status of the account.
   D. rely on forecasts of future economic conditions.

ANSWERS – CONCEPT CHECKERS: THE ASSET ALLOCATION DECISION

1. **C** Return objectives are part of a policy statement's objectives, not constraints.

2. **B** The policy statement should specify objectives and constraints. Return should always be considered with risk. Taxes are a separate constraint, and setting a risk tolerance is an investment policy objective, not constraint.

3. **C** Studies suggest that approximately 90% of a portfolio's returns can be explained by target asset allocation choices.

4. **C** A total return strategy is appropriate for an investor with a longer-term investment horizon who is very risk tolerant. The inclusion of a significant allocation to income producing securities such as bonds and high-dividend stocks makes this a less risky strategy than that for an objective of capital appreciation.

5. **D** An advisor's forecasts of expected returns from and expected volatility (risk) of investing indifferent asset classes are an important part of determining an appropriate asset allocation.

An Introduction to Portfolio Management

Exam Focus

This topic review looks at Markowitz portfolio theory and optimal portfolio choice. The major result is the development of the efficient frontier. Understanding the relationship between portfolio risk and correlation is the key to understanding modern portfolio theory. Be able to discuss diversification, correlation, indifference curves, expected return, and the efficient frontier. A sound grasp of the portfolio theory presented here is essential to an understanding of the capital market theory covered in our next topic review. Additionally, portfolio theory is the heart of much of the portfolio management material essential for the Level 3 exam.

LOS 53.a: Define risk aversion and discuss evidence that suggests that individuals are generally risk averse.

Risk aversion refers to the fact that individuals prefer less risk to more risk. Risk-averse investors:

- Prefer lower to higher risk for a given level of expected returns.
- Will only accept a riskier investment if they are compensated in the form of greater expected return.

In Figure 1, we examine the concept of risk aversion using indifference curves.

Figure 1: Risk Aversion

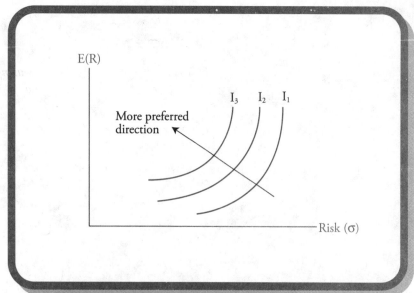

The curved lines, I_1, I_2, and I_3, represent *indifference curves* because all investments (combinations of risk and expected return) that lie along each curve are equally preferred. Because we have a "good" (expected return) and a "bad" (risk), a higher or more preferred indifference curve lies in the northwest direction (more expected return and less risk). Focusing on indifference curve I_1, a risk-averse investor whose preferences are represented by these curves will be equally happy with, or indifferent among, any risk/return combinations on this curve. Notice that as risk increases, a risk-averse investor demands an increasingly higher rate of return as compensation. While an investor would be equally happy with any point on I_1, she prefers all risk/return combinations on I_2 to any combination on I_1. In reality, there are an infinite number of indifference curves, and the indifference curves for any given investor can never cross.

The fact that most individuals buy some sort of insurance, whether auto, health, or homeowners, indicates that they are generally risk averse. Interestingly, however, an individual may exhibit risk-averse tendencies in one area and not in others. For example, many people buy auto insurance to protect against the costs associated with auto accidents but will not buy health insurance or will buy lottery tickets or participate in other forms of gambling.

LOS 53.b: List the basic assumptions behind the Markowitz Portfolio Theory.

In the investment framework he developed, Nobel laureate Harry Markowitz made the following **assumptions about investor behavior:**

- *Returns distribution.* Investors look at each investment opportunity as a probability distribution of expected returns over a given investment horizon.
- *Utility maximization.* Investors maximize their expected utility over a given investment horizon, and their indifference curves exhibit diminishing marginal utility of wealth (i.e., they are convex).
- *Risk is variability.* Investors measure risk as the variance (standard deviation) of expected returns.
- *Risk/return.* Investors make all investment decisions by considering only the risk and return of an investment opportunity. This means that their utility (indifference) curves are a function of the expected return (mean) and the variance of the returns distribution they envision for each investment.
- *Risk aversion.* Given two investments with equal expected returns, investors prefer the one with the lower risk. Likewise, given two investments with equal risk, investors prefer the one with the greater expected return.

Professor's Note: Make sure you understand each of the Markowitz assumptions—it will make asset pricing models easier to grasp.

LOS 53.c: Compute the expected return for an individual investment and for a portfolio.

Professor's Note: It's not obvious whether the exam will require that you describe and calculate expected returns using expectational (probabilistic) data or historical data, so we will do it both ways here and throughout this review wherever appropriate, just to be safe.

Expected Return for an Individual Investment

The *expected rate of return* from *expectational data* for a single risky asset can be calculated as:

$$E(R) = \sum_{i=1}^{n} P_i R_i = P_1 R_1 + P_2 R_2 + \dots + P_n R_n \qquad \text{(using expectational returns)}$$

where:
P_i = probability that state i will occur
R_i = asset return if the economy is in state i

The expected return, based on expectational data, is simply the weighted mean of the distribution of all possible returns.

The *expected rate of return* from *historical data* for a single risky asset can be calculated as:

$$E(R) = \overline{R} = \frac{\sum\limits_{t=1}^{n} R_t}{n} = \frac{(R_1 + R_2 + ... + R_n)}{n}$$

where:
R_t = the return in time period t
n = the number of time periods (using historical returns)

Professor's Note: The expected return with historical data is simply the average return over n years.

Example: Calculating expected return from expectational data

The first three columns of Figure 2 contain the probability of outcomes (states of the world) and the returns for a security in each state of the world. Calculate the expected return on the security.

Answer:

The computation of expected return is illustrated in the fourth column of Figure 2.

Figure 2: Computing Expected Return

State of the World	Probability (P_i)	Return (R_i)	Expected Return ($P_i R_i$)
Expansion	0.25	5.0%	(0.25)(5.0) = 1.25%
Normal	0.50	15.0%	(0.50)(15.0) = 7.50%
Recession	0.25	25.0%	(0.25)(25.0) = 6.25%
			$E(R) = \sum\limits_{i=1}^{3} P_i R_i = 15.00\%$

Example: Calculating expected return from historical data

Assume that the returns on a stock over the first six months of the year are +10%, −15%, +20%, +25%, −30%, and +20%. Compute the expected (average) return.

Answer:

$$\overline{R} = \frac{0.10 - 0.15 + 0.20 + 0.25 - 0.30 + 0.20}{6} = 0.05 = 5.0\%$$

Expected Return for a Portfolio of Risky Assets

The expected return on a portfolio of assets is simply the weighted average of the returns on the individual assets, using their portfolio weights. Thus, for a two-asset portfolio, the expected return is:

$$E(R_p) = w_1E(R_1) + w_2E(R_2)$$

where:
$E(R_1)$ = expected return on asset 1
$E(R_2)$ = expected return on asset 2
w_1 = percentage of the total portfolio value invested in asset 1
w_2 = percentage of the total portfolio value invested in asset 2

LOS 53.d: Compute the variance and standard deviation for an individual investment.

Professor's Note: It's not obvious whether the exam will require you to calculate the variance and standard deviation of returns using expectational (probabilistic) data or historical data, so again we will do it both ways.

In finance, the variance and standard deviation of expected returns are common measures of investment risk. Both of these related measures determine the variability of a distribution of returns about its mean.

The **variance and standard deviation of rates of return** from *expectational data* for an individual investment are calculated as:

$$\text{variance} = \sigma^2 = \sum_{i=1}^{n} P_i[R_i - E(R)]^2$$
$$\text{standard deviation} = \sigma = \sqrt{\sigma^2}$$

where:
R_i = return in state of the world *i*
P_i = probability of state *i* occurring
$E(R)$ = expected return

Example: Calculating variance with expectational data

The returns expectations from the previous example are reproduced in the first three columns of Figure 3. Using this expectational data, calculate the variance and standard deviation of expected returns. Recall that the expected return is 15%.

Answer:

Based on the computations illustrated in Figure 3, the variance and standard deviation are 0.0050 and 7.07%, respectively.

Figure 3: Variance and Standard Deviation Computation

State i	Probability P_i	Return R_i	Expected Return $E(R)$	$[(R_i) - E(R)]^2$	$P_i[(R_i) - E(R)]^2$
Expansion	0.25	0.05	0.15	0.01	$(0.25)(0.01) = 0.0025$
Normal	0.50	0.15	0.15	0.00	$(0.50)(0.00) = 0.0000$
Recession	0.25	0.25	0.15	0.01	$(0.25)(0.01) = 0.0025$
Variance = $\Sigma P_i[(R_i) - E(R)]^2 = 0.0025 + 0.0000 + 0.0025 = 0.0050$					
Standard deviation = $(0.0050)^{1/2} = 0.0707 = 7.07\%$					

The variance and standard deviation of returns from *historical data* are calculated as:

$$\text{variance} = \sigma^2 = \frac{\sum_{t=1}^{n}\left(R_t - \bar{R}\right)^2}{n}$$

$$\text{standard deviation} = \sigma = \sqrt{\sigma^2}$$

where:
R_t = return in period t
$\bar{R}$ = average return (expected return)
n = number of returns

Example: Calculating variance with historical data

The historical returns from the previous example are reported in the first column of Figure 4. Compute the variance and standard deviation.

Answer:

As shown in Figure 4, the computations of the variance and standard deviation result in 0.0417 and 20.41%, respectively.

Figure 4: Variance and Standard Deviation Using Historical Data

R_t	$(R_t - \bar{R})$	$(R_t - \bar{R})^2$
+0.1000	+0.0500	0.0025
−0.1500	−0.2000	0.0400
+0.2000	+0.1500	0.0225
+0.2500	+0.2000	0.0400
−0.3000	−0.3500	0.1225
+0.2000	+0.1500	0.0225
$\bar{R} = 0.0500$		$\Sigma = 0.2500$
		$\sigma^2 = 0.2500/6 = 0.0417$ $\sigma = 0.2041 = 20.41\%$

LOS 53.e: Compute the covariance of rates of return, and show how it is related to the correlation coefficient.

Covariance measures the extent to which two variables move together over time. A positive covariance means that the variables (e.g., rates of return on two stocks) tend to move together. Negative covariance means that the two variables tend to move in opposite directions. A covariance of zero means there is no relationship between the two variables.

The covariance between two assets computed from **expectational data** is equal to:

$$\text{Cov}_{1,2} = \sum_{i=1}^{n} \left\{ P_i \left[R_{i,1} - E(R_1) \right] \left[R_{i,2} - E(R_2) \right] \right\}$$

where:
$R_{t,1}$ = return on asset 1 in state i
$R_{t,2}$ = return on asset 2 in state i
P_i = probability of state i occurring
$E(R_1)$ = expected return on asset 1
$E(R_2)$ = expected return on asset 2

Example: Calculating covariance with expectational data

Calculate the covariance between Asset 1 and Asset 2 with the returns distribution described in the first three columns of Figure 5.

Answer:

First, we must compute the expected return for each of the assets as follows:

$$E(R_1) = \sum_{i=1}^{n} P_i R_{i,1} = 0.25(0.05) + 0.50(0.15) + 0.25(0.25) = 0.0125 + 0.0750 + 0.0625 = 0.15$$

$$E(R_2) = \sum_{i=1}^{n} P_i R_{i,2} = 0.25(0.32) + 0.50(0.14) + 0.25(0.04) = 0.08 + 0.07 + 0.01 = 0.16$$

Armed with the asset's expected returns, we can compute the covariance following the procedure illustrated in Figure 5.

Figure 5: Computing Covariance

P_i	$R_{i,1}$	$R_{i,2}$	$(R_{i,1}) - E(R_1)$	$(R_{i,2}) - E(R_2)$	$P_i[(R_{i,1}) - E(R_1)][(R_{i,2}) - E(R_2)]$
0.25	0.05	0.32	−0.10	+0.16	−0.004
0.50	0.15	0.14	+0.00	−0.02	0.000
0.25	0.25	0.04	+0.10	−0.12	−0.003
				$Cov_{1,2} = \Sigma P_i[(R_{i,1}) - E(R_1)][(R_{i,2}) - E(R_2)] = -0.007$	

The covariance between two asset returns using **historical data** is computed as:

$$Cov_{1,2} = \frac{\sum_{t=1}^{n}\left\{\left[R_{t,1} - \bar{R}_1\right]\left[R_{t,2} - \bar{R}_2\right]\right\}}{n}$$

where:
$R_{i,1}$ = return on asset 1 in period t
$R_{i,2}$ = return on asset 2 in period t
$\bar{R}_1$ = mean return on asset 1
$\bar{R}_2$ = mean return on asset 2
n = number of returns

Professor's Note: There is a similar formula for the covariance in the quantitative methods material that has n − 1 in the denominator. The difference is that the formula we are working with here is a population measure, whereas in the quant material, n − 1 is used because the covariance there is a sample statistic.

Example: Calculating covariance with historical data

Calculate the covariance for the returns of Stock 1 and Stock 2 given the six months of historical returns presented in the first three columns of Figure 6.

Answer:

The covariance calculation is demonstrated in the right side of Figure 6.

Figure 6: Calculating Covariance From Historical Returns

Year	Stock 1	Stock 2	$(R_t - \bar{R}_1)$	$(R_t - \bar{R}_2)$	$(R_t - \bar{R}_1)(R_t - \bar{R}_2)$
1998	+0.10	+0.20	+0.05	+0.10	+0.005
1999	−0.15	−0.20	−0.20	-0.30	+0.060
2000	+0.20	−0.10	+0.15	-0.20	−0.030
2001	+0.25	+0.30	+0.20	+0.20	+0.040
2002	−0.30	−0.20	−0.35	−0.30	+0.105
2003	+0.20	+0.60	+0.15	+0.50	+0.075
	$\bar{R}_1 = 0.05$	$\bar{R}_2 = 0.10$			$\Sigma = 0.255$ Cov = 0.255/6 = 0.0425

Correlation. The magnitude of the covariance depends on the magnitude of the individual stocks' standard deviations and the relationship between their co-movements. The covariance is an absolute measure and is measured in return units squared.

Covariance can be standardized by dividing by the product of the standard deviations of the two securities being compared. This standardized measure of co-movement is called *correlation* and is computed as:

$$\rho_{1,2} = \frac{Cov_{1,2}}{\sigma_1 \sigma_2}$$

or $Cov_{1,2} = \rho_{1,2}\sigma_1\sigma_2$

Professor's Note: The calculation of correlation is the same whether we are using expectational or historical data.

The term $\rho_{1,2}$ is called the *correlation coefficient* between the returns of securities 1 and 2. The correlation coefficient has no units. It is a pure measure of the co-movement of the two stocks' returns and is bounded by −1 and +1.

How should you interpret the correlation coefficient?

- A correlation coefficient of +1 means that returns always move together in the same direction. They are perfectly positively correlated.
- A correlation coefficient of −1 means that returns always move in the exact opposite direction. They are perfectly negatively correlated.
- A correlation coefficient of zero means that there is no relationship between the two stocks' returns. They are uncorrelated. One way to interpret a correlation (or covariance) of zero is that, in any period, knowing the actual value of one variable tells you nothing about the other.

Example: Computing correlation

The covariance between the returns on two stocks is 0.0425. The standard deviations of stocks 1 and 2 are 0.2041 and 0.2944, respectively. Calculate and interpret the correlation between the two assets.

Answer:

$$\rho_{1,2} = \frac{0.0425}{0.2041 \times 0.2944} = 0.71$$

The returns from the two stocks are positively correlated, meaning they tend to move in the same direction at the same time. However, the correlation is not perfect because the correlation coefficient is less than one.

Example: Computing covariance

The correlation between the returns on two stocks is 0.56. The standard deviations of the returns from Stock 1 and Stock 2 are 0.1544 and 0.0892, respectively. Calculate and interpret the covariance between the two assets.

Answer:

$$\text{Cov}_{1,2} = 0.56 \times 0.1544 \times 0.0892 = 0.0077$$

The covariance between the returns from Stock 1 and Stock 2 shows that the two securities' returns tend to move together. However, the strength of this tendency cannot be measured using the covariance—we must rely on the correlation to provide us with an indication of the relative strength of the relationship.

LOS 53.f: List the components of the portfolio standard deviation formula, and explain which component is most important to consider when adding an investment to a portfolio.

Earlier in this review, we showed that the expected return for a portfolio of risky assets is the weighted average of the expected returns of the individual assets in the portfolio. This is not the case for the variance and standard deviation of a portfolio of risky assets. The variance and, by association, the standard deviation of a portfolio of two assets are *not* simple weighted averages of the asset variances (standard deviations). Portfolio variance (standard deviation) is not only a function of the variance (standard deviation) of the returns of the individual assets in the portfolio. It is also a function of the correlation (covariance) among the returns of the assets in the portfolio.

The general formula for the standard deviation for a portfolio of n risky assets is as follows:

$$\sigma_P = \sqrt{\sigma_P^2} = \sqrt{\sum_{i=1}^{n} w_i^2 \sigma_i^2 + \sum_{\substack{i=1 \\ i \neq j}}^{n} \sum_{j=1}^{n} w_i w_j \text{Cov}_{i,j}}$$

where :

σ_p^2	=	portfolio variance
w_i	=	the market weight of asset i
σ_i^2	=	variance of returns for asset i
$\text{Cov}_{i,j}$	=	the covariance between the returns of assets i and j

For a portfolio of two risky assets this is equivalent to:

$$\sigma_p = \sqrt{w_1^2 \sigma_1^2 + w_2^2 \sigma_2^2 + 2w_1 w_2 \sigma_1 \sigma_2 \rho_{1,2}} \text{ or } \sqrt{w_1^2 \sigma_1^2 + w_2^2 \sigma_2^2 + 2w_1 w_2 \text{Cov}_{1,2}}$$

For a portfolio of three risky assets, the expanded form is:

$$\sigma_p = \sqrt{w_1^2\sigma_1^2 + w_2^2\sigma_2^2 + w_3^2\sigma_3^2 + 2w_1w_2Cov_{1,2} + 2w_1w_3Cov_{1,3} + 2w_2w_3Cov_{2,3}}$$

Note that in the first formula for a two-asset portfolio we have substituted $\sigma_1\sigma_2\rho_{1,2}$ for $Cov_{1,2}$ (using the definition of $\rho_{1,2}$) because the formula is often written this way as well to emphasize the role of correlation in portfolio risk.

The first part of the formula is intuitive—the risk of a portfolio of risky assets depends on the risk of the assets in the portfolio and how much of each asset is in the portfolio (the σ and w terms). The second part of the formula is there because the risk (standard deviation) of a portfolio of risky assets also depends on how the returns on the assets move in relation to each other (the covariance or correlation of their returns).

Note that if the asset returns are *negatively correlated*, the final term in the formula for a two-asset portfolio is negative and reduces the portfolio standard deviation. If the correlation is zero, the final term is zero, and the portfolio standard deviation is greater than when the correlation is negative. If the correlation is positive, the final term is positive, and portfolio standard deviation is greater still. The maximum portfolio standard deviation for a portfolio of two assets with given portfolio weights will result when the correlation coefficient is +1 (perfect positive correlation). When assets are perfectly positively correlated, there is no diversification benefit.

This is the key point of the Markowitz analysis and the point of this LOS. *The risk of a portfolio of risky assets depends on the asset weights and the standard deviations of the assets' returns, and crucially on the correlation (covariance) of the asset returns.*

Other things equal, the higher (lower) the correlation between asset returns, the higher (lower) the portfolio standard deviation.

PORTFOLIO RISK AND RETURN FOR A TWO-ASSET PORTFOLIO

Before we move on to the next LOS, let's take a minute to show graphically the risk-return combinations from varying the proportions of two risky assets and then to show how the graph of these combinations is affected by changes in the correlation coefficient for the returns on the two assets.

Figure 7 provides the risk and return characteristics for two stocks, Sparklin' and Caffeine Plus. Figure 8 shows the calculation of portfolio risk and expected return for portfolios with different proportions of each stock (calculated from the formula in the previous LOS).

Figure 7: Risk/Return Characteristics for Two Individual Assets

	Caffeine Plus	*Sparklin'*
Expected return (%)	11%	25%
Standard deviation (%)	15%	20%
Correlation	0.3	

Figure 8: Possible Combinations of Caffeine Plus and Sparklin'

$W_{Caffeine\ Plus}$	100%	80%	60%	40%	20%	0%
$W_{Sparklin'}$	0%	20%	40%	60%	80%	100%
$E(R_p)$	11.0%	13.8%	16.6%	19.4%	22.2%	25.0%
σ_p	15.0%	13.7%	13.7%	14.9%	17.1%	20.0%

The plot in Figure 9 represents all possible expected return and standard deviation combinations attainable by investing in varying amounts of Caffeine Plus and Sparklin'. We'll call it the *risk-return tradeoff curve*.

Figure 9: Risk-Return Tradeoff Curve

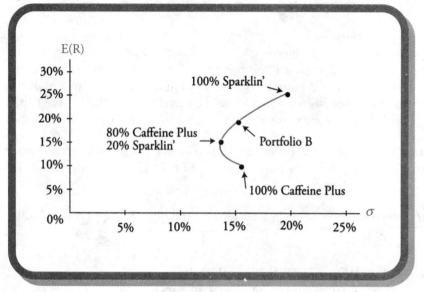

If you have all your investment in Caffeine Plus, your "portfolio" will have an expected return and standard deviation equal to that of Caffeine Plus, and you will be at one end of the curve (at the point labeled "100% Caffeine Plus"). As you increase your investment in Sparklin' to 20% and decrease your investment in Caffeine Plus to 80%, you will move up the risk-return tradeoff curve to the point where the expected return is 13.8% with a standard deviation of 13.7% (labeled "80% Caffeine Plus/20% Sparklin"). Moving along the curve (and changing the expected return and standard deviation of the portfolio) is a matter of changing your portfolio allocation between the two stocks.

We can create portfolios with the *same* risk level (i.e., same standard deviation) and *higher* expected returns by diversifying our investment portfolio across many stocks. We can even benefit by adding just Sparklin' to a portfolio of only Caffeine Plus stock. We can create a combination of Caffeine Plus and Sparklin' (portfolio B) that has the same standard deviation but a higher expected return. Risk-averse investors would always prefer that combination to Caffeine Plus by itself.

Let's take an analytical look at how diversification reduces risk by using the portfolio combinations in Figure 9. As indicated, the end points of this curve represent the risk/return combination from a 100% investment in either Sparklin' or Caffeine Plus. Notice that as Sparklin' is added to Caffeine Plus, the frontier "bulges" up and to the left (i.e., northwesterly, if you think of the plot as a map and north as up). This bulge is what creates the diversification benefits because portfolios with between 100% and 80% allocations to Caffeine Plus have both less risk and greater expected return than a portfolio of Caffeine Plus only.

The Special Role of Correlation

As the correlation between the two assets decreases, the benefits of diversification increase. That's because, as the correlation decreases, there is less of a tendency for stock returns to move together. The separate movements of each stock serve to reduce the volatility of the portfolio to a level that is less than that of its individual components.

Figure 10 illustrates the effects of correlation levels on diversification benefits. We've created the risk-return trade-off line for four different levels of correlation between the returns on the two stocks. Notice that the amount of bulge in the risk-return trade-off line is a function of the correlation between the two assets: the lower the correlation (closer to –1), the greater the bulge; the larger the correlation (closer to +1), the smaller is the bulge.

Figure 10: Effects of Correlation on Diversification Benefits

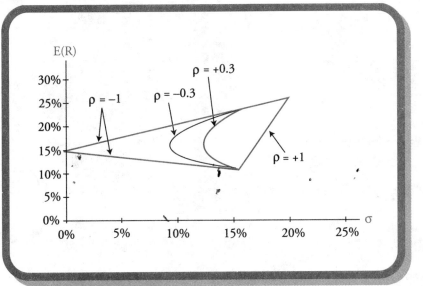

What does all this tell us? *The lower the correlation between the returns of the stocks in the portfolio, all else equal, the greater the diversification benefits.* This principle also applies to portfolios with many stocks, as we'll see next.

LOS 53.g: Describe the efficient frontier and explain the implications for incremental returns as an investor assumes more risk.

The calculations required to generate what we called the risk-return trade-off curve for a two-asset portfolio are not too difficult to do with a spreadsheet. However, the statistical input requirements to apply Markowitz portfolio theory in a large portfolio are significant. Specifically, we must estimate:

- The expected return for each asset available for investment.
- The standard deviation for each asset.
- The correlations between every pair of assets.

This need for correlations can be particularly onerous. For example, if the universe of potential securities includes 100 different stocks, then there are 4,950 pairwise correlation coefficients that must be estimated.

However, with enough computer power, we can generate the set of efficient portfolios from among all the possible combinations of all the assets available for investment. A portfolio is considered to be *efficient* if no other portfolio offers a higher expected return with the same (or lower) risk or if no other portfolio offers lower risk with the same (or higher) return. The concept of efficient portfolios is a key concept in portfolio theory (and capital market theory, discussed in the next topic review).

The efficient frontier represents the set of portfolios that will give you the highest return at each level of risk (or, alternatively, the lowest risk for each level of return). The efficient frontier is portrayed graphically in Figure 11.

Figure 11: Markowitz Efficient Frontier

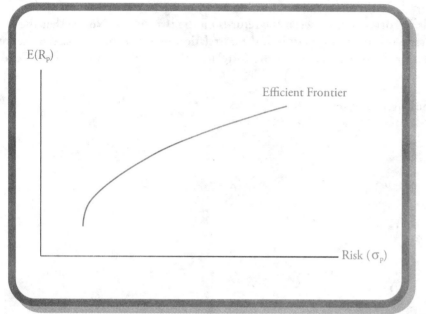

LOS 53.h: Define optimal portfolio and show how each investor may have a different optimal portfolio.

We can combine the concepts of the efficient frontier and indifference curve analysis to describe how a risk averse investor selects his optimal portfolio. Steep indifference curves for Investor A in Figure 12 (I_1 and I_2) indicate greater risk aversion than Investor B, who has relatively flat indifference curves (I'_1 and I'_2). The *optimal portfolio* for each investor is at the point where the investor's (highest) indifference curve is tangent to the efficient frontier. The optimal portfolio is the portfolio that is the most preferred of the possible portfolios (i.e., the one that lies on the highest indifference curve).

Investor A, the more risk-averse investor, has portfolio X as his most preferred portfolio, while Investor B, the less risk-averse investor, has portfolio Y as his most preferred portfolio. Investor B will expect more return than Investor A but is also willing to assume more risk than Investor A to get a higher expected return. The bottom line here is simple—the less risk-averse investor will have a most-preferred portfolio that is riskier, compared to the more risk-averse investor.

Figure 12: Locating the Optimal Portfolio

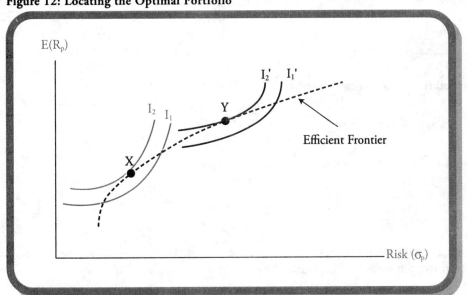

Professor's Note: The steeper the slope at the point of tangency, the greater the level of risk aversion because it takes more additional return to accept a unit of increased risk. If you think this was a lot of work to show that a less risk-averse investor chooses a riskier portfolio, you may be right, but we will use this analysis shortly to extend the model.

KEY CONCEPTS

1. A risk-averse investor prefers higher expected returns for the same level of expected risk and prefers lower risk for a given level of expected returns.

2. The Markowitz assumptions are:
   - Investors see a probability distribution of expected returns for every investment.
   - Investors maximize one-period expected utility, and their indifference curves exhibit diminishing marginal utility of wealth.
   - Investors measure risk as the variance (standard deviation) of expected returns.
   - Investors make all investment decisions only on the basis of risk and return.
   - Investors are risk averse.

3. The expected rate of return from expectational data for a single risky asset is:

$$E(R) = \sum_{i=1}^{n} P_i R_i$$

   The expected rate of return on a single risky asset from historical data is:

$$\bar{R} = \frac{\sum_{t=1}^{n} R_t}{n}$$

4. The variance of rates of return from expectational data for an individual investment is calculated as:

$$\text{variance} = \sigma^2 = \sum_{i=1}^{n} \left\{ \left[R_i - E(R) \right]^2 \times P_i \right\}$$

From historical data, variance is calculated as:

$$\text{variance} = \sigma^2 = \frac{\sum\limits_{t=1}^{N}\left(R_t - \bar{R}\right)^2}{n}$$

5. The covariance from expectational data is calculated as:

$$Cov_{1,2} = \sum_{i=1}^{n}\left\{P_i\left[R_{i,1} - E(R_1)\right]\left[R_{i,2} - E(R_2)\right]\right\}$$

The covariance calculation using historical data is:

$$Cov_{1,2} = \frac{\sum\limits_{t=1}^{n}\left\{\left[R_{t,1} - \bar{R}_1\right]\left[R_{t,2} - \bar{R}_2\right]\right\}}{n}$$

6. The correlation coefficient can take values from −1 to +1 and is a standardized measure of how two random variables change in relation to each other. It is calculated as:

$$\rho_{1,2} = \frac{Cov_{1,2}}{\sigma_1 \times \sigma_2} \text{ so that } Cov_{1,2} = \rho_{1,2}\sigma_1\sigma_2$$

7. The variance of a portfolio of two assets is a function of the correlation between the returns of the two assets, the asset weights, and the standard deviations of the asset returns. It is calculated as:

$$\sigma_p^2 = w_1^2\sigma_1^2 + w_2^2\sigma_2^2 + 2w_1w_2\rho_{1,2}\sigma_1\sigma_2$$

8. The efficient frontier represents the set of portfolios that will give you the highest return at each level of risk and shows the increases in expected return that an investor can expect in equilibrium for taking on more portfolio risk (standard deviation) in an efficient portfolio.

9. The optimal portfolio for an investor is at the point of where an investor's (highest) risk-return indifference curve is tangent to the efficient frontier.

CONCEPT CHECKERS: AN INTRODUCTION TO PORTFOLIO MANAGEMENT

Use the following data to answer Questions 1 through 3.

An investment has a 50% chance of a 20% return, a 25% chance of a 10% return, and a 25% chance of a –10% return.

1.   What is the investment's expected return?
        A. 5.0%.
        B. 10.0%.
        C. 12.5%.
        D. 15.0%.

2.   What is the investment's variance of returns?
        A. 0.005.
        B. 0.010.
        C. 0.015.
        D. 0.150.

3.   What is the investment's standard deviation of returns?
        A. 1.225%.
        B. 1.500%.
        C. 2.250%.
        D. 12.250%.

4.   Which of the following statements about covariance and correlation is **FALSE**?
        A. Positive covariance means that asset returns move together.
        B. A zero covariance implies there is no linear relationship between the two variables.
        C. If two assets have perfect negative correlation, it is impossible to reduce the portfolio's overall variance.
        D. The covariance of a two-stock portfolio is equal to the correlation coefficient times the standard deviation of one stock times the standard deviation of the other stock.

Use the following data to answer Questions 5 and 6.

A portfolio was created by investing 25% of the funds in asset A (standard deviation = 15%) and the balance of the funds in asset B (standard deviation = 10%).

5.   If the correlation coefficient is 0.75, what is the portfolio's standard deviation?
        A. 11.2%.
        B. 10.6%.
        C. 12.4%.
        D. 15.0%.

6.   If the correlation coefficient is –0.75, what is the portfolio's standard deviation?
        A. 2.8%.
        B. 4.2%.
        C. 5.3%.
        D. 10.6%.

7. Which of the following statements about correlation is **FALSE**?
    A. Potential benefits from diversification arise when correlation is less than +1.
    B. If the correlation coefficient were 0, a zero variance portfolio could be constructed.
    C. If the correlation coefficient were –1, a zero variance portfolio could be constructed.
    D. The lower the correlation coefficient, the greater the potential benefits from diversification.

8. A measure of how well the returns of two risky assets move together is the:
    A. range.
    B. covariance.
    C. semivariance.
    D. standard deviation.

9. A portfolio manager adds a new stock to a portfolio that has the same standard deviation of returns as the existing portfolio but has a correlation coefficient with the existing portfolio that is less than +1. If the new stock is added, the portfolio's standard deviation will:
    A. decrease.
    B. not change.
    C. increase by the amount of the new stock's standard deviation.
    D. increase by less than the amount of the new stock's standard deviation.

10. An investor currently owns Brown Co. and is thinking of adding either James Co. or Beta Co. to his holdings. All three stocks offer the same expected return and total risk. The covariance of returns between Brown Co. and James Co. is –0.5 and the covariance between Brown Co. and Beta Co. is +0.5. Which of choices below *best describes* the portfolio's risk? The portfolio's risk would:
    A. decline more if only Beta Co. is purchased.
    B. decline more if only James Co. is purchased.
    C. increase if only Beta Co. is purchased.
    D. remain unchanged if both stocks are purchased.

11. Which of the following portfolios falls *below* the Markowitz efficient frontier?

	Portfolio	Expected Return	Expected Standard Deviation
A.	A	7%	14%
B.	B	9%	26%
C.	C	12%	22%
D.	D	15%	30%

12. In time 1, Stock A's return was 10% and Stock B's return was 15%. In time 2, Stock A's return was 6% and Stock B's return was 9%. What is the covariance of returns between A and B?
    A. 2.
    B. 3.
    C. 6.
    D. 12.

13. The standard deviation of returns is 0.30 for Stock A and 0.20 for Stock B. The covariance between the returns of A and B is 0.006. The return correlation between A and B is:
    A. 0.10.
    B. 0.20.
    C. 0.30.
    D. 0.35.

ANSWERS – CONCEPT CHECKERS: AN INTRODUCTION TO PORTFOLIO MANAGEMENT

1. **B** $(0.5 \times 0.2) + (0.25 \times 0.1) + (0.25 \times -0.1) = 0.1$, or 10%

2. **C** $[0.5(0.2 - 0.1)^2] + [0.25(0.1 - 0.1)^2] + [0.25(-0.1 - 0.1)^2] = 0.005 + 0 + 0.01 = 0.015$

3. **D** $\sqrt{0.015} = 0.1225 = 12.25\%$

4. **C** If two assets have perfect negative correlation, it is possible to reduce the overall risk to zero. Note that positive correlation means that assets move together, a zero correlation implies no relationship, and covariance is defined as the correlation coefficient times the standard deviation of the two stocks in a two-stock portfolio.

5. **B** $\sqrt{[(0.25)^2(0.15)^2] + [(0.75)^2(0.10)^2] + [2(0.25)(0.75)(0.15)(0.10)(0.75)]} = \sqrt{(0.001406) + (0.005625) + (0.004219)}$

   $= \sqrt{(0.01125)} = 0.106 = 10.6\%$

6. **C** $\sqrt{[(0.25)^2(0.15)^2] + [(0.75)^2(0.10)^2] + [2(0.25)(0.75)(0.15)(0.10)(-0.75)]} = \sqrt{(0.001406) + (0.005625) - (0.004219)}$

   $= \sqrt{(0.002812)} = 0.053 = 5.3\%$

7. **B** A zero-variance portfolio can only be constructed if the correlation coefficient between assets is negative. Note that benefits can arise from diversification when correlation is less than +1, and the lower the correlation, the greater the potential benefit.

8. **B** The covariance is defined as the co-movement of the returns of two assets, or how well the returns of two risky assets move together. Note that range, semivariance, and standard deviation are measures of dispersion and measure risk, not how assets move together.

9. **A** There are potential benefits from diversification anytime the correlation coefficient with the existing portfolio is less than one. Because the correlation coefficient of the asset being added with the existing portfolio is less than one, the overall risk of the portfolio should decrease, resulting in a lower standard deviation.

10. **B** The overall risk would decline if either asset were added to the portfolio because both assets have correlation coefficients of less than one. The risk would decline the most if James Co. were added because it has the lowest correlation coefficient.

11. **B** Portfolio B must be the portfolio that falls below the Markowitz efficient frontier because there is a portfolio (Portfolio C) that offers a higher return and lower risk.

12. **C** Mean return A $= \dfrac{10 + 6}{2} = 8\%$; mean return B $= \dfrac{15 + 9}{2} = 12\%$

    $\text{Cov}_{A,B} \dfrac{(10 - 8)(15 - 12) + (6 - 8)(9 - 12)}{2} = 6$

13. **A** Correlation $= 0.006 / [(0.30)(0.20)] = 0.10$

AN INTRODUCTION TO ASSET PRICING MODELS

EXAM FOCUS

This topic review picks up where our review of the work of Prof. Markowitz left off. Adding a riskless asset to the opportunity set transforms portfolio theory into capital market theory. Key concepts in this topic review include the development of the capital market line, the separation of risk into systematic and unsystematic components, and the development of the capital asset pricing model. Be sure that you can discuss each of the major concepts and that you can value an asset using the capital asset pricing model. You should also be familiar with the difference between the necessary assumptions for these pricing models.

LOS 54.a: List the assumptions of the capital market theory.

The assumptions of capital market theory are:

- *Markowitz investors.* All investors use the Markowitz mean-variance framework to select securities. This means they want to select portfolios that lie along the efficient frontier, based on their utility functions.
- *Unlimited risk-free lending and borrowing.* Investors can borrow or lend any amount of money at the risk-free rate.
- *Homogeneous expectations.* This means that when investors look at a stock, they all see the same risk/return distribution.
- *One-period horizon.* All investors have the same one-period time horizon.
- *Divisible assets.* All investments are infinitely divisible.
- *Frictionless markets.* There are no taxes or transaction costs.
- *No inflation and constant interest.* There is no inflation, and interest rates do not change.
- *Equilibrium.* The capital markets are in equilibrium.

LOS 54.b: Explain what happens to the expected return, the standard deviation of returns, and possible risk-return combinations when a risk-free asset is combined with a portfolio of risky assets.

Markowitz's efficient frontier did not consider the existence of a risk-free asset. **Adding a risk-free asset** to the Markowitz portfolio construction process allows portfolio theory to develop into capital market theory. Here's the bottom line (no pun intended):

The introduction of a risk-free asset changes the Markowitz efficient frontier from a curve into a straight line called the **capital market line** (CML). Let's see how this conclusion is derived.

If you invest a portion of your total funds in a risky portfolio M and the remaining portion in the risk-free asset, the equation for the expected return of the resulting portfolio will be:

$$E(R_p) = (1 - w_M)RFR + w_M E(R_M) = RFR + w_M[E(R_M) - RFR]$$

where:

RFR = the risk-free rate

$E(R_M)$ = the expected return on portfolio M

w_M = percentage (weight) of the total portfolio value invested in portfolio M

$1 - w_M$ = the percentage (weight) of the total portfolio value invested in the risk-free asset

Professor's Note: You do not need to memorize the preceding formula! We are going to use it to derive the equation for the CAPM, but on the exam, you can always determine the $E(R_p)$ for a two-stock portfolio (even if it contains the risk-free asset) using the equation: $E(R_p) = w_{RFR}RFR + w_M E(R_M)$.

If you combine the risk-free asset with a risky portfolio, the equation for the expected standard deviation of the resulting portfolio will be the same as for a two-risky-asset portfolio:

$$\sigma_P = \sqrt{(1 - w_M)^2 \sigma_{RFR}^2 + w_M^2 \sigma_M^2 + 2(1 - w_M)w_M \sigma_{RFR} \sigma_M \rho_{RFR,M}}$$

where:

σ_{RFR} = standard deviation of the risk-free asset

σ_M = standard deviation of the expected returns on portfolio M

$\rho_{RFR,M}$ = correlation between the risk-free asset and portfolio M

When one of the assets is risk-free, the calculation is much easier! By definition, under the assumptions of portfolio theory and capital market theory, if an asset is risk-free, its return does not vary. Thus, its variance and standard deviation are zero. If an asset has no variance, its expected return doesn't move. If the risk-free rate, RFR, is constant, it can't co-vary with other assets. In other words, the risk-free rate is stationary. Thus, its correlation coefficient with all other assets is zero.

Since $\sigma_{RFR} = \rho_{RFR,M} = 0$, the equation for portfolio standard deviation simplifies to:

$$\sigma_P = w_M \sigma_M$$

If we put 40% of our portfolio assets in the risky portfolio and the remainder in the risk-free asset, the resulting portfolio has 40% of the standard deviation of the risky portfolio! The risk/return relationship is now linear.

Combining this with our expected return equation gives us the following linear equation for the expected portfolio return as a function of portfolio standard deviation:

$$E(R_P) = RFR + \sigma_P \left\{ \frac{[E(R_M) - RFR]}{\sigma_M} \right\}$$

This is the equation for the capital market line (CML). The CML represents all possible portfolio allocations between the risk-free asset and a risky portfolio. The CML has an intercept of RFR and a slope equal to:

$$\frac{[E(R_M) - RFR]}{\sigma_M}$$

How do we select the optimal risky portfolio when a risk-free asset is also available? First, let's pick a risky portfolio (like portfolio X in Figure 1) that's on the Markowitz efficient frontier, since we know that these efficient portfolios dominate everything below them in terms of return offered for risk taken. Now, let's combine the risk-free asset with portfolio X. Remember, the risk/return relationship resulting from the combination of the risk-free asset and a risky portfolio is a straight line.

Now, choose a risky portfolio that is above portfolio X on the efficient frontier, such as portfolio Y. Portfolios on the line from RFR to Y will be preferred to portfolios on the line from RFR to X because we get more return for a given amount of risk. Actually, we can keep getting better portfolios by moving up the efficient frontier. At point M you reach the best possible combination. Portfolio M is at the point where the risk-return tradeoff line is just tangent to the efficient frontier. The line from RFR to M represents portfolios that are preferred to all the portfolios on the "old" efficient frontier, except M.

Figure 1: Capital Market Lines

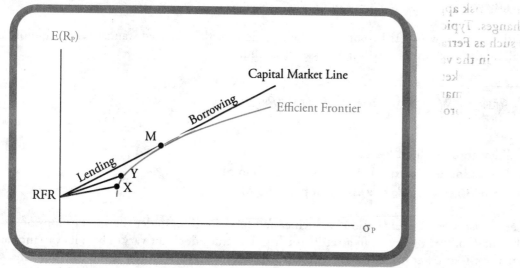

Investors at point RFR have 100% of their funds invested in the risk-free asset. Investors at point M have 100% of their funds invested in portfolio M. Between RFR and M, investors hold both the risk-free asset and portfolio M. This means investors are *lending* some of their funds at the risk-free rate (i.e., buying the risk-free asset) and investing the rest in portfolio M. To the right of M, investors hold more than 100% of portfolio M. This means they are *borrowing* funds to buy more of portfolio M. The *levered positions* represent a 100% investment in portfolio M and borrowing to buy even more of portfolio M.

The introduction of a risk-free asset changes the Markowitz efficient frontier into a straight line called the CML.

LOS 54.c: Identify the market portfolio, and describe the role of the market portfolio in the formation of the capital market line (CML).

All investors have to do to get the risk and return combination that suits them is to simply vary the proportion of their investment in the risky portfolio M and the risk-free asset. So, in the CML world, all investors will hold some combination of the risk-free asset and portfolio M. Since all investors will want to hold the same risky portfolio, **risky portfolio M must be the market portfolio.**

The market portfolio is the portfolio consisting of every risky asset; the weights on each asset are equal to the percentage of the market value of the asset to the market value of the entire market portfolio. For example, if the market value of a stock is $100 million and the market value of the market portfolio is $5 billion, that stock's weight in the market portfolio is 2% ($100 million / $5 billion).

Logic tells us that the market portfolio, which will be held by all investors, has to contain all the stocks, bonds, and risky assets in existence because all assets have to be held by someone. This portfolio theoretically includes all risky assets, so it is completely diversified.

LOS 54.d: Define systematic and unsystematic risk and explain why an investor should not expect to receive additional return for assuming unsystematic risk.

When you diversify across assets that are not perfectly correlated, the portfolio's risk is less than the weighted sum of the risks of the individual securities in the portfolio. The risk that disappears in the portfolio construction process is called the asset's **unsystematic risk** (also called *unique, diversifiable, or firm-specific risk*). Since the market portfolio contains *all* risky assets, it must represent the ultimate in diversification. All the risk that can be diversified away must be gone. The risk that is left cannot be diversified away, since there is nothing left to add to the portfolio. The risk that remains is called the **systematic risk** (also called *nondiversifiable risk* or *market risk*).

The concept of systematic risk applies to individual securities as well as to portfolios. Some securities are very sensitive to market changes. Typical examples of firms that are very sensitive to market movements are luxury goods manufacturers such as Ferrari automobiles and Harley Davidson motorcycles. Small changes in the market will lead to large changes in the value of luxury goods manufacturers. These firms have high systematic risk (i.e., they are very responsive to market, or systematic, changes). Other firms, such as utility companies, respond very little to changes in the overall market. These firms have very little systematic risk. Hence, total risk (as measured by standard deviation) can be broken down into its component parts: unsystematic risk and systematic risk. Mathematically:

total risk = systematic risk + unsystematic risk

Professor's Note: Know this concept!

Do you actually have to buy all the securities in the market to diversify away unsystematic risk? No. Academic studies have shown that as you increase the number of stocks in a portfolio, the portfolio's risk falls toward the level of market risk. One study showed that it only took about 12 to 18 stocks in a portfolio to achieve 90% of the maximum diversification possible. Another study indicated it took 30 securities. Whatever the number, it is significantly less than *all* the securities. Figure 2 provides a general representation of this concept. Note, in the figure, that once you get to 30 or so securities in a portfolio, the standard deviation remains constant. The remaining risk is systematic, or nondiversifiable, risk. We will develop this concept later when we discuss beta, a measure of systematic risk.

Figure 2: Risk vs. Number of Portfolio Assets

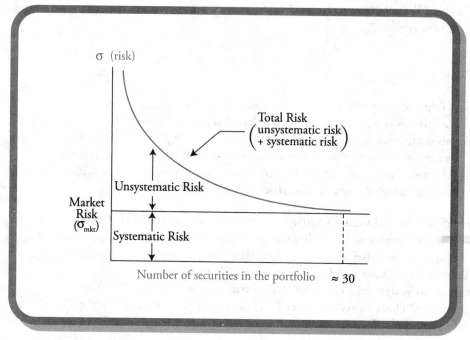

Systematic Risk is Relevant in Portfolios

One important conclusion of capital market theory is that equilibrium security returns depend on a stock's or a portfolio's systematic risk, not its total risk as measured by standard deviation. One of the assumptions of the model is that diversification is free. The reasoning is that investors will not be compensated for bearing risk that can be eliminated at no cost. If you think about the costs of a no-load index fund compared to buying individual stocks, diversification is actually very low cost if not actually free.

The implications of this conclusion are very important to asset pricing (expected returns). The riskiest stock, with risk measured as standard deviation of returns, does not necessarily have the greatest expected return. Consider a biotech stock with one new drug product that is in clinical trials to determine its effectiveness. If it turns out that the drug is effective and safe, stock returns will be quite high. If, on the other hand, the subjects in the clinical trials are killed or otherwise harmed by the drug, the stock will fall to approximately zero and returns will be quite poor. This describes a stock with high standard deviation of returns (i.e., high total risk).

The high risk of our biotech stock, however, is primarily from firm-specific factors, so its unsystematic risk is high. Since market factors such as economic growth rates have little to do with the eventual outcome for this stock, systematic risk is a small proportion of the total risk of the stock. Capital market theory says that the equilibrium return on this stock may be less than that of a stock with much less firm-specific risk but more sensitivity to the factors that drive the return of the overall market. An established manufacturer of machine tools may not be a very risky investment in terms of total risk, but may have a greater sensitivity to market (systematic) risk factors (e.g., GDP growth rates) than our biotech stock. Given this scenario, the stock with more total risk (the biotech stock) has less systematic risk and will therefore have a lower equilibrium rate of return according to capital market theory.

Note that holding many biotech firms in a portfolio will diversify away the firm-specific risk. Some will have blockbuster products and some will fail, but you can imagine that when 50 or 100 such stocks are combined into a portfolio, the uncertainty about the portfolio return is much less than the uncertainty about the return of a single biotech firm stock.

To sum up, unsystematic risk is not compensated in equilibrium because it can be eliminated for free through diversification. Systematic risk is measured by the contribution of a security to the risk of a well diversified portfolio and the expected equilibrium return (required return) on an individual security will depend on its systematic risk.

LOS 54.e: Describe the capital asset pricing model, diagram the security market line (SML), and define beta.

Given that the only relevant risk for an individual asset i is the covariance between the asset's returns and the return on the market, $Cov_{i,mkt}$, we can plot the relationship between risk and return for individual assets using $Cov_{i,mkt}$ as our measure of systematic risk. The resulting line, plotted in Figure 3, is one version of what is referred to as the **security market line** (SML).

Figure 3: Security Market Line

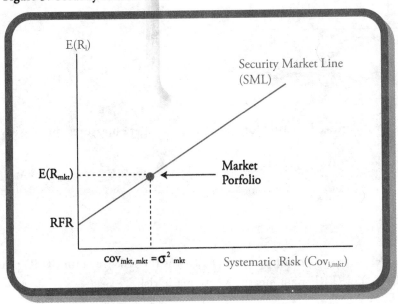

The equation of the SML is:

$$E(R_i) = RFR + \frac{E(R_{mkt}) - RFR}{\sigma^2_{mkt}}\left(Cov_{i,mkt}\right)$$

which can be rearranged and stated as:

$$E(R_i) = RFR + \frac{Cov_{i,mkt}}{\sigma^2_{mkt}}\left[E(R_{mkt}) - RFR\right]$$

The line described by this last equation is presented in Figure 4, where we let the standardized covariance term, $\frac{Cov_{i,mkt}}{\sigma^2_{mkt}}$, be defined as beta, β_i. This is the most common means of describing the SML, and this relation between beta (systematic risk) and expected return is known as the **capital asset pricing model** (CAPM).

Figure 4: The Capital Asset Pricing Model

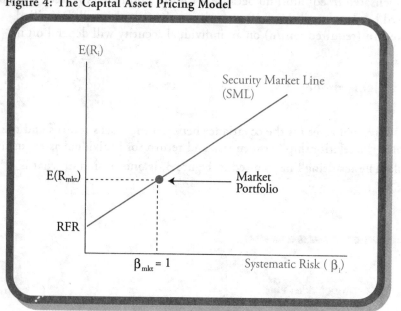

So, we can **define beta**, $\beta = \dfrac{\text{Cov}_{i,mkt}}{\sigma_{mkt}^2}$, as a standardized measure of systematic risk. Beta measures the sensitivity of a security's returns to changes in the market return.

Formally, the CAPM is stated as:

$$E(R_i) = RFR + \beta_i[E(R_{mkt}) - RFR]$$

The CAPM holds that, in equilibrium, the expected return on risky asset $E(R_i)$ is the risk-free rate (RFR) plus a beta-adjusted market risk premium, $\beta_i[E(R_{mkt}) - RFR]$. Beta measures systematic risk.

It is important that you recognize that the CML and SML are very different. Recall the equation of the CML:

$$E(R_P) = RFR + \sigma_P\left\{\frac{\left[E(R_M) - RFR\right]}{\sigma_M}\right\}$$

The CML uses total risk = σ_p on the X-axis. Hence, only efficient portfolios will plot on the CML. On the other hand, the SML uses beta (systematic risk) on the X-axis. So in a CAPM world, *all properly priced securities and portfolios of securities will plot on the SML.*

The CAPM is one of the most fundamental concepts in investment theory. The CAPM is an equilibrium model that predicts the expected return on a stock, given the expected return on the market, the stock's beta coefficient, and the risk-free rate.

Example: Capital asset pricing model

The expected return on the market is 15%, the risk-free rate is 8%, and the beta for stock A (β_A) is 1.2. Compute the rate of return that would be expected (required) on this stock.

Answer:

$E(R_A) = 0.08 + 1.2 (0.15 - 0.08) = 0.164$

Note: $\beta_A > 1$ so $E(R_A) > E(R_{mkt})$

Professor's Note: Know this calculation!

Example: Capital asset pricing model

The expected return on the market is 15%, the risk-free rate is 8%, and the beta for stock B (β_B) is 0.8. Compute the rate of return that would be expected (required) on this stock.

Answer:

$E(R_B) = 0.08 + 0.8 (0.15 - 0.08) = 0.136$

Note: Beta < 1 so $E(R_B) < E(R_{mkt})$

LOS 54.f: Calculate and interpret using the SML, the expected return on a security, and evaluate whether the security is undervalued, overvalued, or properly valued.

Let's clarify some terminology before we continue. The LOS asks for expected return based on the SML. You should also think of this as the "required return." There is another type of "expected return" which is based on *opinions* of the returns that can be earned on the stock given our future price and dividend forecasts. To keep this straight, we will refer to the expected return based on the theory of the CAPM as the *required* return, and the expected return based on perception and opinion as an *estimated* or *forecast* return.

In a CAPM world, all asset returns should fall on the SML. The SML tells us an asset's *required return* given its level of systematic risk (as measured by beta). The way we can use the CAPM to identify mispriced securities is to compare an asset's *estimated return* (given our forecasts of future prices and dividends) to the required return according to the SML. If the returns are not equal, the asset is either overvalued or undervalued and an appropriate trading strategy may be implemented.

- An asset with an estimated return greater than its required return from the SML is undervalued; we should buy it (return too high, price too low).
- An asset with an estimated return less than its required return from the SML is overvalued; we should sell it (return too low, price too high).
- An asset with an estimated return equal to its required return from the SML is properly valued; we're indifferent between buying or selling it.

Professor's Note: This is the most important LOS in this review. You are likely to see this material on the exam. Make sure you know it and nail the exam question!

Example: Identifying mispriced securities

Figure 5 contains information based on analyst's forecasts for three stocks. Assume a risk-free rate of 7% and a market return of 15%. Compute the expected and required return on each stock, determine whether each stock is undervalued, overvalued, or properly valued, and outline an appropriate trading strategy.

Figure 5: Forecast Data

Stock	Price Today	E(Price) in 1 Year	E(Dividend) in 1 Year	Beta
A	$25	$27	$1.00	1.0
B	40	45	2.00	0.8
C	15	17	0.50	1.2

Answer:

Expected and required returns computations are shown in Figure 6.

Figure 6: Forecasts vs. Required Returns

Stock	Forecast Return	Required Return
A	($27 – $25 + $1) / $25 = 12.0%	0.07 + (1.0)(0.15 – 0.07) = 15.0%
B	($45 – $40 + $2) / $40 = 17.5%	0.07 + (0.8)(0.15 – 0.07) = 13.4%
C	($17 – $15 + $0.5) / $15 = 16.6%	0.07 + (1.2)(0.15 – 0.07) = 16.6%

- Stock A is *overvalued*. It is expected to earn 12%, but based on its systematic risk it should earn 15%. It plots *below* the SML.
- Stock B is *undervalued*. It is expected to earn 17.5%, but based on its systematic risk it should earn 13.4%. It plots *above* the SML.
- Stock C is *properly valued*. It is expected to earn 16.6%, and based on its systematic risk it should earn 16.6%. It plots *on* the SML.

The appropriate trading strategy is:

- Short sell stock A.
- Buy stock B.
- Buy, sell, or ignore stock C.

We can do this same analysis graphically. The expected return/beta combinations of all three stocks are graphed in Figure 7 relative to the SML.

Figure 7: Identifying Mispriced Securities

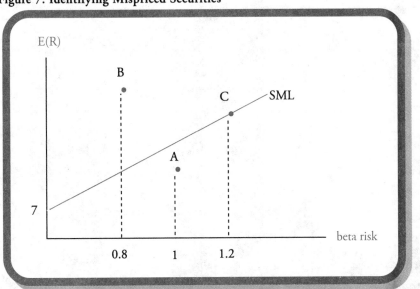

Professor's Note: A trick to use when working these types of problems is: if the estimated return plots "over" the SML, the security is "under" valued. If the estimated return plots" under" the SML, the security is "over" valued.

Remember, all stocks should plot on the SML; any stock not plotting on the SML is mispriced. Notice that Stock A falls below the SML, Stock B lies above the SML, and Stock C is on the SML. If you plot a stock's expected return and it falls below the SML, the stock is overpriced. That is, the stock's expected return is too low given its systematic risk. If a stock plots above the SML, it is underpriced and is offering an expected return greater than required for its systematic risk. If it plots on the SML, the stock is properly priced.

Since the equation of the SML is the capital asset pricing model, you can determine if a stock is over- or underpriced graphically or mathematically. Your answers will always be the same.

LOS 54.g: Describe the effect on the SML of relaxing each of its main underlying assumptions line.

The CAPM requires a number of assumptions, many of which do not reflect the true nature of the investment process. This section addresses the impact on the CAPM of relaxing some of the assumptions required in the derivation of the model.

Different borrowing and lending rates. One of the key assumptions of the CAPM is the ability of investors to lend and borrow at the risk-free rate. This assumption is what makes the CML straight. A straight CML allows risk to be separated into its systematic and unsystematic components. Without an equal lending and borrowing rate, you cannot determine a security's systematic risk, and, therefore, you cannot derive the SML. Without the SML, you cannot derive the CAPM.

Investors can lend all they want by buying investments at the risk-free rate, but investors must pay a premium over the risk-free rate to borrow. The graph in Figure 8 shows what this does to the CML. With unequal borrowing and lending rates, the CML follows the Markowitz efficient frontier (i.e., the no risk-free asset efficient frontier) between points A and B. Essentially, this puts a kink in the CML.

Figure 8: CAPM with Unequal Borrowing and Lending Rates

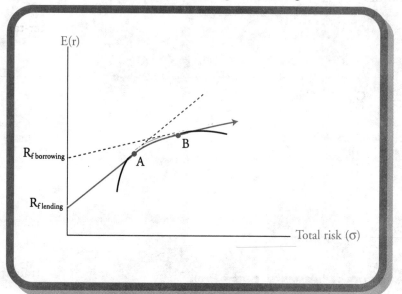

Without borrowing and lending at the same rate, can the validity of the CAPM be maintained? Yes, by the introduction of the **zero-beta portfolio**. The CAPM cannot be derived without equal borrowing and lending rates or some substitute for equal borrowing and lending rates. Fortunately, we have a substitute—the zero-beta model. The zero-beta version of the CAPM assumes that investors can find a *portfolio of securities with returns that are uncorrelated with market returns*. Since the portfolio is uncorrelated with the market, the portfolio will have a beta of zero, that is, no systematic risk.

As long as the expected return on the zero-beta portfolio is assumed to be greater than the risk-free lending rate, the resulting security market line will have a smaller risk premium (i.e., a flatter slope). With the introduction of a zero-beta portfolio with expected returns greater than those of the risk-free asset, we can still derive a linear relation between systematic risk and expected returns, a zero-beta CAPM. This relation can be expressed as:

$$E\left(R_{stock}\right) = E\left(R_{zero\ beta\ portfolio}\right) + \left(Beta_{stock}\right)\left[E\left(R_{market}\right) - E\left(R_{zero\ beta\ portfolio}\right)\right]$$

Transaction costs. The no-transaction-costs assumption guarantees that all securities move to the SML. Why? Securities below the SML are overpriced, and securities above the SML are underpriced. Investors will buy the underpriced securities and sell the overpriced securities until no excess return opportunities exist. When all excess return opportunities have been eliminated, all securities will lie on the SML.

However, with transaction costs, securities that are just slightly mispriced will not be brought back to the SML, because the transaction costs will be greater than the profit potential. This will allow a band of expected returns to exist around the SML. The width of the band is a function of the size of the transaction costs: the higher the costs the wider the band.

Heterogeneous expectations and planning periods. If investors have different risk and return expectations or project their expectations over different time horizons, each investor will have a unique view of the SML. The homogeneous expectations and single holding period assumptions are necessary to bring the multitude of individual security market lines together into one SML and one CML. If these assumptions are not valid, there will be many SMLs and CMLs. The composite graph would be a band of lines with the width of the band determined by the divergence of expectations and time horizons; the greater the divergence of expectations and planning periods, the wider the band. The impact of heterogeneous expectations and multiple planning periods on the CAPM is similar to the impact of transactions costs—the SML becomes a band rather than a line.

Taxes. The expected after-tax returns for taxable investors are usually much different from the pre-tax returns we used in developing the CAPM. Individual investors pay ordinary income tax on dividend income and capital gains tax on realized gains. Individual investors facing different marginal tax rates will have different after-tax return expectations, so their security market lines and capital market lines will be quite different.

KEY CONCEPTS

1. The assumptions of capital market theory are:
   - All investors use the Markowitz mean-variance framework to select securities.
   - Investors can borrow or lend any amount of money at the risk-free rate.
   - All investors have homogeneous expectations.
   - All investors have the same one-period time horizon.
   - All investments are infinitely divisible.
   - There are no taxes or transaction costs.
   - There is no inflation, and interest rates do not change.
   - Capital markets are in equilibrium.

2. The introduction of a risk-free asset changes the Markowitz efficient frontier from a curve into a straight line called the CML. The equation of the CML is:

$$E(R_P) = RFR + \sigma_P \times \left\{ \frac{\left[E(R_M) - RFR \right]}{\sigma_M} \right\}$$

   where R_M and σ_M are the return and standard deviation of the market portfolio

3. The market portfolio is the tangent point where the CML touches the Markowitz efficient frontier. The market portfolio consists of every risky asset; the weights on each asset are equal to the percentage of the market value of the asset to the market value of the entire market portfolio.

4. Total risk is equal to systematic risk plus unsystematic risk.
   - Market or systematic risk cannot be diversified away.
   - Unique or company risk is unsystematic and can be diversified away.

5. The equation of the SML shows the conclusion of the CAPM; expected security returns depend only on systematic risk as measured by beta:

   $$E(R_i) = RFR + \beta_i [E(R_{mkt}) - RFR]$$

6. Beta (β) is a standardized measure of systematic risk. It is calculated as:

   $$\beta_i = \frac{Cov_{i,mkt}}{\sigma^2_{mkt}} = \left(\frac{\sigma_i}{\sigma_{mkt}} \right) \times \rho_{i,mkt}$$

7. The SML will tell us assets' required returns given their level of systematic risk (as measured by beta). We can compare this to the assets' expected returns (given our forecasts of future prices and dividends) to identify undervalued assets and overvalued assets.

8. The graph of the SML is:

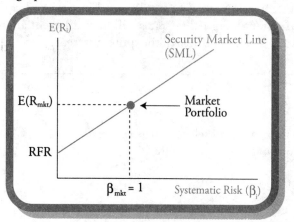

9. Relaxing the CAPM assumptions changes the model's implications.
   * The CAPM cannot be derived without equal borrowing and lending rates, unless investors can create a zero-beta portfolio.
   * The existence of transactions costs means that the SML is a band (with fairly tight upper and lower bounds on prices) rather than a line.
   * The impact of heterogeneous expectations and multiple planning periods on the CAPM is similar to the impact of transactions costs—the SML becomes a band rather than a line.
   * Individual investors facing different marginal tax rates will have different after-tax return expectations, so their security market lines (SML) and capital market lines (CML) will be quite different.

CONCEPT CHECKERS: AN INTRODUCTION TO ASSET PRICING MODELS

1. An investor put 60% of his money into a risky asset offering a 10% return with a standard deviation of returns of 8%, and he put the balance of his funds in the risk-free asset offering 5%. What is the expected return and standard deviation of his portfolio?

Expected Return	Standard Deviation
A. 6.0%	6.8%
B. 8.0%	8.0%
C. 8.0%	4.8%
D. 10.0%	6.6%

2. What is the risk measure associated with the capital market line (CML)?
   A. Beta.
   B. Covariance.
   C. Market risk.
   D. Standard deviation.

3. A portfolio to the right of the market portfolio on the CML is:
   A. a lending portfolio.
   B. a borrowing portfolio.
   C. an inefficient portfolio.
   D. an impossible portfolio.

4. As you increase the number of stocks in a portfolio, the systematic risk will:
   A. remain constant.
   B. increase at a decreasing rate.
   C. decrease at a decreasing rate.
   D. decrease at an increasing rate.

5. Total risk equals:
   A. unique plus diversifiable risk.
   B. market plus nondiversifiable risk.
   C. systematic plus unsystematic risk.
   D. systematic plus nondiversifiable risk.

6. What is the required rate of return for a stock with a beta of 1.2, when the risk-free rate is 6% and the market is offering 12%?
   A. 6.0%.
   B. 7.2%.
   C. 12.0%.
   D. 13.2%.

7. What is the required rate of return for a stock with a beta of 0.7, when the risk-free rate is 7% and the market is offering 14%?
   A. 11.9%.
   B. 14.0%.
   C. 14.9%.
   D. 16.8%.

8.   The risk-free rate is 6% and the expected market return is 15%. An investor sees a stock with a beta of 1.2 selling for $25 that will pay a $1 dividend next year. If he thinks the stock will be selling for $30 at year end, he thinks it is:
     A. overpriced, so buy it.
     B. overpriced, so short it.
     C. underpriced, so buy it.
     D. underpriced, so short it.

9.   A stock with a beta of 0.7 currently priced at $50 is expected to increase in price to $55 by year end and pay a $1 dividend. The expected market return is 15%, and the risk-free rate is 8%. The stock is:
     A. overpriced, so do not buy it.
     B. underpriced, so buy it.
     C. properly priced, so buy it.
     D. properly priced, so do not buy it.

10. The market is expected to return 15% next year and the risk-free rate is 7%. What is the expected rate of return on a stock with a beta of 1.3?
     A. 10.4%.
     B. 16.3%.
     C. 17.1%.
     D. 17.4%.

11. The market is expected to return 12% next year and the risk free rate is 6%. What is the expected rate of return on a stock with a beta of 0.9?
     A. 10.8%.
     B. 11.4%.
     C. 13.0%.
     D. 16.2%.

12. The covariance of the market's returns with the stock's returns is 0.005 and the standard deviation of the market's returns is 0.05. What is the stock's beta?
     A. 0.1.
     B. 1.0.
     C. 1.5.
     D. 2.0.

13. The covariance of the market's returns with the stock's returns is 0.008. The standard deviation of the market's returns is 0.08 and the standard deviation of the stock's returns is 0.11. What is the correlation coefficient between the returns of the stock and returns of the market?
     A. 0.50.
     B. 0.91.
     C. 1.00.
     D. 1.25.

14. Which of the following statements about the SML and the CML is **FALSE**?
     A. Securities that plot above the SML are undervalued.
     B. Investors expect to be compensated for systematic risk.
     C. The market portfolio consists of all the risky assets in the universe.
     D. Securities that fall on the SML have no intrinsic value to the investor.

15. Susan Kinicki is an analyst. She is talking with a colleague, Charles Riker, about how to determine whether a security is undervalued or overvalued. After meeting with her supervisor, she meets Riker for lunch. During lunch, she makes the following statements:

i) "I'm not recommending ONJ stock because the expected return is greater than the return I calculated using the CAPM."

ii) "Relaxing the standard assumptions of homogeneous expectations and zero transactions costs have the same effect on the SML—the SML becomes a band rather than a straight line."

Riker considers Kinicki's statements and then replies, "I agree with you about the ONJ stock; I don't intend to recommend it either. However, I thought that heterogeneous expectations and positive transactions costs affected the SML differently. I know that transactions costs result in a band, but I don't think introducing heterogeneous expectations has that effect."

Answer this question in context of the SML. Riker is correct with regard to:
A. statement (i), but not statement (ii).
B. statement (ii), but not statement (i).
C. both statement (i) and (ii).
D. neither statement (i) or (ii).

ANSWERS – CONCEPT CHECKERS: AN INTRODUCTION TO ASSET PRICING MODELS

1. **C**   Expected return: $(0.60 \times 0.10) + (0.40 \times 0.05) = 0.08$, or 8.0%.

   Standard deviation: $0.60 \times 0.08 = 0.048$, or 4.8%.

2. **D**   Remember that the capital market line (CML) plots return against *total risk* which is measured by standard deviation.

3. **B**   A portfolio to the right of a portfolio on the CML has more risk than what is offered by the market. Investors seeking to take on more risk will *borrow* at the risk-free rate to purchase more of the market portfolio.

4. **A**   When you increase the number of stocks in a portfolio, *unsystematic risk* will decrease at a decreasing rate; however, *systematic risk* cannot be diversified away and will remain constant no matter how many assets are added to the portfolio.

5. **C**   Because unsystematic risk can be diversified away, investors only expect to be compensated for taking on *systematic risk*.

6. **D** $6 + 1.2(12 - 6) = 13.2\%$

7. **A** $7 + 0.7(14 - 7) = 11.9\%$

8. **C**   Required rate = $6 + 1.2(15 - 6) = 16.8\%$

   Return on stock = $(30 - 25 + 1) / 25 = 24\%$

   Based on risk, the stock plots above the SML and is underpriced, so buy it!

9. **A**   Required rate = $8 + 0.7(15 - 8) = 12.9\%$

   Return on stock = $(55 - 50 + 1) / 50 = 12\%$

   The stock falls below the SML so it is *overpriced*.

10. **D** $7 + 1.3(15 - 7) = 17.4\%$

11. **B** $6 + 0.9(12 - 6) = 11.4\%$

12. **D**   Beta = covariance / market variance

   Market variance = $0.05^2 = 0.0025$

   Beta = $0.005 / 0.0025 = 2.0$

13. **B** $\rho_{1,2} = \dfrac{Cov_{1,2}}{\sigma_1 \sigma_2} = \dfrac{0.008}{(0.08)(0.11)} = 0.909$

14. **D**   Securities that fall on the SML are expected to earn the market rate of return and, therefore, do have intrinsic value to the investor (and may have diversification benefits). The other statements are true.

15. **D**   Riker is incorrect to agree with Kinicki about ONJ stock—a stock with an expected return greater than that calculated with the CAPM is undervalued. He is incorrect with respect to statement ii) as well. Introducing heterogeneous expectations and positive transactions costs both make the SML relationship a band rather than a line.

ORGANIZATION AND FUNCTIONING OF SECURITIES MARKETS

Study Session 13

EXAM FOCUS

This review covers securities markets, explains how and where securities are traded, and introduces much of the terminology of securities trading. It's all testable material and you should pay special attention to the calculations dealing with margin accounts. The other important topic areas here include the difference between primary and secondary markets, the mechanics of short sales, the difference between a dealer market and an exchange market, types of orders, and the different arrangements with investment bankers that can be made when issuing new securities.

LOS 55.a: Describe the characteristics of a well-functioning securities market.

A well-functioning securities market will offer the following characteristics:

- **Timely and accurate information** on the price and volume of past transactions and on current supply and demand conditions.
- **Liquidity** (the ability to buy or sell quickly at a known price), which requires *marketability* (the ability to sell the security quickly) and *price continuity* (prices don't change much from one transaction to the next in the absence of news because numerous buyers and sellers are willing to trade at prices above and below the current price).
- **Internal efficiency** refers to low transaction costs.
- **Informational (external) efficiency**, which means that prices adjust rapidly to new information so the prevailing market price reflects all available information regarding the value of the asset.

LOS 55.b: Distinguish between competitive bids, negotiated sales, and private placements for issuing bonds.

A new issue of bonds is usually sold with the help of an investment banker who may or may not *underwrite* the issue (guarantee the sale of the whole issue at an agreed-upon price). The cost of the underwriting and any additional legal and advisory services provided by the investment banker can be determined by negotiation with a single underwriter or by soliciting bids for the services that will be provided.

A **negotiated sale** (most common with corporate bond issues) is one in which the price of the underwriting and advisory services is agreed upon through negotiations between the issuer and an investment banker, usually one with whom the issuing firm has a relationship. The investment banker may suggest types of securities to issue and markets where they should be sold in addition to the normal issuance functions.

A **competitive bid** process is used more in the issuance of municipal bonds, where the securities to be issued have been determined and the issuer solicits bids for the underwriting/sales function from a number of different investment banks.

In a **private placement**, the issue is not registered with the SEC for public sale, but is sold by the investment banker to a small number of buyers or a single buyer. The buyers are typically large institutions, and this method allows for customization of the features of the issue to suit both the buyer's and issuer's needs. There is no underwriting function here. The investment banker facilitates the sale to a third party or parties.

LOS 55.c: Distinguish between primary and secondary capital markets, and explain how secondary markets support primary markets.

Primary capital markets refers to the sale of *new* issues of securities. Most issues are distributed with the aid of an underwriter. The underwriter provides three services to the issuer:

1. *Origination,* which involves the design, planning, and registration of the issue.

2. *Risk bearing,* which means the underwriter insures or guarantees the price by purchasing the securities.

3. *Distribution*, which is the sale of the issue.

Corporate stock or bond issues are almost always sold with the assistance of an investment banking firm.

New equity issues involve either:

- New shares issued by firms whose shares are already trading in the marketplace. These issues are called *seasoned* or *secondary issues.*
- First time issues by firms whose shares are not currently trading in the marketplace. These are called *initial public offerings* (IPOs).

The relationship between the firm and the investment banker underwriting the issue can take one of three forms: competitive bids, negotiation, or best efforts. A *best efforts* underwriting indicates that the investment banker does not take the price risk. That is, the underwriter sells the issue for the best available price with no price guarantees to the issuing firm.

Secondary financial markets are where securities trade after their initial offerings. Secondary markets are important because they provide liquidity. The greater liquidity the securities have, the more willing investors are to buy the securities. Liquid secondary markets also provide investors with continuous information about the market price of their securities. The better the secondary market, the easier it is for firms to raise external capital in the primary market.

LOS 55.d: Distinguish between call and continuous markets.

Securities exchanges are places where buyers and sellers conduct the trade of securities. They may be structured as call markets or continuous markets:

- In *call markets*, the stock is only traded at specific times. All trades, bids, and asks are declared, and then one negotiated price is set that clears the market for the stock. This method is used in smaller markets and to set the opening price in major markets.
- In *continuous markets,* trades occur at any time the market is open. The price is set by either the auction process or by dealer bid-ask quotes.

LOS 55.e: Compare and contrast the structural differences among national stock exchanges, regional stock exchanges, and the over-the-counter (OTC) markets.

National stock exchanges. The major national exchanges trade shares for a large number of prestigious firms that are geographically dispersed to a diverse clientele. The major exchanges are:

- The New York Stock Exchange (NYSE) lists approximately 2,700 firms and has an average daily volume of 1.5 billion shares. The NYSE is a price-driven market.
- The American Stock Exchange (AMEX) lists firms that are not listed on the NYSE, along with foreign shares, warrants, and options. The AMEX is a price-driven market.
- Other national exchanges include the Tokyo, London, and Frankfurt Stock Exchanges and the Paris Bourse.

- The *global 24-hour market* refers to the passing of trading from New York to Tokyo to London and back to New York as the clock rotates.

Over-the-counter market. The over-the-counter (OTC) market includes the trading in all securities not listed on one of the registered exchanges. If any registered dealer is willing to make a market in a security, it can trade in the OTC market.

In the U.S., dealers and market makers list their bid and ask quotes over the National Association of Securities Dealers Automated Quotation (NASDAQ) National Market System (NMS).

The OTC market is the largest market in the U.S. in terms of the number of issues traded. However, in terms of value, the OTC market is about 60% of the size of the NYSE.

The NMS is a negotiated market in which investors negotiate directly with the dealers. In contrast, the registered exchanges are continuous auction markets in which the broker acts as an intermediary between the buyer and seller.

NMS listing requirements are less stringent than those of the registered exchanges. The listing requirements are shown in Figure 1.

Figure 1: NYSE and NMS Listing Requirements

	NYSE	*NMS*
Pretax income (millions)	$2.5	$1.0
Public shares (millions)	1.1	1.1
Minimum stockholders	2,000	400

Regional exchanges. Regional exchanges serve smaller local firms within various countries. The listing requirements for regional exchanges are usually much less stringent than large national exchanges. U.S. regional exchanges include the Chicago and Pacific exchanges. Japan has seven regional stock exchanges. Although regional exchanges list smaller firms, the exchanges often have the same operating procedures as the large national exchanges.

Third market. Stocks listed on a registered exchange may also be traded in the OTC market. Nonmember investment firms can make markets in and trade registered securities without going through the exchange. This segment of the OTC market is called the *third market*.

Fourth market. The *fourth market* describes the direct exchange of securities between investors without using the services of a broker as an intermediary. Directly negotiated sales are done by investors to save transactions costs.

LOS 55.f: Compare and contrast major characteristics of exchange markets, including exchange membership, types of orders, and market makers.

A *pure auction market* is an exchange system where buyers and sellers submit their bid and ask prices to a central location, and transactions are matched by brokers who do not have a position in the stock. An auction market is a *price-driven market*.

An *order-driven* system is one in which buyers and sellers submit their orders to dealers, who either buy the stock for their own inventory or sell the stock from their own inventory. An order-driven system is called a *dealer market*.

Professor's Note: The New York Stock Exchange and many other national and regional exchanges are auction markets. The U.S. over-the-counter market and other "exchanges" throughout the world are dealer markets.

Exchange membership. Membership on the U.S. exchanges falls into one of four categories:

- The *specialist* controls the limit order books, posts bid and ask prices, and trades for his own account.
- The *commission broker* executes customer trades for a brokerage firm.
- *Floor brokers* act as freelance brokers for other commission brokers.
- *Registered traders* trade for their own accounts.

Types of orders. There are four types of orders: market orders, limit orders, short sale orders, and stop loss orders.

- *Market orders* are orders to buy or sell at the best price available.
- *Limit orders* are orders to buy or sell away from the current market price. A *limit buy order* is placed below the current price. A *limit sell order* is placed above the current price. Limit orders have a time limit, such as instantaneous, one day, one week, one month, or good till canceled (GTC). Limit orders are turned over to the specialist by the commission broker.
- *Short sale orders* are orders where a trader borrows stock, sells it, and then purchases the stock later to return the stock back to the original owner. Short sales are discussed in greater detail later in this review.
- *Stop loss orders* are used to prevent losses or to protect profits. Suppose you own a stock currently selling for $40. You are afraid that it may drop in price, and if it does, you want your broker to sell it, thereby limiting your losses. You would place a *stop loss sell* order at a specific price (e.g., $35); if the stock price drops to this level, your broker will place a sell market order. A *stop loss buy* order is usually combined with a short sale to limit losses. If the stock price rises to the "stop" price, the broker enters a market order to buy the stock.

Market makers. Specialists are the *exchange market makers* on the U.S. exchanges. Specialists provide two basic functions to the exchange:

- They act as brokers handling the *limit order book*, where limit and stop orders are maintained.
- They act as dealers by buying and selling stocks for their own accounts to maintain an orderly market and provide liquidity to the market if there is an inadequate order flow.

The specialist has sole access to the information in the limit order book and is expected to use this information to add liquidity and help stabilize the market. The specialist provides *bridge liquidity* to the market by acting as a seller in an up market and as a buyer in a down market. This will tend to narrow the bid-ask spread and improve market continuity. The specialist's income comes from broker commissions on the limit order book trades and from the dealer bid-ask spread on the liquidity trades.

The Tokyo Stock Exchange (TSE) has 124 regular members (100 Japanese and 24 foreigners) and one *Saitori* member. The regular members act as brokers, and the Saitori member acts as an intermediary broker between regular members and maintains the limit order book. Saitori members are similar to U.S. specialists, but they do not have to maintain an orderly market.

London Stock Exchange members include brokers and jobbers. The brokers trade shares for the public and make markets in listed securities. The jobbers trade for themselves or the public and institutions.

LOS 55.g: Describe the process of selling a stock short and discuss an investor's likely motivation for selling short.

Short sales are orders to sell securities that the seller does not own. For a short sale, the short seller (1) simultaneously borrows and sells securities through a broker, (2) must return the securities at the request of the lender or when the short sale is closed out, and (3) must keep a portion of the proceeds of the short sale on deposit with the broker.

Why would anyone ever want to sell securities short? The seller thinks the current price is too high and that it will fall in the future, so the short seller hopes to sell high and then buy low. If a short sale is made at $30 per share and the price falls to $20 per share, the short seller can buy shares at $20 to replace the shares borrowed and keep $10 per share as profit.

Three rules apply to short selling:

- The **uptick rule** states that stocks can only be shorted in an up market. Thus, a short sale can only trade at a price higher than the previous trade. Zero ticks, where there is no price change, keep the sign change of the previous order.
- The short seller must pay all dividends due to the lender of the security.
- The short seller must deposit collateral to guarantee the eventual repurchase of the security.

LOS 55.h: Describe the process of buying a stock on margin, compute the rate of return on a margin transaction, define maintenance margin and determine the stock price at which the investor would receive a margin call.

Margin transactions involve buying securities with borrowed money. Brokerage firms can lend their customers money and keep the securities as collateral. The margin lending rate is about 1.5 percentage points above the bank *call money rate* (which is about 1 percentage point below the prime rate). In the U.S., margin lending limits are set by the Federal Reserve Board under Regulations T and U. The required equity position is called the *margin requirement*. The *initial margin* requirement is currently 50%. This means the borrower must provide 50% of the funds in the trade. An initial margin requirement of 40% would mean that the investor must put up 40% of the funds, and the brokerage firm may lend the 60% balance.

After the trade, the price of the stock will change, causing the balance of the margin account to fluctuate. Should the stock price go up, the customer's profits accumulate at a faster pace than a 100% equity position. This leverage is the benefit of margin trading. It is also the risk. Just as leverage may enhance returns, it can also magnify losses.

> **Example: Return on margin trade**
>
> Assume that an investor purchases 100 shares of a stock for $75 per share (total cost of $7,500). Compute the investor's return if the stock is sold for $150 per share (total value of $15,000) and the transaction was:
>
> (a) 100% cash.
>
> (b) A margin purchase with an initial margin requirement of 60%.
>
> **Answer:**
>
> (a) As a 100% cash (equity) transaction, the investor would have had a return equal to:
>
> $$\frac{\$15,000}{\$7,500} - 1 = 100\%$$
>
> (b) With an initial margin of 60%, the cost of the investment (equity in the position) would be only $4,500 = 0.6 × ($75 × 100). The other $3,000 of the purchase will be borrowed from the brokerage firm. If the shares were then sold at $150 per share, the position would be worth $12,000 (i.e., $15,000 – $3,000). In this situation, the investor would have a return equal to:
>
> $$\frac{\$12,000}{\$4,500} - 1 = 167\%$$

Professor's Note: The calculated return in this example is artificially high because we ignored commissions and interest paid on the margin loan. Nevertheless, the potential gains from leverage for a margined investment remain substantial.

The **maintenance margin** for an investment account is the investor's required equity position in the account. It is applicable to both margin purchases and short sales. The Federal Reserve sets maintenance margins in the U.S., but brokerage firms can increase them. For stock transactions, the maintenance margin is currently 25%. If an investor's margin account balance falls below the maintenance margin, the investor will receive a *margin call* and will be required to either liquidate the position or bring the account back to its maintenance (minimum) margin requirement. The following formulas indicate the stock price at which a margin account is just at the maintenance margin. A price below this price, P_0, will trigger a margin call for margin purchases, and a price above P_0 will trigger a margin call for short sales.

$$\text{trigger price (margin purchases)} = P_0 \left(\frac{1 - \text{initial margin}}{1 - \text{maintenance margin}} \right)$$

$$\text{trigger price (short sales)} = P_0 \left(\frac{1 + \text{initial margin}}{1 + \text{maintenance margin}} \right)$$

where:
P_0 = initial purchase price

Example: Margin call price for a long position

Assume you bought a stock for $40 per share. If the initial margin requirement is 50% and the maintenance margin requirement is 25%, at what price will you get a margin call?

Answer:

$$\frac{\$40(1-0.5)}{1-0.25} = \$26.67$$

Since this is a margin purchase, a margin call is triggered at a price below $26.67.

Example: Margin call price for a short sale

Assume you short a $40 stock. If the initial margin requirement is 50% and the maintenance margin requirement is 30%, at what price will you get a margin call?

Answer:

$$\frac{\$40(1+0.5)}{1+0.30} = \$46.15$$

Since this is a short sale, a margin call is triggered at a price above $46.15.

LOS 55.i: Discuss major effects of the institutionalization of securities markets.

The main cause of change in the markets has been the increasing number of participating financial institutions. The **effects of institutionalization** have been:

Commissions. The old fixed commission system fostered many of the problems in the market today. One is the practice where one brokerage house gives up some of its commissions to another firm for research and sales services (this is also referred to as *soft dollar* transfers). The fixed commission system also promoted the growth of the third and fourth markets. Negotiated commission rates started in 1975 by mandate of the SEC and have caused a significant decrease in commission rates.

Block trading. Institutions frequently deal in large trades called block trades. Since Rule 113 prevents specialists from contacting institutions directly to sell any blocks they acquire, specialists prefer not to buy large blocks from institutions. Because of this, large-block trading houses have developed to handle these trades. *Block houses* are also called *upstairs traders.* For example, Institution A wants to sell 100,000 shares of XYZ. Institution A calls Block Co. and arranges for Block Co. to buy the shares. After buying the shares, Block Co. contacts Institutions B and C and sells them the shares. Block Co. gets a negotiated fee from Institution A and potentially some price appreciation on the sale to B and C. If Block Co. is a member of the exchange, the trade will be listed (crossed) as a trade on the exchange floor.

Stock price volatility. Empirical evidence does *not* support the hypothesis that the presence of institutions has increased price volatility in the markets.

National market system. A national market system has been proposed. If developed, it will provide for the centralization of trade reporting, quotations, limit order book, and enhanced competition among all qualified market members.

New trading systems. NYSE average daily trading volume, now exceeds 1 billion shares. Some of the new technologies developed to handle this volume are:

- The *super dot* system, which allows electronic market orders (for up to 2,099 shares) and limit orders (for up to 30,099 shares) to be transmitted directly to the specialist trading post or the exchange's order management system.
- The opening *automated report service,* which matches opening orders for the specialist.
- The *display book*, which keeps track of all limit orders and incoming market orders for the specialist.

KEY CONCEPTS

1. Four characteristics of a well-functioning market are timely and accurate information, liquidity, low transactions costs (internal efficiency), and rapid price adjustment to new information (external efficiency).

2. A new issue may be sold through an underwriter chosen by competitive bidding (underwriters bid for the business), a negotiated sale (the cost of issuance is negotiated with the underwriter), or through a private placement where the issue is not registered for public sale but sold directly to a small number of buyers.

3. The secondary market is largely a dealer market (over-the-counter market). Secondary trading also takes place on exchanges (e.g., NYSE and AMEX).

4. Primary markets refer to the sale of newly issued securities, and secondary markets refer to the markets for previously issued securities (e.g., the New York Stock Exchange). These markets provide investors with liquidity and continuous price information, increasing the attractiveness of security ownership.

5. In call markets, securities are traded at specific times at a single price after bids and offers have accumulated, while in continuous markets trading takes place at various prices and times as bids and offers for the securities arrive.

6. Stock exchanges are physical places where traders and dealers gather to trade with each other. The over-the-counter market is a network of dealers (called market makers) in various locations who stand ready to purchase or sell securities at posted prices.

7. Exchange markets have members with different roles (specialists, commission brokers, floor brokers and traders), and the types of orders are market orders, limit orders, stop (loss) orders, and short sales.

8. Selling short refers to borrowing securities and selling them at the market price in an attempt to profit by buying (and returning) the securities at a lower price in the future.

9. A short seller may only sell on an "uptick," must pay any dividends to the lender of the securities as they are due, and must deposit collateral to provide funds for any losses on the short position if share price goes up.

10. In a margin transaction, investors can borrow against securities to purchase them, leaving the securities at the brokerage house as collateral for the loan.

11. The rate of return on a margin transaction is calculated as the profit or loss on the security position divided by the equity or margin deposited to make the trade (the cost of the position minus the margin loan).

12. The maintenance margin percentage (typically 25%) is the minimum that the equity in a margin account can reach before the deposit of more funds is required.

13. The stock price at which an investor who purchases a stock on margin will receive a margin call can be calculated as:

$$\text{trigger price (margin purchases)} = P_0 \left(\frac{1 - \text{initial margin}}{1 - \text{maintenance margin}} \right)$$

14. The price at which a short seller will receive a margin call can be calculated as:

$$\text{trigger price (short sales)} = P_0 \left(\frac{1 + \text{initial margin}}{1 + \text{maintenance margin}} \right)$$

15. The institutionalization of securities markets has led to lower negotiated commissions on trades, an increase in the number and overall importance of block trades, and movement toward a national market system, but it has not increased the volatility of stock prices as some have claimed.

CONCEPT CHECKERS: ORGANIZATION AND FUNCTIONING OF SECURITIES MARKETS

1. A well-functioning market will:
   A. provide liquidity.
   B. provide timely and accurate information.
   C. have good internal and external efficiency.
   D. all of the above.

2. An underwriter provides:
   A. origination.
   B. risk bearing.
   C. distribution.
   D. all of these.

3. New shares of firms already trading on the exchange are called:
   A. liquidity trades.
   B. seasoned issues.
   C. continuous trades.
   D. competitive trades.

4. Which of the following is NOT a characteristic of a well-functioning market?
   A. Liquidity.
   B. Seasoned issues.
   C. Continuous information.
   D. Lowest possible transaction costs.

5. To be traded on the over-the-counter markets, a stock must have:
   A. a market maker.
   B. 1,000 shareholders.
   C. net assets of $20 million.
   D. 1 million publicly held shares.

6. The sale of shares between two investors is called:
   A. block trade.
   B. the third market.
   C. the fourth market.
   D. the over-the-counter market.

7. The requirement that a short sale can only occur at a higher price than the last previously changed price is known as:
   A. rule 415.
   B. limit trading.
   C. the uptick rule.
   D. the stop loss rule.

8. The current market price of the XYZ Company stock is $40. An order to sell at $45 would be a:
   A. buy order.
   B. stop order.
   C. limit order.
   D. market order.

9. A stock is selling at $50. An investor's valuation model predicts that it should be selling at $40. If she believes her model, she would *most likely* place a:
    A. short sale order.
    B. stop order to buy.
    C. limit order to sell.
    D. market order to buy.

Use the following data to answer Questions 10 through 13.

- An investor buys 100 shares of XYZ.
- The market price is $50 on full margin.
- The initial margin requirement is 40%.
- The maintenance margin requirement is 25%.

10. How much equity must the investor have in the account?
    A. $2,000.
    B. $3,000.
    C. $4,000.
    D. $5,000.

11. At what price will the investor get a margin call?
    A. $26.67.
    B. $37.50.
    C. $40.00.
    D. $62.50.

12. If the price of the stock falls to $45, what is the equity balance in the margin account?
    A. $1,000.
    B. $1,500.
    C. $2,000.
    D. $2,500.

13. If the stock is sold one year later for $60, what is the investor's rate of return?
    A. 20%.
    B. 33%.
    C. 50%.
    D. 100%.

Use the following data to answer Questions 14 and 15.

An investor sells 100 shares of a $50 stock short. The initial margin requirement is 40%, and the maintenance margin requirement is 30%.

14. How much money must the investor have in the margin account for this trade?
    A. $2,000.
    B. $3,000.
    C. $4,000.
    D. $5,000.

15. At what price will the investor get a margin call?
    A. $35.71.
    B. $53.85.
    C. $57.69.
    D. $69.33.

16. In the U.S., who sets the initial margin requirements?
    A. The Justice Department.
    B. The Federal Reserve Board.
    C. The New York Stock Exchange.
    D. The Securities Exchange Commission.

17. At U.S. stock exchanges, the limit order book is controlled by:
    A. specialists.
    B. floor brokers.
    C. registered traders.
    D. commission brokers.

18. In which of the following market types can stocks trade anytime the market is open?
    A. Rule 415.
    B. Call markets.
    C. Market orders.
    D. Continuous markets.

ANSWERS – CONCEPT CHECKERS: ORGANIZATION AND FUNCTIONING OF SECURITIES MARKETS

1. **D**   Providing liquidity, providing timely and accurate information, and having good internal and external efficiency are all characteristics of a well-functioning market.

2. **D**   Providing origination, risk bearing, and distribution are all functions of an underwriter for an initial offering of a security.

3. **B**   Issues of new shares of firms whose shares are already trading in the marketplace are called seasoned issues.

4. **B**   Seasoned issues are new issues of shares of firms whose shares are already trading in the market and have nothing to do with a well-functioning market. A well-functioning market should provide liquidity and continuous information. A market is internally efficient if it provides the lowest possible transaction costs.

5. **A**   As long as a security has a market maker, it can trade in the OTC market. The OTC market is not subject to the rules of large exchanges.

6. **C**   In the fourth market, where no broker/dealer is present to serve as an intermediary, securities are exchanged directly between investors.

7. **C**   The uptick rule states that stocks can only be shorted in an up market. Thus, a short sale can only trade at a price higher than the previous trade.

8. **C**   Limit orders are timed orders placed away from the market price. Note the difference between a limit order and stop order limit: limit buys are placed below the current price while a limit sell is placed above the current price; stop sells are placed below the market price and stop buys are placed above the market price. Because the order is to sell XYZ at $45 when the current price is $40, the order would be a limit sell order.

9. **A**   If the investor believes the stock is overvalued, the investor should place a short sale order, which would benefit the investor if the stock declined to its equilibrium value.

10. **A**   Initial margin requirement ($) = (initial margin %)(number of shares × price per share) = 0.4 × (100 × $50.00) = $2,000.

11. **C**   For a long position, the formula for the margin call $= \dfrac{\text{original price} \times (1 - \text{initial margin \%})}{1 - \text{maintenance margin \%}} = \dfrac{50 \times (1 - 0.4)}{1 - 0.25} = \$40.00.$

12. **B**   The new margin account balance = initial margin balance − change in stock value = 2,000 − 500 = $1,500 (note the $2,000 equity balance comes from the answer to question 10). The $500 represents the $5 loss per share.

13. **C**   First, determine the sales proceeds: ($60 × 100 shares) = $6,000. Then, calculate the loan payoff = total cost of purchase − initial margin amount) = 5,000 − 2,000 = 3,000. The return = [(proceeds from sale − loan payoff) / equity] − 1 = [(6,000 − 3,000) / 2,000] − 1 = 1.50 − 1 = 0.50, or 50%. An alternative is to divide the profit by the initial equity $= \dfrac{6,000 - 5,000}{2,000} = 0.50$, or 50%.

14. **A**   100 × 50 = $5,000. $5,000 × 0.4 margin requirement = $2,000

15. **B**   (50 × 1.4) / 1.3 = $53.85 (remember with a short sale, the investor is hurt by *rising* prices).

16. **B**   In the U.S., margin lending limits are set by the Federal Reserve Board under Regulations T and U.

17. **A**   Specialists are exchange market makers who handle the limit order book and act as dealers, buying and selling their specific stocks to provide market liquidity. Floor brokers, registered traders, and commission brokers only trade for various accounts.

18. **D**   Continuous markets are defined as markets where stocks can trade anytime the market is open.

©2007 Schweser

Bond indexes fall into three basic categories:

- Investment-grade bond indexes include those provided by Lehman Brothers, Merrill Lynch, Salomon Brothers, and Ryan. The correlation between investment-grade bond returns is 0.95, as bond returns are driven by aggregate interest rates changes.
- High-yield bond indexes are maintained by First Boston, Lehman Brothers, Merrill Lynch, Salomon Brothers, and academics Blume-Keim. Merrill Lynch also does a series of indexes on convertible securities. The correlation between the high-yield indexes is much weaker than between the investment-grade indexes.
- Global bond indexes are made available by Lehman Brothers, Merrill Lynch, and Salomon Brothers. These indexes show long-run risk return performance differences, low correlation between countries, and a significant exchange rate effect on volatility and correlations.

Composite stock-bond indexes. Composite stock-bond indexes are developed to measure the performance of all securities in a given country. The Merrill Lynch-Wilshire Capital Markets Index is an example of one of these indexes. The Brinson Partner Global Securities Market Index contains U.S. stocks and bonds, non-U.S. equities and nondollar bonds, and cash.

Comparison of indexes over time. The risk/return performances of indexes are different. This is explained by the fact that different indexes represent different asset classes (stocks versus bonds). Also, within a given asset class, there are indexes for different subclasses (e.g. small-cap indexes versus large-cap equity indexes). Studies have found a low correlation to exist between indexes within a given country and between different countries. These findings support the argument for diversification, both domestically and globally.

KEY CONCEPTS

1. A price-weighted index is a simple average of the prices of the stocks in the index and gives the most weight to higher-priced stocks. The divisor must be adjusted over time for stock splits, and the index is biased downward because faster-growth firms tend to split their shares, decreasing the weights of the most successful companies in the index.
2. A value-weighted index shows the change in the total market value of all index stocks relative to a base year value of 100 and can exhibit bias because stocks with the largest market capitalizations can have a disproportionate influence on the index.
3. An equal-weighted (unweighted) index can be calculated as a simple average of the percentage holding period returns on each index stock or as the geometric average of the holding period returns, but the geometric average puts a downward bias on the index returns.
4. The DJIA and Nikkei indexes are domestic stock indexes. Global stock indexes are calculated for companies in many different countries. Bond indexes are challenging to create due to pricing difficulties on individual issues and a changing universe of bonds. Composite indexes have both stock and bond components and can be domestic or international.

CONCEPT CHECKERS: SECURITY-MARKET INDEXES

1. Which of the following will have the *least effect* on index returns?
    A. How the sample is chosen.
    B. How the data are collected.
    C. The weighting scheme for the index firms.
    D. The computational procedure for calculating the index.

2. Which of the following is a price-weighted index?
    A. The NYSE Index.
    B. The Standard and Poor's 500.
    C. The Value Line Composite Average.
    D. The Dow Jones Industrial Average.

3. In which of the following weighting schemes do firms with greater market capitalizations have a greater impact on the index than do firms with less market capitalization?
    A. Price-weighted.
    B. Value-weighted.
    C. Equal-weighted.
    D. The Dow Jones Industrial Average.

4. Stock splits potentially cause a downward bias in which of the following index weighting schemes?
    A. Price-weighted.
    B. Value-weighted.
    C. Equal-weighted.
    D. The Standard and Poor's 500.

5. Which index weighting scheme would produce returns *closest* to those of a portfolio of index stock with an equal dollar investment in each stock in the index?
    A. Unweighted.
    B. Price-weighted.
    C. Value-weighted.
    D. The Standard and Poor's 500.

6. Which index weighting scheme would produce returns *closest* to those of a portfolio of index stocks with an equal number of shares of each index stock?
    A. Unweighted.
    B. Price-weighted.
    C. Value-weighted.
    D. The NYSE Index.

7. Which of the following is a reason why creating bond market indexes is more difficult than creating stock market indexes?
    A. The price volatility of a bond is constant.
    B. The universe of bonds is much smaller than that of stocks.
    C. Bond markets have continuous trade data unlike stock markets.
    D. The universe of bonds is constantly changing because of numerous new issues, bond maturities, calls, and bond sinking funds.

Use the information in the following table to answer Questions 8 through 11.

	As of January 1		As of December 31	
	Share Price	Number of Shares Outstanding (000's)	Share Price	Number of Shares Outstanding (000's)
Stock A	$22	1,500	$28	1,500
Stock B	$40	10,000	$50	10,000
Stock C	$34	3,000	$30	3,000

8. The 1-year return on a price-weighted index of these three stocks is *closest* to:
   A. 12.0%.
   B. 12.5%.
   C. 13.5%.
   D. 18.0%.

9. The 1-year return on an unweighted index of these three stocks using the arithmetic mean is *closest* to:
   A. 12.0%.
   B. 12.5%.
   C. 13.5%.
   D. 18.0%.

10. The 1-year return on a value-weighted index of these stocks is *closest* to:
    A. 12.0%.
    B. 12.5%.
    C. 13.5%.
    D. 18.0%.

11. The 1-year return on an unweighted index of these three stocks using the geometric mean is *closest* to:
    A. 12.0%.
    B. 12.5%.
    C. 13.5%.
    D. 18.0%.

ANSWERS – CONCEPT CHECKERS: SECURITY-MARKET INDEXES

1. **B** Collecting the data for a market index is simply recording security prices. Selecting the sample, weighting the sample, and the method of computation are the key factors that influence index returns.

2. **D** The DJIA is a price-weighted index. The NYSE and the S&P 500 are market value-weighted, while the Value Line Composite is an unweighted price index.

3. **B** Market capitalization has a large effect on value-weighted indexes because firms with the largest market cap may dominate the index.

4. **A** Stock splits potentially introduce a downward bias in a price-weighted index. Large, successful firms splitting their stock and, hence, lowering their representative weight in the index, cause the downward bias. Value- and equal-weighted indexes are not affected by stock splits.

5. **A** An unweighted price series assumes that the investor makes and maintains an equal dollar investment in each stock in the index. Don't confuse this with a price-weighted index, which assumes that an investor invests in an equal number of shares of each stock.

6. **B** A price-weighted series is an arithmetic average of the current prices of a sample of securities. A price-weighted index assumes an investor purchases an equal number of shares of each stock represented in the index.

7. **D** New issues, maturities, calls and sinking funds cause the universe of bonds to change constantly. The price volatility of bonds is always changing; the universe of bonds is much larger than that of stocks; and bond markets do not have continuous trade data.

8. **B** $\dfrac{22+40+34}{3}=32$, $\dfrac{28+50+30}{3}=36$, $\dfrac{36}{32}-1=0.125=12.5\%$

9. **C** $\left[\left(\dfrac{28}{22}-1\right)+\left(\dfrac{50}{40}-1\right)+\left(\dfrac{30}{34}-1\right)\right]\left(\dfrac{1}{3}\right)=0.135=13.5\%$

10. **D** Total portfolio value January 1:

$$\left[22(1,500)+40(10,000)+34(3,000)\right](1,000)=\$535,000,000$$

Total portfolio value December 31:

$$\left[28(1,500)+50(10,000)+30(3,000)\right](1,000)=\$632,000,000$$

$$\dfrac{632}{535}-1=0.1813\approx18\%$$

From a base value of 100, the December 31 index value would be:

$$\dfrac{632}{535}\times100=118.13$$

11. **A** $\left[\left(\dfrac{28}{22}\right)\left(\dfrac{50}{40}\right)\left(\dfrac{30}{34}\right)\right]^{\frac{1}{3}}-1=0.1197\approx12\%$

EFFICIENT CAPITAL MARKETS

EXAM FOCUS

Market efficiency is a key concept. It has been tested extensively and has important implications for investment strategy. You must know the three forms of market efficiency and what the evidence from tests of the three forms has been. Know the types of tests for the various forms of market efficiency. Finally, you must understand the implications of the various forms of market efficiency, technical analysis, fundamental analysis, and the role of portfolio managers in the investment process.

LOS 57.a: Define an efficient capital market, discuss arguments supporting the concept of efficient capital markets, describe and contrast the forms of the efficient market hypothesis (EMH): weak, semistrong, and strong, and describe the tests used to examine the weak form, the semistrong form, and the strong form of the EMH.

An **efficient capital market** is one in which the current price of a security fully reflects all the information currently available about that security, including risk. An **informationally efficient capital market** is one in which security prices adjust rapidly and completely to new information. Market efficiency is based on the following set of assumptions:

- A large number of profit maximizing participants are analyzing and valuing securities independent of each other.
- New information comes to the market in a random fashion, and news announcements are independent of each other in regard to timing.
- Investors adjust their estimates of security prices rapidly to reflect their interpretation of the new information received. Market efficiency does not assume that market participants correctly adjust prices, just that their price adjustments are unbiased. Some prices will over-adjust, and some will under-adjust.
- Expected returns implicitly include risk in the price of the security.

Under these assumptions, the competitive behavior of this large group of market participants should cause rapid price adjustments in response to any newly released information. The new price will reflect investors' new estimates of the investment's value and riskiness. Should these assumptions not hold (as in emerging markets), abnormal returns may be possible.

The Forms of the Efficient Market Hypothesis (EMH)

In an influential academic paper, Eugene Fama divided the efficient market hypothesis (EMH) into three categories.

Weak-form efficient markets. The weak form of the EMH states that current stock prices *fully reflect all currently available security market information*. Thus, past price and volume information will have no predictive power about the future direction of security prices. The conclusion is that an investor cannot achieve excess returns using technical analysis.

Semistrong-form efficient markets. The semistrong form of the EMH holds that security prices rapidly adjust to the arrival of all new public information. As such, current security prices *fully reflect all publicly available information*. The semistrong form says security prices include all security market and nonmarket information available to the public. The conclusion is that an investor cannot achieve abnormal returns using fundamental analysis.

Strong-form efficient markets. The strong form of the EMH states that stock prices *fully reflect all information from public and private sources*. The strong form includes all types of information: market, nonmarket public, and private (inside) information. This means that no group of investors has monopolistic access to information relevant to the formation of prices, and none should be able to consistently achieve abnormal returns.

Professor's Note: As a base level knowledge of the EMH, you should know that weak form addresses security market information; the semistrong form addresses security market and nonmarket public information; and the strong form addresses security market, nonmarket, and inside or private information.

Tests Used to Examine the Weak Form, the Semistrong Form, and the Strong Form of the EMH

Since the efficient market hypothesis has major implications as to the value of security analysis, there have likely been more academic studies in finance on the topic of market efficiency than any other single area.

Weak-Form Tests of the EMH

There have been two types of tests of the weak form of the EMH, statistical tests and trading rule tests.

Statistical tests for independence. The weak form contends that, over time, security returns are independent of each other. Statistical tests have been conducted to test for this independence.

- Autocorrelation tests indicate that security returns are not significantly correlated over time.
- Runs tests also indicate that stock price changes (upticks and downticks) are independent over time.

Trading rule tests. A lot of EMH studies have been conducted to see if investors can earn abnormal returns following mechanical trading rules (filter rules) based on price data.

- Tests of filter rules show that investors cannot earn abnormal returns after accounting for the impact of transactions costs. (Filter rules entail trading stocks when prices move up or down certain amounts.)
- Researchers have tested other trading rules and generally found that such activity does not outperform a buy-and-hold policy on a risk-adjusted basis after taking account of commissions.

Semistrong-Form Tests of the EMH

Semistrong-form tests require that security returns be adjusted to reflect market returns and risk.

Early tests looked at a security's performance in excess of the market return. Abnormal returns were measured as the stock's actual return less the market's actual return.

$$\text{abnormal return} = R_{actual} - R_{mkt}$$

Later tests looked at the security's performance in excess of market returns adjusted for the security's volatility (beta risk): Abnormal returns are measured as the stock's actual return less the stock's expected return based on its beta risk.

$$\text{abnormal return} = R_{actual} - E(R) = R_{actual} - \{RFR + \beta[E(R_{mkt}) - RFR]\}$$

Example: Abnormal returns

A stock has a 10% return when the market return is 5% and the risk-free rate (RFR) is 2%. The stock's beta is 1.2. Compute the unadjusted and adjusted abnormal return for this security.

Answer:

The stock's non-risk-adjusted abnormal return is 10% – 5% = 5%. The stock's risk-adjusted abnormal return is 10% – [2% + 1.2(5% – 2%)] = 4.4%.

Time-series tests are based on the assumption that, in efficient markets, the best estimate of future returns is the long-run historical rate of return. So if markets are semistrong-form efficient, an investor should not be able to outperform these estimates in the short or long term.

Cross-sectional tests of the semistrong-form of the EMH are based on the assumption that markets are efficient when all securities' returns lie along the security market line. That is, a security's rate of return should be directly related to its level of market risk (i.e., beta). So after adjusting returns for risk, all security returns should be equivalent or comparable. The hypothesis is that firm characteristics such as size, analyst coverage, or book value to market value ratios should not be useful in predicting abnormal returns. Note that the results of these tests depend on the effectiveness of the asset pricing model employed.

Event studies examine abnormal returns before and after the release of information about a significant firm-related event. The hypothesis is that investors should not be able to earn positive abnormal returns on average by buying or selling based on types of firm events.

Strong-Form Tests of the EMH

In addition to informational efficiency, the strong-form EMH implies that no group of investors has access to private information that would allow the group to consistently experience above-average profits. (This implies perfect markets in addition to efficient markets.) Academic tests of the strong form look at the legal use of private information and exclude illegal insider trading. The reported tests identify and study four groups of investors who are expected to be able to outperform the market, or who claim to be able to do so because of their access to private information.

Insider trading. Tests of Securities Exchange Commission (SEC) insider trading filings indicate that inside purchasers have made above-average profits. Other tests show that public traders tracking the purchases of insiders via SEC filings were able to earn excess returns. However, studies conducted after 1976 indicate that this inefficiency seems to have been eliminated.

Exchange specialists. Stock exchange specialists, by the very nature of their membership on the exchange, have access to information in the limit order book that is only available to them. Tests show that specialists derive above-average returns from this information.

Security analysts. Some strong-form tests have addressed the question of whether analysts and their advice can provide excess returns. These tests are based on the assumption that analysts may have information that the rest of the market does not have.

- *The Value Line (VL) enigma.* Studies indicate that VL rankings of 1 and 5 contain significant information (stocks rated 1 are the most attractive). Changes in the rankings from 2 to 1 also appear to be significant. Recent studies, however, show that any information in the VL reports is already reflected in price by the second day after publication.
- *Analyst recommendations.* Studies of the "Heard on the Street" column in *The Wall Street Journal* show that stocks have a significant price change on the day they appear in the column.

Professional money managers. Tests indicate that mutual funds, bank trust departments, pension plans, and endowment funds are *not* able to match the performance of a simple buy-and-hold policy.

LOS 57.b: Identify various market anomalies and explain their implications for the EMH, and explain the overall conclusions about each form of the EMH.

An anomaly is something that deviates from the common rule. The common rule here is the efficient market hypothesis. Tests of the EMH are frequently called "anomaly studies," so in the efficient markets literature, an anomaly is something that helps to disprove the efficient markets hypothesis.

The following are **documented market anomalies:**

1. *Earnings surprises to predict returns.* Studies of quarterly earnings reports indicate that the markets have not adjusted stock prices to reflect the release of quarterly earnings surprises as fast as would be expected based on the semistrong EMH. As a result, it appears that earnings surprises can be used to identify individual stocks that will produce abnormal returns.
2. *Calendar studies.* The "January Anomaly" shows that, due to tax-induced trading at year-end, an investor can profit by buying stocks in December and selling them during the first week in January. The "weekend effect" shows that the average return for weekdays is positive but that a negative return is associated with the Friday close to the Monday open. Also, prices tend to rise on the last trade of the day.
3. *Price-earnings ratio* (P/E) tests indicate that low P/E ratio stocks experienced superior results relative to the market, while high P/E ratio stocks have significantly inferior results.
4. *Small firm effect.* Small firms consistently experienced significantly larger risk-adjusted returns than larger firms. This is called the *small firm effect.* Many academics claim these results reflect the inability of the asset-pricing model to provide a complete measure of risk for small-firm stocks.
5. The *neglected firms effect* is a result of tests of the small firm effect. Small firm tests also found that firms that have only a small number of analysts following them have abnormally high returns. These excess returns appear to be caused by the lack of institutional interest in the firms. The neglected firm effect applies to all sizes of firms.
6. *Book value/market value ratios* have been associated with abnormal returns. It has been found that the greater the ratio of book value/market value, the greater the risk-adjusted rate of return, regardless of firm size.

Overall Conclusions About the EMH

Most, but not all, evidence generated by testing the weak form of the EMH indicates that, after incorporating trading costs, simple trading rules cannot generate positive abnormal returns on average. Hence the results support the weak-form of the EMH.

The results are mixed for the semistrong form of the EMH. Event studies strongly support the EMH, while time-series and cross-sectional tests give evidence that markets are not always semistrong-form efficient.

Aside from the results on corporate insiders and specialists, the tests support the strong form of the EMH. It appears that corporate insiders and exchange specialists have monopolistic access to highly valuable information.

LOS 57.c: Explain the implications of stock market efficiency for technical analysis and fundamental analysis, discuss the implications of efficient markets for the portfolio management process and the role of the portfolio manager, and explain the rationale for investing in index funds.

If weak-form market efficiency holds, technical analysis (based on past price and volume information) has no value, and it cannot be used to earn positive abnormal returns on average.

If semistrong-form efficiency holds, neither technical nor fundamental analysis has any value because both are based on public information. Remember, semistrong-form efficiency is based on market information and other publicly available information, so it includes weak-form efficiency.

Implications of Efficient Markets, the Portfolio Management Process, and the Role of the Portfolio Manager

Portfolio management. In an efficient market, portfolio managers must create and maintain the appropriate mix of assets to meet their clients' needs. In other words, portfolio management should be centered on client objectives and constraints and the construction of the appropriate portfolio through effective asset allocation decisions.

Portfolio managers should help:

- Quantify their clients' risk tolerances and return needs within the bounds of the client's liquidity, income, time horizon, and legal and regulatory constraints.
- Verbalize their clients' portfolio policies and strategies needed to meet the client's needs, then construct an optimal portfolio by allocating funds between financial and real assets. This is referred to as asset allocation.
- Diversify their clients' portfolios (on a global basis) to eliminate unsystematic risk.
- Monitor and evaluate changing capital market expectations as they affect the risk/return expectations of the assets in the client's portfolio.
- Monitor their clients' needs and circumstances.
- Rebalance their clients' portfolios when changes are necessary.

Portfolio managers should also help their clients minimize their total transaction costs. There are three ways to lower costs: minimize taxes, reduce trading turnover, and minimize liquidity costs by trading relatively liquid stocks.

Performance measurement. One of the major outcomes of the EMH tests is that the proper way to gauge performance is to measure investment professionals against a randomly selected buy-and-hold strategy of stocks within the same risk class.

Tests do show that it may be possible to achieve above-average performance by selecting stocks that are neglected by other analysts, have high book value/market value ratios, and are small market capitalization firms. Also, strong-form tests of the Value Line enigma indicate that analysts have outperformed expectations in the past.

Money managers. The implication of the strong-form tests is that money managers as a group have not outperformed the buy-and-hold policy. It is argued that the investor's job is to separate good managers from average and poor managers. This approach is supported by the research showing that some analysts (e.g., Value Line) have the ability to separate the best and the worst stocks from a universe of stocks.

The rationale for investing in index funds. The conclusion you might draw from the efficient market literature is that since you cannot, in general, expect to beat the market, you should attempt to match the market while minimizing your costs. One way to match the market's performance is to put your money into an index fund. An index fund is designed to duplicate the composition and performance of a specific index or market segment. There are index funds for domestic and international markets and for various market segments.

Proper diversification is the key to utilizing index funds. Most investors do not have the resources to purchase individual securities in the correct proportions so that their portfolio mimics the market. Moreover, certain securities may lack proper market liquidity to warrant inclusion in a market replication strategy. The result is that market index funds like the Vanguard 500 (which mimics the S&P 500) or unit trusts such as the Standard and Poor's Depositary Receipts (SPDRs or "spiders") are an easy, cost-effective way for most investors to gain the proper exposure to a market index.

KEY CONCEPTS

1. A market is (informationally) efficient with respect to a particular set of information if no positive abnormal (risk-adjusted) returns can be earned on average by trading based on that information.

2. The concept of informational efficiency of markets is supported by the large number of market participants seeking to gain a trading advantage and the fact that new, relevant information arrives randomly (is unpredictable).

3. The three forms of efficiency refer to efficiency with respect to different information sets. The three forms and the respective information they refer to are:
   • Weak—market information, including all past price and volume information.
   • Semistrong—public information, including market and fundamental information.
   • Strong—all information, including private, insider, fundamental, and market information.

4. The tests of the three forms of market efficiency can be categorized as:
   • Weak—statistical tests of independence and mechanical trading rules (filter rules).
   • Semistrong—time series tests, cross-sectional tests, event studies.
   • Strong—test the performance of insiders, specialists, analyst recommendations, and money manager performance.

5. Six anomalies with respect to semistrong-form efficiency have been well supported. Abnormal returns have been shown to be predictable using earnings surprises, calendar effects, P/E ratios, firm size, analyst neglect, and book-to-market ratios.

6. Overall tests have supported weak-form efficiency, offered mixed results with respect to semistrong-form efficiency, and shown violations of strong-form efficiency for corporate insiders and exchange specialists.

7. If weak-form efficiency holds, technical analysis has no value. If semistrong-form efficiency holds, neither technical nor fundamental analysis has any value in stock selection and portfolio construction.

8. Even if markets are informationally efficient, portfolio mangers can still add value by matching portfolios to each client's constraints and risk tolerance, providing diversification and minimizing transactions costs.

9. Index funds provide broad diversification at very low cost. To the extent that markets are efficient, index funds will outperform the average money manager who devotes time and resources to "beating the market."

CONCEPT CHECKERS: EFFICIENT CAPITAL MARKETS

1. The two major tests employed to test the weak-form efficient market hypothesis (EMH) are:
    A. event studies and runs tests.
    B. autocorrelation tests and runs tests.
    C. event studies and performance tests.
    D. time-series tests and cross-sectional tests.

2. Which of the following forms of the EMH assumes that no group of investors has monopolistic access to relevant information?
    A. Weak form.
    B. Strong form.
    C. Semistrong-form.
    D. Both weak and semistrong form.

3. The strong-form EMH asserts that stock prices fully reflect which of the following types of information?
    A. Market.
    B. Market and public.
    C. Public and private.
    D. Public, private, and future.

4. The strong-form EMH goes beyond the semistrong-form in that it calls for:
    A. perfect markets.
    B. a large number of profit-maximizing participants.
    C. information to come to the market on a random basis.
    D. all nonmarket public information should be incorporated into security prices.

5. A stock's abnormal rate of return is defined as the:
    A. rate of return during abnormal price movements.
    B. the market rate of return less the actual rate of return.
    C. actual rate of return less the expected risk-adjusted rate of return.
    D. expected risk-adjusted rate of return minus the market rate of return.

6. Which of the following is **NOT** an assumption behind the semistrong form of the EMH?
    A. A large number of profit-maximizing participants.
    B. In regard to timing, news announcements are independent of each other.
    C. All information is cost free and available to everyone at the same time.
    D. Investors adjust their expectations rapidly when confronted with new information.

7. Research has revealed that the performance of professional money managers compared to the performance of the market is:
    A. equal.
    B. inferior.
    C. superior.
    D. slightly better.

8. Under the EMH, the major effort of the portfolio manager should be:
    A. to maximize transactions costs.
    B. to achieve complete diversification of the portfolio.
    C. to help clients underperform the market benchmark.
    D. all of the above.

9. Which of following efficient market studies suggests that securities markets are semistrong-form efficient?
    A. Small-firm effect studies.
    B. Neglected-firm effect studies.
    C. Price/earnings ratio studies.
    D. Event studies.

10. An analyst has gathered the following data about a stock:
    *   A beta of 1.375.
    *   An actual return of 10.5%.
    *   The market rate of return is 6%.
    *   The risk-free rate is 2%.

    Compute the stock's abnormal return.
    A. 2%.
    B. 3%.
    C. 4%.
    D. 5%.

11. Assume the following data:

	Beginning Price	Ending Price	Cash Flow During the Year
Analyst's portfolio	$40	$41	$6.00
Risk-matched market portfolio	$10	$11	$0.25

    How does the analyst's portfolio performance compare to the risk-matched portfolio performance?
    A. Equal.
    B. Inferior.
    C. Superior.
    D. Slightly worse.

12. The implication of the weak-form EMH is:
    A. insider information is of no value for obtaining excess abnormal returns.
    B. all public and private information is rapidly incorporated into security prices.
    C. technical analysts can make excess returns on filter rules but not runs rules.
    D. there should be no relationship between past price changes and future price changes.

13. The January anomaly, the neglected firm effect, and the book value/market value ratio are studies examining which form of the EMH?
    A. Weak form of the EMH.
    B. Strong form of the EMH.
    C. Semistrong form of the EMH.
    D. Both the weak and semistrong forms of the EMH.

14. If a firm announces an unexpected large cash dividend, the EMH would predict which of the following price changes at the announcement?
    A. No price change.
    B. An abnormal price change to occur before the announcement.
    C. An abnormal price change to occur at the time of the announcement.
    D. A gradual price change to occur for several weeks after the announcement.

15. Which of the following is **NOT** one of the three assumptions that underlie an efficient capital market?
    A. Expected returns implicitly include risk in the price of the security.
    B. A large number of profit-maximizing participants are analyzing and valuing securities independent of each other.
    C. Investors adjust their estimates of security prices slowly to reflect their interpretation of the new information received.
    D. New information comes to the market in a random fashion, and the timing of news announcements is independent.

16. Autocorrelation tests and tests of the predictive power of earnings surprises apply to which forms of the EMH?

	Autocorrelation	Earnings surprises
A.	Weak	Strong
B.	Semistrong	Strong
C.	Weak	Semistrong
D.	Semistrong	Weak

ANSWERS – CONCEPT CHECKERS: EFFICIENT CAPITAL MARKETS

1. **B** The two types of tests used to examine the weak form of the EMH are:

   1. Statistical tests of the independence of security returns (runs and autocorrelation tests).

   2. Trading rule tests to examine if mechanical trading rules can generate excess returns.

2. **B** Strong-form EMH states that stock prices fully reflect all information from public and private (inside) sources. Thus, no group of investors has an advantage. Note that the semistrong form only deals with public information.

3. **C** Strong-form EMH states that stock prices fully reflect all information from public and private (inside) sources.

4. **A** The strong-form EMH assumes perfect markets in which all information is cost free and available to everyone at the same time. The other answer choices apply to any market.

5. **C** Abnormal returns are measured by taking the security's actual return less the security's expected return based on its beta risk.

6. **C** The semistrong form of EMH assumes that stock prices reflect all public information. The semistrong form of EMH does not dispute that information could be held by insiders. All information being cost free and available to everyone at the same time is actually an assumption of strong-form EMH.

7. **B** Tests indicate that mutual funds, bank trust departments, pension plans, and endowment funds are not able to match the performance of a simple buy-and-hold policy. The performance of professionals has been inferior to that of the market.

8. **B** Portfolio managers should minimize transaction costs, help clients try to outperform the market benchmark, and diversify the portfolio to minimize risk.

9. **D** The majority of studies that have looked at firm-related events have concluded that there are no predictable short-run or long-run impacts on security returns because of these events. This supports the EMH. The neglected firm, small firm, and P/E ratio studies have found significant positive risk-adjusted abnormal returns to small, underfollowed, and low P/E firms, results which do not support the semistrong form of the EMH.

10. **B** $10.5\% - [2\% + 1.375(6\% - 2\%)] = 3\%$

11. **C** Analyst: $\dfrac{\$41 - \$40 + \$6}{\$40} = 0.175$; Market: $\dfrac{\$11 - \$10 + \$0.25}{\$10} = 0.125$

12. **D** Weak-form EMH states that security prices reflect all historical market information, meaning that there should be no relationship between past price changes and future price changes.

13. **C** The January anomaly, neglected firm effect, and book/market value ratio all deal with public information and are studies of semistrong-form EMH.

14. **C** EMH would suggest that stock prices adjust rapidly to new information—this implies that the stock dividend would cause an abnormal change in price to occur at the time of the announcement.

15. **C** Investors adjust rapidly (not slowly) to new information.

16. **C** Autocorrelation tests test the weak form (past price information), and tests of the predictive power of earnings surprises test the semistrong form (publicly available information).

MARKET EFFICIENCY AND ANOMALIES

EXAM FOCUS

This topic review is fairly straightforward. Know two limitations to the claim that market prices should be perfectly efficient, and know the limitations on arbitrage as a mechanism for forcing securities prices to their informationally efficient levels. Know the main reasons that research evidence suggesting anomalous returns behavior may be misleading.

LOS 58.a: Explain limitations to fully efficient markets.

LOS 58.b: Describe the limits of arbitrage to correct anomalies.

There are three primary limitations on the market's ability to produce informationally efficient prices.

1. Processing new information entails costs and takes at least some time. If market prices are efficient, there are no returns to the time and effort spent on fundamental analysis. But if no time and effort is spent on fundamental analysis, there is no process for making market prices efficient. We can resolve this apparent conundrum by looking to the time lag between the release of new value-relevant information and the adjustment of market prices to their new efficient levels.

   There must be an adequate return to fundamental analysis and trading based on new information to compensate analysts and traders for their time and effort. Those who act rapidly and intelligently to the release of new information will be rewarded. If stock prices adjust to their new efficient levels within minutes or hours of the release of new information, we can consider markets to be efficient. If this price-adjustment process takes days or weeks, stock prices are not efficient. In this case we expect that more activity by analysts, traders, and arbitrageurs will tend to reduce the adjustment period over time.

2. Market prices that are not precisely efficient can persist if the gains to be made by information trading are less than the transaction costs such trading would entail. The difficulties associated with short sales can be viewed as relatively high transaction costs. This means that deviations from efficient prices on the upside (overvalued stocks) may be more prevalent than downside deviations (undervalued stocks) since the transaction costs of increasing long positions are low relative to those of short selling. In general, for securities with larger transaction costs, the deviations from informationally efficient prices should be greater.

3. There are limits on the ability of the process of arbitrage to bring about efficient prices. Arbitrage is frequently not riskless. Just because fundamentals indicate that one stock is overpriced relative to another, or absolutely over- or underpriced, does not mean that trading based on this information will be immediately profitable. For example, one risk of shorting overvalued stocks during the internet stock bubble of the late 1990s was that a shorted company might be taken over at a significantly higher stock price than the one at which a trader sold short. The fact that the acquiring firm paid too much for the shares offers no solace to short sellers who have to cover their positions at the takeover price.

Even in **pairs trading**, where an arbitrageur buys the underpriced security and shorts the overpriced security, significant risk from stock-specific factors remains. Additionally, there is no guarantee that even correctly-identified relative mispricings of similar stocks will be corrected in the near term. Investors of the funds that arbitrageurs and traders use can be notoriously impatient, removing funds when trades go against them or if results are not consistently good. Since capital is limited, in periods where there are many apparent mispricings, money will be used only to pursue the most attractive trades, leaving other mispricings unexploited.

LOS 58.c: Illustrate why investors should be skeptical of anomalies.

Investors should be skeptical of many "identified" anomalies. There are several issues concerning research methods and statistical significance to consider.

Measurement of Abnormal Returns

One of the most persistent criticisms of studies that document anomalous returns based on firm characteristics is that the model used to estimate normal returns may be flawed. Researchers often use the CAPM to model normal returns based on estimated firm betas. The fact that small firms show positive abnormal (risk-adjusted) returns on average may indicate that small firms are persistently underpriced, or that investing in small firms entails risk that is not captured by the firms' betas. This is especially problematic when tests for abnormal returns involve returns over longer periods. Since normal returns over a day or a week are close to zero, measuring abnormal returns is not as heavily influenced by the returns model used. Using such factors as firm size and price-book values may mitigate such problems, but the theoretical support for these characteristics as risk factors is weak.

The bottom line here is that we must be aware that firm characteristics associated with positive abnormal returns may be characteristics associated with a type of risk that is not captured by the returns model estimates to which actual returns are compared.

Strategy Risk

In addition to the concerns with the inadequate specification of firm risk in estimating normal returns, investors should consider strategy risk. Capturing the abnormal returns of a trading strategy is not without risk, even if the anomalous returns behavior persists. If the strategy is based on returns over a 20-year period, abnormal returns may be positive in only some of those years. Investors seeking to exploit the predictability of abnormal returns may have one or more down years in a row, even if the firm characteristics upon which the strategy is based continue to have predictive power over the long term. Any strategy designed to exploit anomalous returns behavior has the inherent risk that the behavior will either not continue, or be significantly reduced by other investors pursuing similar or identical strategies. Additional strategy risk such as this must be rewarded with higher returns and should not be disregarded.

Data Mining

Recall from quantitative methods, that statistical tests have a probability of a type I error equal to their significance level. A test of the hypothesis that stock prices are efficient (no abnormal returns) at the 5% level of significance will be rejected at the 5% level of significance 1 out of 20 times by chance, even when it is actually true.

Consider a researcher who tests 20 different factors using the same sample of data. In each test he tries to determine whether abnormal returns could have been earned by forming portfolios based on one of these factors. Even if none of the factors actually is valuable in predicting abnormal returns, chances are that one of the tests will show a statistically significant relation between a factor and subsequent abnormal returns. Now imagine thousands of researchers doing a hundred thousand tests all on the same data sample. This results in a data mining problem.

There are certainly many relationships in the data resulting purely from chance. Standard statistical tests will identify these as statistically significant when they are in fact not driven by any real characteristics of markets and are unlikely to be repeated outside the sample period. While a less-than-ethical researcher could be guilty of purposely mining the data, a large number of independent skilled researchers who just use the same data (e.g., U.S. stock returns) can also be mining the data.

Survivorship Bias

When constructing samples, researchers must be careful not to include just surviving companies, mutual funds, or investment newsletters. Since survivors tend to be those that have done well (by skill or chance), samples of mutual funds that have 10-year track records, for example, will exhibit performance histories with upward bias. Mutual fund companies regularly discontinue funds with poor performance histories or roll their assets into better-performing funds.

Sample Selection Bias

Sample selection bias (of the unintentional variety) occurs when the method of selecting a sample is not truly random. It is present when the researcher has inadvertently selected a sample that exhibits characteristics that are not present, or not present to the same degree of significance, in the overall population. If a researcher finds evidence of an anomaly in sample data, but the data are predominantly from small firms because that was the only information available to the researcher, it could be a mistake to make inferences about characteristics of the whole population of publicly-traded firms based on that sample.

Small Sample Bias

Inferences about an entire population drawn from tests on a small sample may be incorrect. One type of small sample bias is to use a short time period. What is true over one time period is not necessarily true over longer periods.

Nonsynchronous Trading

Closing stock prices in market data may be actual trading prices very close to the market close for large-cap, heavily traded stocks. For stocks that trade infrequently, closing prices may be prices from much earlier in the day. Using these "stale" prices can make strategies appear more attractive than they really are. Assuming that one could actually trade at closing prices at or near the close of the market, may make a strategy look profitable when the strategy could not really be implemented.

KEY CONCEPTS

1. Market prices are generated by the activities of researchers and traders who analyze and react to new information. There must be some reward for this effort, but that reward may be earned only by those who process and act on the new information rapidly and skillfully.
2. Transaction costs prevent trading and arbitrage from resulting in perfectly efficient securities prices. Securities and strategies with higher transaction costs permit greater deviations from perfectly efficient prices.
3. Information-based trading is not without risks. Arbitrageurs have no guarantee that prices will move to "more rational" levels or that strategies will consistently perform well, have limited capital, and constraints imposed on them by the suppliers of investment capital.
4. Research purporting to have identified anomalous returns behavior may be subject to data mining bias, incorrect measurement of risk and abnormal returns, small sample bias, survivor bias, sample selection bias, or the use of stale prices due to nonsynchronous trading.

CONCEPT CHECKERS: MARKET EFFICIENCY AND ANOMALIES

1. The effect on market efficiency of restricting short sales is *most likely* to:
    A. create a band of efficient prices.
    B. improve market efficiency.
    C. lead to upside bias in stock prices.
    D. reduce the speed of adjustment to new information.

2. A researcher has examined the performance of the shares of firms that went public during the period 1998–1999 and found evidence of positive abnormal returns over the three months after the firms' shares began trading. This evidence of anomalous returns behavior is *least likely* subject to:
    A. measurement problems for abnormal returns.
    B. sample selection bias.
    C. small sample bias.
    D. survivorship bias.

3. A researcher has examined a sample of shares of smaller firms that trade infrequently and found that they have had greater volatility of the price change between the market closing price and the opening price the next trading day than large-cap stocks in similar industries. Based on this information, he suggests entering into an options trading strategy to exploit the differences in overnight volatility. The researcher has *most likely:*
    A. misestimated normal returns.
    B. confused price change with volatility.
    C. overestimated overnight volatility of his sample.
    D. introduced small sample bias into his results.

ANSWERS – CONCEPT CHECKERS: MARKET EFFICIENCY AND ANOMALIES

1. **C**   The best answer here is "lead to upside bias." The higher the transactions costs of short sales, the more security prices may be above efficient levels without causing short sales to drive them down to efficient levels. This will not necessarily reduce the speed of adjustment to new information as much as it will limit adjustment when stocks are overpriced.

2. **D**   The researcher has used a relatively small time period during which the post-initial public offering (IPO) returns of new issues may not have been representative of those over longer time periods. There is potential bias in the sample because the selection criterion may have produced a sample that is highly concentrated in one, or a few, industries that were experiencing unexpectedly rapid growth. Any time abnormal returns are being measured over longer periods, such as three months, there are potential measurement errors. Additionally, since the stocks had no trading history, estimating risk is problematic. There is no indication that the sample suffers from survivorship bias, since IPOs were included regardless of their fates.

3. **C**   The estimating of normal returns is not an issue here and we have no information suggesting that his sample or sample period is necessarily small. The most likely problem here is one of nonsynchronous trading. For stocks that trade infrequently, market closing prices may be those from trades many hours earlier and the opening trades the next day may come many hours after the opening. The problem, then, is that he is measuring volatility over a potentially much longer period for the small-cap stocks than for the large-cap stocks that likely trade near both the close and the opening.

AN INTRODUCTION TO SECURITY VALUATION AND INDUSTRY ANALYSIS

Study Session 14

EXAM FOCUS

To estimate the market value of any investment, find the present value of its future cash flows: estimate the number and dollar amount of future cash flows, estimate when they will be received and what form they will take, and discount these cash flows to the present using the required rate of return. The required return on any investment is the real rate of interest plus premiums for inflation and risk. To make an investment decision, compare the estimated value of the security to its current market price. For success on the Level 1 exam, candidates should be prepared to calculate the value of an investment with the valuation formulas presented in this review. All of them are variations of the same discounted cash flow technique. The single LOS for Reading 60 is included here.

LOS 59.a: Explain the top-down approach, and its underlying logic, to the security valuation process.

The **top-down, three-step approach** to security valuation starts with a forecast of the direction of the general economy. Next, based on this economic forecast, project the outlook for each industry under review. Third, within each industry, select the firms most likely to perform the best given these economic and industry forecasts. As indicated, this approach is a three-step analytical process:

economic analysis → industry analysis → stock analysis

Step 1: Forecast macroeconomic influences

Fiscal policy is a direct approach to affect aggregate demand in an attempt to manage the rate of economic growth. Tax cuts encourage spending (demand) and speed up the economy; tax increases discourage spending and slow economic growth. Government spending creates jobs, thus increasing aggregate demand.

Monetary policy is used by the central bank to manage economic growth. Decreasing the money supply causes interest rates to rise, putting upward pressure on costs and downward pressure on demand. Increasing the money supply reduces interest rates and increases demand. Inflation can result from increasing the money supply too fast. Rising interest rates reduce the demand for investment funds and rising consumer prices reduce product demand.

From a global (import/export) perspective, the potential domestic economic impact from political changes in major international economies must be considered.

Step 2: Determine industry effects

Identify industries that should prosper or suffer from the economic outlook identified in Step 1. Consider how these industries react to economic change: some industries are cyclical, some are counter-cyclical, and some are noncyclical.

Consider global economic shifts: an industry's prospects within the global business environment determine how well or poorly individual firms in the industry will do. Thus, industry analysis should precede company analysis.

Step 3:   Perform firm analysis

After performing an industry analysis, compare firms within each attractive industry using financial ratios and cash flow analysis. For stock purchases, identify the company with the most upside potential. For short selling, identify the firm whose stock should perform the worst. This involves not only examining a firm's past performance, but also its prospects.

LOS 59.b: Explain the various forms of investment returns.

The returns (broadly defined) on an investment can be measured in several ways, including cash flows from projects, interest income on bonds, and dividend income on stocks. Capital gains, the increase in the price of an asset, are another form of investment returns.

We might also measure investment returns as earnings (per share of common stock), operating cash flow, or some other cash flow measure. In this topic review, we focus on dividends and capital gains as the relevant return measures for valuing shares of stock. Based on the dividend discount model's assumptions, we will also value a share of stock based on its earnings per share.

LOS 59.c: Calculate and interpret the value of a preferred stock, or of a common stock, using the dividend discount model (DDM).

Valuing preferred stock is easy since the dividend is fixed and the income stream (dividends) is theoretically infinite (it's a perpetuity):

$$\text{preferred stock value} = \frac{D_p}{(1 + k_P)^1} + \frac{D_p}{(1+k_P)^2} + \ldots + \frac{D_p}{(1+k_P)^\infty} = \frac{D_p}{k_P}$$

Again, the only problem is determining the required return, k_P. Because of default risk factors, the firm's required rate on preferred (k_p) should be above the firm's bond rate (k_d). However, since dividends paid to corporate investors are subject to the *dividends received deduction* (i.e., 80% of dividends paid are tax exempt), preferred yields are below the yields on the firm's highest grade bonds.

Throughout this review, we will be computing "values," all of which are simply the present value of expected future dividends and an eventual sale price, or of an infinite stream of expected cash dividends. Keep in mind that value is the same as price if markets are in equilibrium (efficient), so we are essentially calculating what the price "should" be. This is often referred to as intrinsic value.

Example: Preferred stock valuation

A company's bonds are currently yielding 8.5%, and its preferred shares are selling to yield 50 basis points (0.5%) below the firm's bond yield. Calculate the value of the company's 5%, $100 par preferred stock.

Professor's Note: The dividend on preferred stock is usually expressed as a percentage of par. If CFA Institute gives you a preferred dividend in this manner, take care not to confuse the dividend rate with the discount rate, or the par value with the price.

Answer:

Determine the discount rate: 8.5% – 0.5% = 8.0%

Value the preferred stock: $D_p/k_P = \$5.00/0.08 = \$62.50$

The general DDM. Valuing common stock is more difficult than valuing bonds and preferred stock because the size and timing of future cash flows are uncertain, and the required rate of return on common equity, k_e, is unknown. However, a stock's value is still the PV of its future expected cash flows. Since the only cash flows a stockholder ever receives from the firm are dividends (cash or liquidating), the model used is called the *dividend discount model* (DDM).

$$value = \frac{D_1}{(1+k_e)^1} + \frac{D_2}{(1+k_e)^2} + \frac{D_3}{(1+k_e)^3} + ... + \frac{D_\infty}{(1+k_e)^\infty}$$

A couple of important comments must be made here. First, if an investor sells the stock, the purchaser is buying the remaining dividend stream, so a stock's value at any point in time is still determined by the dividends it is expected to pay after that point.

Second, if a company declares it will never pay dividends, its shares should be worthless because the stockholders would never receive anything of value from the firm. However, since we see shares of firms that pay no dividends being actively traded in the market, investors must expect to receive something of value, like a liquidating dividend, at some point in the future.

One-year holding period. If your holding period is one year, the value you will place on the stock today is the PV of any dividends you will receive during the year plus the PV of the price you can sell the stock for at the end of the year. The valuation equation is:

$$value = \frac{dividend\ to\ be\ received}{(1+k_e)^1} + \frac{year\text{-}end\ price}{(1+k_e)^1}$$

Steps used to determine a stock's value:

- Identify all expected future cash flows (dividends and future price).
- Estimate the equity discount rate: $k_e = RFR + \beta (R_{mkt} - RFR)$.
- Discount the expected dividend and selling price at the required return.

Example: One-period DDM valuation

Calculate the value of a stock that paid a $1 dividend last year. You think next year's dividend will be 5% higher (g = 0.05), and the stock will sell for $13.45 at year end. The risk-free rate of interest is 6%, the market return is 12%, and the stock's beta is 1.2.

Answer:

The next dividend is the current dividend increased by the estimated growth rate. In this case, we have:

$$D_1 = D_0 \times (1 + g) = \$1.00 \times (1 + 0.05) = \$1.05$$

Next, we must estimate the required return on equity. Using the CAPM we have:

$$k_e = RFR + \beta (R_{mkt} - RFR)$$
$$= 0.06 + 1.2(0.12 - 0.06)$$
$$= 13.2\%$$

Now we can compute the present value of the expected future cash flows as follows:

Dividend: $\dfrac{\$1.05}{1.132} = \$0.93$

Year-end price: $\dfrac{\$13.45}{1.132} = \$11.88$

Add the PV estimates. The current value based on the investor's expectations is:

Stock value = \$0.93 + \$11.88 = \$12.81

Multiple-year holding period DDM. With a multiple-year holding period, we simply estimate all the dividends to be received as well as the expected selling price at the end of the holding period. For a 2-year holding period, we have:

$$value = \frac{D_1}{(1 + k_e)^1} + \frac{D_2}{(1 + k_e)^2} + \frac{P_2}{(1 + k_e)^2}$$

Professor's Note: It is useful to think of the subscript, t, on dividends (D_t) and prices (P_t) as the "end" of period t. For example, in the preceding equation, P_2 is the price at the end of period (year) 2. Think of it as the price you can sell the stock for, just after you collect D_2.

Example: Multiple period DDM valuation

Using the stock in the preceding example, we had a current dividend of \$1.00, an expected growth rate of 5%, and the CAPM-determined required rate of return of 13.2%. Calculate the value of this stock assuming that you expect to sell it for \$14.12 in two years.

Answer:

Find the PV of the future dividends:

D_1 : $\dfrac{\$1.05}{1.132} = \$0.93$

D_2 : $\dfrac{\$1.05(1.05)}{(1.132)^2} = \dfrac{\$1.103}{1.2814} = \$0.86$

PV of dividends = 0.93 + 0.86 = \$1.79

Find the PV of the future price:

$$\frac{\$14.12}{(1.132)^2} = \$11.02$$

Add the present values. The current value based on the investor's expectations is $1.79 + $11.02 = $12.81.

The **infinite period DDM** assumes the growth rate, g, in dividends from year to year is constant. Hence, next period's dividend, D_1, is $D_0(1 + g_c)$, the second year's dividend, D_2, is $D_0(1 + g_c)^2$, and so on, where g_c is a constant growth rate. The extended equation using this assumption is as follows:

$$\text{value} = \frac{D_0(1+g_c)^1}{(1+k_e)^1} + \frac{D_0(1+g_c)^2}{(1+k_e)^2} + \frac{D_0(1+g_c)^3}{(1+k_e)^3} + \ldots + \frac{D_0(1+g_c)^\infty}{(1+k_e)^\infty}$$

Thank goodness this equation simplifies to:

$$\text{value} \doteq \frac{D_0(1 + g_c)}{k_e - g_c} = \frac{D_1}{k_e - g_c}$$

This is the infinite period dividend discount model.

Professor's Note: In much of the finance literature, you will see this model referred to as the constant growth DDM, the constant growth dividend valuation model, or the Gordon Growth Model. Whatever you call it, D_1 over k minus g should be permanently tattooed on your brain. Note that our valuation model for preferred stock is the same as the constant growth model with no growth (g = 0).

Example: Infinite period DDM valuation

Calculate the value of a stock that paid a $2 dividend last year, if dividends are expected to grow at 5% forever. The risk-free rate is 6%, the expected return on the market is 11%, and the stock's beta is 1.2.

Answer:

Determine D_1: $D_0(1 + g_c) = \$2(1.05) = \$2.10$

Determine k_e: RFR + $\beta(R_{mkt} - RFR)$
= 0.06 + 1.2(0.11 − 0.06)
= 12%

Calculate the stock's value = $D_1/(k_e - g_c)$
= $2.10/(0.12 − 0.05)
= $30.00

This example demonstrates that the stock's value is determined by the relationship between the investor's required rate of return on equity, k_e, and the projected growth rate of dividends, g_c.

Notice the critical relationship between k_e and g_c:

- As the difference between k_e and g_c widens, the value of the stock falls.
- As the difference narrows, the value of the stock rises.
- Small changes in the difference between k_e and g_c cause large changes in the stock's value.

Also, remember the assumptions of the infinite period DDM:

- The stock pays dividends, and they grow at a constant rate.
- The constant growth rate, g_c, is never expected to change.
- k_e must be greater than g_c. If not, the math will not work.

If any one of these assumptions is not met, the model breaks down.

Professor's Note: When doing stock valuation problems on the exam, watch for words like forever, infinitely, indefinitely, etc. This will tell you that the infinite period DDM should be used. Also watch for words like "just paid" or "recently paid." These will refer to the last dividend, D_0. Words like "will pay" or "is expected to pay" refer to D_1.

Value of a Common Stock for a Company Experiencing Temporary Supernormal Growth

A firm may temporarily experience a growth rate that exceeds the required rate of return on the firm's equity, but no firm can maintain this relationship indefinitely. We must assume the firm will return to a more sustainable rate of growth at some point in the future. Since the assumptions of the infinite period model (constant g and $k_e > g_c$) don't hold, the infinite period DDM cannot be used to value growth companies that are experiencing very rapid growth that will not continue forever.

A valuation approach for supernormal growth companies (and companies that don't currently pay dividends) is to combine the multi-period and infinite period models. This is referred to as the **multistage dividend discount model** in many finance textbooks.

$$\text{value} = \frac{D_1}{(1 + k_e)} + \frac{D_2}{(1 + k_e)^2} + \ldots + \frac{D_n}{(1 + k_e)^n} + \frac{P_n}{(1 + k_e)^n}$$

where:
D_n = last dividend of the supernormal growth period
D_{n+1} = first dividend affected by the constant growth rate, g_c

P_n = $\dfrac{D_{n+1}}{k_e - g_c}$, the first period's dividend after constant growth begins

Steps in using the temporary supernormal growth model:

- Project the size and duration of the supernormal dividend growth rate, g^*.
- Using this supernormal growth rate, estimate dividends during the supernormal period.
- Forecast what the normal (constant) growth rate will be at the end of the supernormal growth period, g_c.
- Project the first dividend at the resumption of normal growth.
- Estimate the price of the stock at the end of the supernormal growth period.
- Determine the discount rate, k_e.
- Add the PV of all dividends and the terminal stock price.

Example: Supernormal growth

Consider a stock with dividends that are expected to grow at 20% per year for four years, after which they are expected to resume their normal growth rate of 5% per year, indefinitely. The last dividend paid was $1.00, and k_e = 10%. Calculate the value of this stock.

Answer:

Calculate the dividends during the supernormal growth period using g^*:

$D_1 = D_0(1 + g^*) = 1.00(1.20) = \$1.20$

$D_2 = D_1(1 + g^*) = 1.20(1.20) = \$1.44$

$D_3 = D_2(1 + g^*) = 1.44(1.20) = \$1.73$

$D_4 = D_3(1 + g^*) = 1.73(1.20) = \$2.08$

Calculate the first dividend at the resumption of normal constant growth using g_c:

$D_5 = D_4(1 + g_c) = 2.08(1.05) = \$2.18$

Find the value of the stock at the end of the supernormal growth period using the infinite period DDM:

$$P_4 = \frac{D_5}{k_e - \overline{g}_c} = \frac{2.18}{0.10 - 0.05} = \$43.60$$

Remember, P_4 is the value at the end of period 4, which is the PV of all of the expected dividends from period 5 (D_5) through infinity. D_5 is the first dividend that grows at the normal, constant growth rate.

Calculate the PV of the cash flows (discounted at k_e):

$$\frac{1.20}{1.1} + \frac{1.44}{1.1^2} + \frac{1.73}{1.1^3} + \frac{2.08}{1.1^4} + \frac{43.60}{1.1^4} = \$34.78$$

Professor's Note: A common mistake with supernormal growth problems is to calculate the future price, P_4 in this example, then forget to discount it back to the present. Don't make this mistake because CFA Institute is sure to present this common error as one of the choices.

Example: Delayed dividend payments

This example reflects the fact that high growth firms normally don't pay dividends during their supernormal growth phase.

The firm will have three years of extraordinary growth during which no dividends will be paid. Beginning in year 4, earnings will stabilize and grow at a sustainable 5% rate indefinitely, and the firm will pay out 50% of its earnings in dividends. Given $E_4 = \$1.64$ and $k_e = 10\%$, calculate the value of this stock.

Answer:

Project the dividend that will be paid at the end of year 4:

$D_4 = (\text{dividend payout ratio})(E_4) = (0.5)(1.64) = \$0.82$

Find the value of the stock at the end of year 3. Remember, P_3 is the value of dividends 4 through infinity at the end of year 3, one period *before* the firm resumes normal growth.

$P_3 = D_4 / (k_e - g_c) = \$0.82 / (0.1 - 0.05) = \$16.40$

Find P_0: I/Y = 10%; N = 3; FV = \$16.40; CPT $\rightarrow$ PV = \$12.32 = P_0

Remember, there can be two types of supernormal growth problems:

- The company pays dividends, and there are two or more growth rates that are not zero. To work these problems, you find the PV of all the projected dividends, and the PV of $P_n = D_{n+1} / (k - g_c)$.
- The company initially pays no dividends but then pays out some or all of its earnings as dividends at the resumption of normal growth. In this type of problem, you find the PV of the future price, $P_n = D_{n+1} / (k - g_c)$, which is determined by the delayed dividend stream.

Professor's Note: I am placing subscript "c" under the constant growth g_c to help distinguish it from other growth rates. CFA Institute will not likely do this, so you should be sure that you identify which growth rate is the constant one on the exam when you are working with different growth rates.

LOS 59.d: Show how to use the DDM to develop an earnings multiplier model, and explain the factors in the DDM that affect a stock's price-to-earnings (P/E) ratio.

How does the DDM relate to the P/E ratio? Start with the general form of the infinite period DDM:

$$P_0 = \frac{D_1}{k-g}$$

Divide both sides of the equation by next year's projected earnings, E_1:

$$\frac{P_0}{E_1} = \frac{D_1 / E_1}{k-g}$$

This demonstrates that the P/E ratio is a function of:

- D_1/E_1 = the expected dividend payout ratio.
- k = the required rate of return on the stock.
- g = the expected constant growth rate of dividends.

Example: P/E valuation method

A firm has an expected dividend payout ratio of 60%, a required rate of return of 11%, and an expected dividend growth rate of 5%. Calculate the firm's expected P/E ratio. If you expect next year's earnings (E_1) to be \$3.50, what is the value of the stock today?

Answer:

Expected P/E ratio: $0.6/(0.11 - 0.05) = 10$.

Value of the stock: $(E_1)(P/E_1) = (\$3.50)(10) = \$35.00$.

What you should know about the earnings multiplier approach to valuation is that:

- The main determinant of the size of the P/E ratio is the difference between k and g, which, as shown earlier, has a significant impact on stock price.
- The relevant P/E ratio you should study is the expected (P_0/E_1) ratio, *not* the historical (P_0/E_0) ratio.
- The P/E ratio is just a restatement of the DDM, so anything that influences stock prices in the DDM will have the same effect on the P/E ratio.

There are several problems with using P/E analysis:

- Earnings are historical cost accounting numbers and may be of differing quality.
- Business cycles may affect P/E ratios. Currently reported earnings may be quite different from your expectations of earnings in the future (E_1).
- Also, like the infinite growth model, when k < g, the model cannot be used.

LOS 59.e: Explain the components of an investor's required rate of return (i.e., the real risk-free rate, the expected rate of inflation, and a risk premium) and discuss the risk factors to be assessed in determining a country risk premium for use in estimating the required return for foreign securities.

As we have discussed, the required rate of return on equity, k, is influenced by:

- The real risk-free rate (RFR_{real}), which is determined by the supply and demand for capital in the country. The real risk-free rate is the rate investors would require if there were absolutely no risk or inflation.
- An inflation premium (IP), which investors require to compensate for their expected loss of purchasing power.
- A risk premium (RP) to compensate investors for the uncertainty of returns expected from an investment. Since different investments have different patterns of return and different guarantees, risk premiums can differ substantially.

$$k = \text{required rate of return} = (1 + RFR_{real})(1 + IP)(1 + RP) - 1$$
$$k = \text{required rate of return (approximate)} \approx RFR_{real} + IP + RP$$

The real risk-free rate and the inflation premium together comprise the nominal risk-free rate, $RFR_{nominal}$. That is:

$$RFR_{nominal} = (1 + RFR_{real})(1 + IP) - 1$$

This may be approximated as:

$$RFR_{nominal} = RFR_{real} + IP$$

Professor's Note: A real rate is a rate that does not include inflation, while a nominal rate does. If a rate is not specified as being a real rate on the exam, it is safe for you to assume that it is a nominal rate.

The risk premium, RP, is a premium demanded for internal and external risk factors. *Internal risk factors* are diversifiable and include business risk, financial risk, liquidity risk, exchange-rate risk, and country risk. *External risk factors*, known as market risk factors, are macroeconomic in nature and are nondiversifiable.

Example: Computing the nominal risk-free rate

Calculate the nominal risk-free rate if the real risk-free rate is 4% and the expected inflation rate is 3%.

Answer:

$$RFR_{nominal} = (1.04)(1.03) - 1$$
$$= 1.0712 - 1$$
$$= 7.12\%$$

Alternatively, the nominal rate is frequently approximated by summing the real rate and expected inflation:

$$RFR_{nominal} = 4\% + 3\% = 7\%$$

The required rate of return on *any* investment is a combination of the nominal risk-free rate plus a risk premium. For equity investments, the risk premium can be determined by reference to a risk premium curve or by using the capital asset pricing model (CAPM):

$$k = RFR_{nominal} + RP$$

Using the CAPM, we have:

$$k = RFR + \beta[E(R_{mkt}) - RFR]$$

Professor's Note: Notice here that RFR is a nominal rate.

Estimating the Required Return for Foreign Securities

Security valuation models and their variables are essentially the same all over the world. However, there are significant differences in the determination of these variables.

To estimate the required rate of return for foreign securities, we can calculate the real risk-free rate, adjust it for the expected inflation rate, then determine the risk premium.

The **country risk premium** is estimated with consideration of five types of risk that will differ substantially from country to country.

- *Business risk* represents the variability of a country's economic activity, along with the degree of operating leverage for firms within the country.
- *Financial risk* will be different in countries throughout the world.
- *Liquidity risk* is often found in countries with small or inactive capital markets.
- *Exchange rate risk*, the uncertainty in exchange rates, must always be taken into account when considering foreign investments.
- *Country risk* arises from unexpected economic and political events.

LOS 59.f: Estimate the implied dividend growth rate, given the components of the required return on equity and incorporating the earnings retention rate and current stock price.

Assuming past investments are stable and dividends are calculated to allow for maintenance of past earnings power, the firm's earnings growth rate, g, can be defined as the firm's earnings plowback or retention rate (RR) times the return on the equity (ROE) portion of new investments.

$$g = (RR)(ROE)$$

Note that if RR is the earnings retention rate, (1 – RR) must be the firm's dividend payout rate.

Professor's Note: Recall that we used the DuPont method to decompose ROE into its component parts: net profit margin × asset turnover × financial leverage = ROE. You can use these components, along with the retention rate, to calculate ROE × RR = g, the implied (sustainable) growth rate.

Let's work through an example to illustrate why g equals RR × ROE for a stable but expanding company.

Example: Sustainable growth

Assume ROE is constant and that new funds come solely from earnings retention. Calculate the firm's growth rate, given that the firm earns 10% on equity of $100 per share and pays out 40% of earnings in dividends.

Answer:

Period 1 per share earnings = EPS_1 = ROE × Equity per share = (0.10)($100) = $10 per share
Period 1 dividend per share = D_1 = payout × EPS_1 = (0.40)($10) = $4.00 per share
Period 1 retained earnings = RR_1 × EPS_1 = ($10)(1 − 0.4) = $6.00 per share

so,

Period 2 earnings per share = (0.10)($100) + (0.10)($6) = $10.60 per share
Period 2 dividend per share = D_2 = (0.40)($10.60) = $4.24 per share

Analysis of growth:

Earnings growth = (EPS_2 − EPS_1) / EPS_1 = ($10.60 − $10) / $10 = 6%
Dividend growth = ($4.24 − $4) / $4 = 6%
Analysis of stock price: assume k = 10%
Price at the beginning of period 1 = D_1 / (k − g_c) = $4.00 / (0.10 − 0.06) = $100
Price at the beginning of period 2 = D_2 /(k − g_c) = $4.24 / (0.10 − 0.06) = $106

The stock's price will grow at a 6% rate, just as earnings and dividends will.

growth = g_c = (ROE)(Retention rate) = (0.1)(1 − 0.4) = 6%

The growth rate here, g_c = ROE × RR, is called the *internal* or *sustainable* growth rate—the rate of growth sustainable without resorting to external sources of capital (relying on retained earnings only).

So, what we know about dividend growth can be summarized as follows:

- If a firm's profit margin increases, ROE will increase.
- If ROE increases, g, which is (ROE)(RR), will increase.
- If g increases, the difference between k and g will decrease.
- If k − g decreases, the price of the stock will increase.

LOS 59.g: Describe a process for developing estimated inputs to be used in the DDM, including the required rate of return and expected growth rate of dividends.

As we have indicated, the DDM holds that the value of a share of stock is the present value of its cash flows. Thus, the DDM requires the following three inputs:

- An estimate of the stock's future cash flows, which are dividends and future price.
- A dividend growth rate, g.
- A discount rate, which is the appropriate required return on equity, k.

Once the present value of the asset has been estimated, compare it to the current market price.

Example: Application of DDM

Assume you are analyzing the XYZ company. Its current stock price is $18.00. After reviewing XYZ's financial data, you find that last year's earnings were $2.00 per share. The firm's ROE is 10%, and you expect it to stay that way for the foreseeable future. The firm has a stable dividend payout policy of 40%. The current nominal risk-free rate is 7%, the expected market return is 12%, and XYZ's beta is 1.2. Calculate the value of XYZ and indicate whether this stock is a "buy" based on your estimate.

Answer:

Step 1: Determine the required rate of return:

$$k = 0.07 + 1.2(0.12 - 0.07) = 13\%$$

Step 2: Determine the growth rate:

Step 2a: RR = (1 – dividend payout) = 1 – 0.4 = 0.6

Step 2b: g = (RR)(ROE) = (0.6)(0.10) = 0.06 or 6%

Step 3: Determine last year's dividend:

$$D_0 = E_0(\text{dividend payout ratio}) = \$2(0.4) = \$0.80$$

Step 4: Determine next year's dividend:

$$D_1 = D_0(1 + g_c) = \$0.80(1 + 0.06) = \$0.85$$

Step 5: Estimate the value:

$$V_0 = D_1/(k - g_c) = \$0.85/(0.13 - 0.06) = \$12.14$$

Professor's Note: Rounding differences may occur, not unlike those you might encounter on the exam.

Step 6: Compare the stock's value to its current market price:

$$\$12.14 \text{ vs. } \$18.00$$

Do not buy and possibly sell this stock short.

If estimated value > market price → buy
If estimated value < market price → don't buy

LOS 60: Describe how structural economic changes (e.g., demographics, technology, politics, and regulation) may affect industries.

An analyst should take into account how broad structural changes will affect specific industries over time. Four types of structural changes are:

- **Demographics.** Demographic factors include age distribution and population changes, as well as changes in income distribution, ethnic composition of the population, and trends in the geographical distribution of the population. As a large segment of the population reaches their twenties, residential construction, furniture, and related industries see increased demand. An aging of the overall population can mean significant growth for the health care industry and developers of retirement communities.
- **Lifestyles.** Examples of the effect of changing lifestyles on industry growth prospects are the increases in meals consumed outside the home and catalog sales, as the percentage of families with two employed spouses has increased. Consumption patterns are also affected by current perceptions of what is "in style" and trends in consumer tastes in recreation, entertainment, and other areas of discretionary expenditure.

- **Technology.** Changes in technology have had very important consequences for many industries over time. Change in the technology of transportation and communications has certainly had important effects on these industries, both in terms of products and services consumed but also in their production and pricing. Technological advances in computers and microprocessors in general have lead to sweeping changes in how inventory is managed and how products are distributed in many industries, particularly in the retailing industry.

- **Politics and regulation.** Changes in the political climate and changes in specific government regulations can also have significant effects on particular industries. The imposition of tariffs on steel will lead to increased domestic production and profitability; the rise of terrorist activity has helped some industries and imposed costs on others, such as the airline and shipping industries; and requirements of a minimum wage and the widespread expectation of employment benefits packages have affected hiring practices and production methods, especially in labor intensive industries. Regulation of the introduction and sale of everything from new drugs to genetically engineered crops has important implications for many industries as well.

KEY CONCEPTS

1. The top-down approach to security valuation has three steps:
    - Forecast the influence of the general economy on the securities markets.
    - Analyze the prospects for the various industries under your economic forecast.
    - Analyze the individual firms in the industries under your economic forecast.
2. The returns from any investment can be measured as price change (capital gain/loss), cash income (i.e., interest, dividends, rental income, etc.), earnings, or a variety of cash flow measures for equities.

3. The preferred stock valuation model: $P_0 = V_0 = \dfrac{D_{ps}}{K_{ps}}$

4. The calculation of the value of common stock can take different forms:

    - One period stock valuation model: $P_0 = V_0 = \dfrac{D_1}{1 + k_e} + \dfrac{P_1}{1 + k_e}$

    - A multiple-year holding period:

    $$\text{stock value} = \frac{D_1}{(1 + k_e)^1} + \frac{D_2}{(1 + k_e)^2} + \ldots + \frac{D_n}{(1 + k_e)^n} + \frac{P_n}{(1 + k_e)^n}$$

    - Infinite period model: $P_0 = V_0 = \dfrac{D_0 \times (1 + g)}{k_e - g}$ or $\dfrac{D_1}{k_e - g}$

5. For a firm with supernormal growth (g_1) over n periods followed by a constant growth rate of dividends forever (g_2) can be valued as:

    $$\frac{D_1}{1 + k_e} + \frac{D_2}{(1 + k_e)^2} + \ldots + \frac{D_n}{(1 + k_e)^n} + \frac{\dfrac{D_{n+1}}{k_e - g_2}}{(1 + k_e)^n}$$

    where : $D_1 = D_0 (1 + g_1) \ldots D_n = D_0 (1 + g_1)^n$
    and $D_{n+1} = D_n (1 + g_2)$

6. By dividing both sides of the infinite period DDM by E_1, it can be used as an earnings multiplier model:

$$\frac{P_0}{E_1} = \frac{\dfrac{D_1}{E_1}}{k-g}$$

7. The relationship between the nominal risk-free rate, the real risk-free rate, and the expected rate of inflation is: nominal risk-free rate = (1 + real risk-free rate)(1 + expected inflation) – 1.

8. The firm's internal or sustainable growth rate, g, is equal to ROE × RR. RR is the firm's retention rate, so (1 – RR) is the firm's dividend payout rate.

9. The following five factors are used to estimate a country's risk premium:
   - Business risk.
   - Financial risk.
   - Liquidity risk.
   - Exchange rate risk.
   - Specific country risk that arises from unexpected economic and political events.

10. An analyst should consider structural changes in the economy and how they will affect the growth and profitability of specific industries.

CONCEPT CHECKERS: AN INTRODUCTION TO SECURITY VALUATION AND INDUSTRY ANALYSIS

1. Which of the following describes the flow of the top-down valuation process?
   A. Economic analysis, industry analysis, company analysis.
   B. Company analysis, industry analysis, economic analysis.
   C. Economic analysis, company analysis, industry analysis.
   D. Pick the best stocks regardless of the industry and economic conditions.

2. An analyst used the infinite period valuation model to determine that XYZ Corporation should be valued at $20. The current market price is $30. The analyst should do which of the following?
   A. Issue a buy recommendation on XYZ.
   B. Issue a sell recommendation on XYZ.
   C. Issue a hold recommendation on XYZ.
   D. Do nothing since the results conflict each other.

3. What would an investor be willing to pay for a share of preferred stock that paid an annual $7 dividend if the yield on preferred was 25 basis points *below* the A bond yield of 8%?
   A. $77.50.
   B. $87.50.
   C. $90.32.
   D. $110.71.

4. An analyst projects that a stock will pay a $2 dividend next year and that it will sell for $40 at year-end. If the required rate of return is 15%, what is the value of the stock?
   A. $25.00.
   B. $33.54.
   C. $36.52.
   D. $43.95.

5. An analyst expects a stock selling for $25 per share to increase to $30 by year-end. The dividend last year was $1, but the analyst expects next year's dividend to be $1.50. What is the expected holding period yield on this stock?
   A. 20.00%.
   B. 21.67%.
   C. 24.00%.
   D. 26.00%.

6. A stock paid a $2 dividend last year. An investor projects that next year's dividend will be 10% higher and that the stock will be selling for $40 at the end of the year. The risk-free rate of interest is 8%, the market return is 13%, and the stock's beta is 1.2. Determine the value of the stock.
   A. $35.
   B. $37.
   C. $39.
   D. $42.

7. A stock will pay a $2 dividend next year, $2.25 the year after, and $2.50 the following year. An investor believes that she can then sell the stock for $50 at the end of a 3-year holding period. The risk-free rate of interest is 7%, the market return is 13%, and the stock's beta is 1. What is the value of the stock?
   A. $35.76.
   B. $37.44.
   C. $39.92.
   D. $47.99.

8. The infinite period dividend discount model (DDM) implies that a stock's value will be greater:
    A. the larger its expected dividend.
    B. the higher the expected growth rate.
    C. the lower the required rate of return.
    D. all of the above.

9. Holding all other factors constant, which of the following is expected to grow at the same rate as dividends in the infinite period DDM?
    A. Sales.
    B. ROE.
    C. Stock price.
    D. All of the above.

10. The infinite period DDM assumes which of the following?
    A. $g < k$.
    B. $g = k$.
    C. $g > k$.
    D. $g \neq k$.

11. What is the intrinsic value of a company's stock if next year's expected dividend is projected to be 5% greater than today's $1 dividend? The sustainable growth rate is 5%, and investor's required rate of return for this stock is 10%.
    A. $20.00.
    B. $21.00.
    C. $21.05.
    D. $22.05.

12. Next year's dividend is expected to be $2; $g = 7\%$; and $k = 12\%$. What is the stock's intrinsic value?
    A. $16.67.
    B. $28.57.
    C. $40.00.
    D. $42.80.

13. A stock paid a $1 dividend last year. The risk-free rate is 5%; the expected return on the market is 12%; and the stock's beta is 1.5. If dividends are expected to grow at a 5% rate forever, what is the value of the stock?
    A. $10.00.
    B. $15.25.
    C. $21.50.
    D. $25.75.

14. The XX Company paid a $1 dividend last year. The company is expecting dividends to grow at a 6% rate into the future. What is the value of this stock if an investor requires a 15% rate of return on stocks of this risk class?
    A. $10.60.
    B. $11.11.
    C. $11.78.
    D. $12.78.

15. If a company currently has a high and unsustainable g that exceeds k, what is the appropriate valuation model?
    A. Book value model.
    B. Infinite growth DDM.
    C. Price earnings multiple.
    D. Temporary supernormal growth (multistage) DDM.

16. Assume that a stock is expected to pay dividends at the end of year 1 and year 2 of $1.25 and $1.56, respectively. Dividends are expected to grow at a 5% rate thereafter. Assuming that k_e is 11%, the value of the stock is *closest* to which of the following?
    A. $22.30.
    B. $23.42.
    C. $24.55.
    D. $30.11.

17. An analyst feels that Brown Company's earnings and dividends will grow at 25% for two years, after which growth will fall to a market-like rate of 6%. If the projected discount rate is 10% and Brown's most recently paid dividend was $1, value Brown's stock using the supernormal growth (multistage) dividend discount model.
    A. $31.25.
    B. $33.54.
    C. $34.22.
    D. $36.65.

18. Firms with abnormally high return on equity (ROE) will probably do which of the following?
    A. Go out of business.
    B. Pay out all earnings in dividends.
    C. Retain a large portion of their earnings.
    D. Be indifferent between retention and payout.

19. How would an investor *best solve* for the intrinsic value of a stock that currently pays no dividends but is expected to start in five years?
    A. Use the P/E ratio.
    B. Equate the intrinsic value to the market price.
    C. Use the infinite period (constant growth) DDM.
    D. Use the temporary supernormal growth (multistage) DDM.

20. The ABC Company will experience a 25% growth rate over the next three years and pay no dividends over that time period. Growth will then fall to 6%, at which time the company will institute a 40% payout ratio. If the expected dividend in year 4 is projected to be $2 per share and the required return is 10%, the firm's intrinsic value today is *closest* to:
    A. $37.57.
    B. $41.66.
    C. $48.00.
    D. $50.00.

21. A firm has an expected dividend payout ratio of 60% and an expected future growth rate of 7%. What should the firm's price-to-earnings (P/E) ratio be if the required rate of return on stocks of this type is 15%?
    A. 5.0X.
    B. 7.5X.
    C. 10.0X.
    D. 15.5X.

22. An investor is analyzing a firm that has a historical earnings retention rate of 60%, which is projected to continue into the future, and a constant ROE of 15%. The stock's beta is 1.2. The nominal risk-free rate is 8%, and the expected market return is 13%. If the investor thinks that next year's earnings will be $3 per share, the stock's value would be *closest* to:
    A. $15.
    B. $24.
    C. $35.
    D. $55.

23. If a company has an earnings retention rate of zero, the firm's P/E ratio will be which of the following?
    A. 1 / g.
    B. 1 / k.
    C. D / P + g.
    D. D / k – g.

24. A stock's P/E ratio based on the DDM is which of the following?
    A. (1 – RR) / [k – RR(ROE)].
    B. (1 + RR) / [k – RR(ROE)].
    C. (1 + RR) / [k + RR(ROE)].
    D. (1 – RR) / [k + (RR)(ROE)].

25. Which of the following yields the growth rate of dividends?
    A. Adding the firm's earnings retention rate to the ROE.
    B. Subtracting the earnings retention ratio from the ROE.
    C. Dividing the firm's earnings retention rate by the ROE.
    D. Multiplying the firm's earnings retention rate by the ROE.

26. A stock just paid a dividend of $1. The dividend for the next three years is expected to grow at a 30% rate, after which the dividend in the fourth year and all future years is expected to grow at a rate consistent with an ROE of 10% and a dividend payout ratio of 60%. If the discount rate is 14%, the value of the stock is *closest* to:
    A. $19.37.
    B. $20.89.
    C. $22.90.
    D. $25.10.

27. Eisen Company paid a $1 dividend last year and is expected to continue to pay out 30% of its earnings as dividends in the foreseeable future. The firm's ROE 10%. What is the value of Eisen stock if you require a 13% return on stocks in Eisen's risk class?
    A. $10.70.
    B. $17.83.
    C. $19.56.
    D. $35.67.

28. The imposition of a tariff on imported aluminum will *most likely* benefit:
    A. domestic aluminum producers.
    B. foreign aluminum producers.
    C. domestic airframe manufacturers.
    D. Brazilian airlines.

ANSWERS – CONCEPT CHECKERS: AN INTRODUCTION TO SECURITY VALUATION AND INDUSTRY ANALYSIS

Professor's Note: Although your answer may vary slightly from the given choices, this is often the case on the actual CFA exam. Pick the closest one and move on!

1. **A**   Top-down analysis works from the macro to the micro level—economic analysis, industry analysis, company analysis.

2. **B**   Because the stock is selling for more than its intrinsic value, the stock is overvalued. The analyst should issue a sell recommendation.

3. **C**   Preferred stock uses the PV of perpetuity model. Required return = $0.08 - 0.0025 = 0.0775$.
$7.0 / 0.0775 = \$90.32$.

4. **C** $(\$40 + \$2) / 1.15 = \$36.52$.

5. **D** $(\$31.50 / \$25) - 1 = 0.26$.

6. **B**   Required return using CAPM = $0.08 + 1.2(0.13 - 0.08) = 14\%$. $[\$40 + \$2(1.1)] / 1.14 = \$37.02$.

7. **C** $k = 0.07 + 1(0.13 - 0.07)$, $V_0 = (\$2 / 1.13) + [\$2.25 / (1.13)^2] + [(\$2.50 + \$50) / (1.13)^3] = \$39.92$.

8. **D**   A larger expected dividend, a higher expected growth rate, and lower required return will all increase the expected value of a stock.

9. **C**   The infinite period DDM implies that the stock price will grow at the (constant) growth rate of dividends. A crucial assumption of the DDM is that ROE is constant; sales growth rate could be the same as the growth rate of dividends and earnings, but this is not required.

10. **A**   For the infinite period DDM, the constant growth rate must be less than the required rate of return or else the math will not work. *Note:* The choice $g \neq k$ is a "trick" distractor. It is incorrect because if $g > k$, the formula does not work.

11. **B**   Using the infinite period DDM, $\$1(1.05) / (0.1 - 0.05) = \$21.00$.

12. **C**   Using the infinite period DDM, $\$2 / (0.12 - 0.07) = \$40.00$.

13. **A** $k = 0.05 + 1.5(0.12 - 0.05) = 15.5\%$, $V_0 = \$1(1.05) / (0.155 - 0.05) = \$10.00$.

14. **C**   Using the infinite period DDM, $\$1(1.06) / (0.15 - 0.06) = \$11.78$.

15. **D**   Companies may sometimes have temporary supernormal growth where $g > k$. If this is the case, the temporary supernormal growth DDM is appropriate.

16. **C** $(\$1.25 / 1.11) + (\$1.56) / (1.11)^2 + (\$1.56)(1.05) / (0.11 - 0.05) / (1.11)^2 = \$24.55$.

17. **D** $1.25 / 1.1 + [\$1(1.25)^2 / (1.1)^2] + [\$1(1.25)^2(1.06) / (0.1 - 0.06) / (1.1)^2] = \$36.65$.

18. **C**   Firms with abnormally high return on equity will likely retain a high portion of their earnings because the firm will likely be able to earn higher returns by reinvesting those earnings than investors could earn if the earnings were paid out in dividends.

19. **D**   If a company does not pay dividends but is expected to in the future, the temporary supernormal growth DDM would be the best method to use. Work with earnings to find the PV of the future price that is determined by the future projected revenue stream.

20. **A**   Note that this problem gives you more information than you need. Simply use the period 4 dividend with the infinite period DDM, and discount that (time 3) value back to the present. $[\$2 / (0.10 - 0.06)] / (1.1)^3 = \$37.57$.

21. **B**   Using the earnings multiplier model, $0.6 / (0.15 - 0.07) = 7.5\text{X}$.

22. **B** $g = 0.6 \times 0.15 = 9\%$; $k = 0.08 + 1.2(0.13 - 0.08) = 14\%$; $P_0 = (\$3 \times 0.4) / (0.14 - 0.09) = \$24.00$.

23. **B**   If a company is paying out all of its earnings as dividends, the constant growth DDM and earnings multiplier model simplify into the PV of a perpetuity formula $= 1/k$, because $g = 0$ (in the denominator) and payout $= 1$ (in the numerator).

24. **A**   The earnings multiplier model calculates P/E as follows: payout $/ k - g$. Substituting terms, payout $= 1 - RR$, and $g = ROE(RR)$.

25. **D** $g = RR \times ROE$.

26. **A** $g = 0.4 \times 0.1 = 4\%$; $P_0 = \$1.30 / 1.14 + \$1.69 / (1.14)^2 + \$2.20 / (1.14)^3 +$
     $[\$2.20(1.04) / (0.14 - 0.04)] / (1.14)^3 = \$19.37$.

27. **B** $g = 0.7 \times 0.1 = 7\%$; $P_0 = \$1(1.07) / (0.13 - 0.07) = \$17.83$.

28. **A**   A structural change involving the imposition of a tariff will benefit domestic producers.

EQUITY: CONCEPTS AND TECHNIQUES

EXAM FOCUS

This topic review focuses on the analysis of global industries and provides a framework for this analysis. You should be able to describe the stages of the business cycle and the stages of the industry life cycle and recognize a stage if given descriptive information about the business environment or industry conditions. There are two measures of industry concentration that you need to be able to interpret. Finally, you should know the risk factors to consider in global industry analysis, and you *must* know Porter's five factors (memorize these) to consider when evaluating the intensity of competition and the nature of competition for profits along the value chain.

LOS 61.a: Classify business cycle stages and identify, for each stage, attractive investment opportunities.

Five stages of the business cycle can be identified. They are:

- *Recovery*—the economy begins to show signs that a recession is ending. Attractive investments include cyclicals, commodities, and commodity-linked equities.
- *Early expansion*—the recovery takes hold and the momentum of the recovery increases. Attractive investments include stocks in general and real estate.
- *Late expansion*—the recovery has continued, and confidence and momentum are high. Attractive investments include bonds and interest-sensitive stocks.
- *Slowing, entering recession*—growth has turned flat and then negative. Attractive investments include bonds and interest-sensitive stocks.
- *Recession*—typically, the money supply will be expanded, but recovery may take time. Attractive investments include commodities and stocks.

LOS 61.b: Discuss, with respect to global industry analysis, the key elements related to return expectations.

Returns, more specifically return on equity (ROE) compared to the cost of capital, and growth opportunities are the key drivers of value creation. Returns expectations are therefore an important element in identifying value and opportunities. **Returns expectations** depend on:

- *Demand.* The analyst must estimate worldwide demand in global industry analysis, which will involve an analysis of the countries that are most important to a firm's business and the relation of product demand to factors such as expected GDP growth and monetary conditions.
- *The value chain.* Creation of value by a firm will likely come from specific stages of the value chain. Value creation takes place in many steps, from the production of raw materials to equipment production (which may involve several intermediate steps), to the production of final goods, and culminating with sales and distribution to consumers or other producers and service after the sale. Where the profits lie along this chain of value creation can change over time. An analyst must be aware of this and form an opinion about a firm's plans to expand upstream or downstream along the value chain and its ability to exploit profitable opportunities, either within the industry or by extending its product line.

LOS 61.c: Describe the industry life cycle and identify an industry's stage in its life cycle.

Figure 1 depicts a general illustration of the **industry life cycle**. This figure shows sales on the vertical axis and the phases of a firm's life cycle on the horizontal axis.

Figure 1: Industry Life Cycle

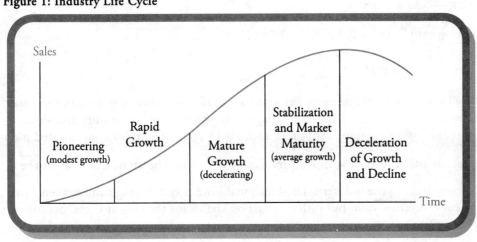

The following descriptions can be used to identify an industry's stage in its life cycle.

- *Pioneering phase.* This is the start-up phase, where the industry experiences limited growth in sales and low, or even negative, profit margins. Demand is low, and firms in the industry are faced with substantial developmental costs.
- *Rapid accelerating growth phase.* During this stage, markets develop for the industry's products, and demand grows rapidly. There is limited competition among the few firms in the industry, and sales growth and profit margins are high and accelerating.
- *Mature growth phase.* Sales growth is still above normal but ceases to accelerate. Competitors enter the market, and profit margins start to decline.
- *Stabilization and market maturity phase.* This is the longest phase. Industry sales growth rates approach the average growth rate of the economy. Fierce competition produces slim profit margins, and ROE becomes normal.
- *Deceleration of growth and decline.* Demand shifts away from the industry. Growth of substitute products causes declining profit margins.

Professor's Note: While we are focused on a sales estimate, please be aware that industry life cycle analysis can also provide us with insights into profit margins and earnings growth.

LOS 61.d: Interpret and explain the significance of a concentration ratio and a Herfindahl index.

A **concentration ratio** is calculated as the percentage market share of the N largest firms in an industry. We would express it as, "the four-firm concentration ratio is 78% for the automobile industry," for example. Knowing that the four largest firms in the industry account for 78% of sales gives us an idea of the competition structure in the industry.

An alternative concentration measure is the **Herfindahl index**. It is calculated as the sum of the squared market shares of the N largest firms (an N-firm Herfindahl index) or of all the firms in the industry (Herfindahl index for the entire industry).

Example: Calculation of concentration ratios

An industry has four firms with market shares of 40%, 30%, 20%, and 10%. Calculate the three-firm concentration ratio and the Herfindahl index for this industry.

Answer:

The three-firm concentration ratio is $0.4 + 0.3 + 0.2 = 90\%$.

The Herfindahl index is $0.4^2 + 0.3^2 + 0.2^2 + 0.1^2 = 0.3$

In practice, an analyst will use both of these measures to get a picture of the structure of competition in the industry. Overall, a Herfindahl index less than 0.1 indicates a lack of concentration in the industry; values between 0.1 and 0.18 indicate some concentration; and values above 0.18 suggest a highly concentrated industry.

An alternative way to interpret the index is to view its reciprocal, $\frac{1}{0.3} = 3.33$ for the above example, as the equivalent number of equal-sized firms in the industry. The Herfindahl index can distinguish between two industries that have the same concentration ratio but different market shares for the largest firms, because it puts more weight on the market shares of the largest firms by its construction.

LOS 61.e: Discuss, with respect to global industry analysis, the elements related to risk, and describe the basic forces that determine industry competition.

The **elements related to risk** in global industry analysis area:

- *Competition in markets*: Looking at the relation of price to average cost can provide information about the strategies that firms are following in an industry. The viability of strategies to keep new competitors out of an industry or to drive existing competitors out of an industry can be a source of risk.
- *Competition along the value chain*: Profits and high rates of return may lead to efforts to share in these profits by labor, suppliers of intermediate products, distributors, buyers, or outsourcing partners.
- *Governmental policies*: Some companies are subsidized or otherwise advantaged by the policies and institutions of the governments in their home countries. In other instances, governmental regulation, such as minimum wage laws or restrictions on the work week, may disadvantage a company. Such governmental participation can be an important factor in the competitive environment of an industry.
- *Market risk factors*: Risk can also be gauged by the returns-based measures of total risk and market risk (covariance risk). These measures may change over a business cycle or in response to a changed competitive structure within the industry. Other standard measures of risk, such as leverage or ROE variability, are incorporated here since they will affect total risk and market risk.

Forces That Determine Industry Competition

In addition to life cycle analysis, industry sales (and earnings) forecasts should be preceded with an evaluation of the competitive structure of the industry. This is necessary because the profitability of a specific firm in an industry is heavily influenced by the competitive environment in which it does business and the profitability of the industry as a whole.

A widely cited author, Michael Porter, believes that the competitive environment of an industry determines the ability of firms within that industry to sustain above-average rates of return on invested capital. In his widely cited book, *Competitive Strategy: Techniques for Analyzing Industries and Competitors* (New York: Free Press, 1980), Porter described five factors for determining the intensity of competition within an industry.

Porter's five factors that determine industry competition are:

- *Rivalry among the existing competitors.* Rivalry is high when many equal-sized firms compete within an industry. Slow growth leads to competition when firms fight for market share, and high fixed costs lead to price cutting as firms try to operate at full capacity.
- *Threat of new entrants.* The easier it is to enter the market, the greater the potential for competition. Barriers to entry (e.g., very high startup costs, regulation, economies of scale) help limit competition.
- *Threat of substitute products.* The profit potential in an industry is limited when many substitute products exist. This availability of substitute products restricts the price that firms may charge. There are higher levels of competition and lower profit margins for more commodity-like products.
- *Bargaining power of buyers.* A limited number of buyers or a high concentration of buyers relative to sellers places the buying firms in an advantageous position over sellers. This means the buying firms have significant control over prices.
- *Bargaining power of suppliers.* A limited number of selling firms or a high concentration of sellers relative to buyers places the selling firms in an advantageous position over buyers. This means the selling firms have significant control over prices. Suppliers are more powerful if there are just a few of them or if they are more concentrated than the buying firms. This enables sellers to control prices.

KEY CONCEPTS

1. The five stages of the business cycle are recovery, early expansion, late expansion, slowing, and recession. Commodities, stocks, and cyclicals are attractive investments during recession and recovery, while bonds and interest-sensitive stocks are attractive investments as expansion slows and interest rates are expected to decline.

2. Returns expectations are based on demand analysis, the sources of value creation, a firm's ability to expand profitably up or down the value chain, and the nature and intensity of competition within an industry.

3. The stages of the industry life cycle are pioneering, rapid growth, mature growth, market maturity, and decline.

4. An N-firm concentration ratio is the total market share of the N largest firms in an industry, and an N-firm Herfindahl index is the sum of the squared market shares of the N largest firms in an industry.

5. Risk analysis focuses on the viability of a firm's competitive strategy, the nature of competition for profits along the value chain, governmental participation as it positively or negatively affects a firm's competitive position, and market risk factors.

6. The five forces that can be used to analyze industry competition are rivalry among competitors, bargaining power of buyers, bargaining power of sellers, the threat of new entrants, and the threat of the introduction of substitute products.

CONCEPT CHECKERS: EQUITY: CONCEPTS AND TECHNIQUES

1. During the late expansion phase of the business cycle, which of the following would be the *most attractive* investment?
    A. Real estate.
    B. Commodities.
    C. Cyclical stocks.
    D. Interest sensitive stocks.

2. Return expectations can be *best determined* by examining:
    A. company leverage.
    B. market risk.
    C. demand.
    D. past cash flows.

3. The phase of the industry life cycle where new entrants to the market arrive and begin to erode profit margins is the:
    A. mature growth phase.
    B. decline.
    C. market maturity.
    D. rapid growth phase.

4. An industry has four firms with market shares of 60%, 20%, 15%, and 5%. The four-firm Herfindahl index for this industry is *closest* to:
    A. 1.
    B. 0.425.
    C. 2.35.
    D. 0.283.

5. Efforts by unions to secure wage increases can be *best viewed* as:
    A. market competition.
    B. competition along the value chain.
    C. downstream expansion.
    D. competition by suppliers.

6. Which of the following is **NOT** one of Porter's "five factors" that determine the intensity of industry competition?
    A. Threat of government regulation.
    B. Threat of substitutes.
    C. Rivalry among competitors.
    D. The bargaining power of buyers.

7. The three largest firms in a $200 billion industry have revenues of $50 billion, $30 billion, and $20 billion. Assuming that there are ten other equal-size firms in the industry, calculate the three-firm concentration ratio and the Herfindahl index for the entire industry.

Concentration	Herfindahl
A. 0.50	0.095
B. 0.50	0.12
C. 0.095	0.12
D. 0.095	0.095

ANSWERS – CONCEPT CHECKERS: EQUITY: CONCEPTS AND TECHNIQUES

1. **D** As the expansion ends and the economy declines, monetary easing and a decreased demand for capital should cause interest rates to go down.

2. **C** Demand analysis is the primary factor in estimating ROE. Past cash flows may be a starting point, but they do not provide expected returns in the future since business cycles and country-specific factors in the firm's primary markets must be considered to estimate future returns on equity.

3. **A** In the mature growth phase, sales growth is still above normal, but the arrival of competition begins to erode profit margins.

4. **B** $0.6^2 + 0.2^2 + 0.15^2 + 0.05^2 = 0.425$

5. **B** There is competition along all the steps in value creation from the producers of raw materials, through the various production steps, to distributors and buyers. Union activity is better described as cooperation among suppliers (of labor) than as competition by suppliers.

6. **A** The threat of government regulation is not one of the five factors.

7. **B** Three-firm concentration ratio $= \dfrac{50 + 30 + 20}{200} = 0.50$

$$\text{Herfindahl} = \left(\frac{50}{200}\right)^2 + \left(\frac{30}{200}\right)^2 + \left(\frac{20}{200}\right)^2 + 10 \times \left(\frac{10}{200}\right)^2 = 0.12$$

COMPANY ANALYSIS AND STOCK VALUATION

EXAM FOCUS

This topic review applies estimated P/Es and earnings to the valuation process for an individual common stock. Candidates should note that the formulas and process behind the calculations are identical whether we are talking about market and industry indices or individual companies. Note well the distinction between "good" companies and "good" (undervalued) stocks.

COMPANY VS. STOCK ANALYSIS

After analyzing the economy and determining which industries offer the most promise, the next step in the top-down approach is selecting stocks. This is not simply a matter of identifying a "good company," defined as one with solid earnings and growth potential.

Company analysis might identify the best firms, but it does not necessarily identify the best investments. A good company might be overpriced in the market, while a bad company might be underpriced and represent a better investment. To select the best stocks, the investor must answer two questions: (1) What are the best companies in the best industries? (2) Are the stocks of these companies priced correctly? This is where the valuation techniques that we have learned come into play.

LOS 62.a: Differentiate between 1) a growth company and a growth stock, 2) a defensive company and a defensive stock, 3) a cyclical company and a cyclical stock, 4) a speculative company and a speculative stock and 5) a value stock and a growth stock.

Growth company vs. growth stock. A *growth company* is one whose management has the ability to consistently select investments (projects) that earn higher returns than required by their risk. A *growth stock* is one that earns higher returns than other stocks of equivalent risk.

Even though a firm might be recognized as a growth company, its price may already reflect those growth expectations, and the stock will earn only the risk-adjusted required return. In addition, investor enthusiasm regarding the stock may be excessive, and this excess buying pressure may have pushed the price too high. In this case, even though the firm earns above-normal returns, its stock can actually earn below-normal returns.

Regardless of whether the firm is defined as a growth company, if a firm's stock price is below its intrinsic value, it can be a *growth stock*. Assuming the market estimates the correct value at some point, the stock price will rise, and the stock will (temporarily) earn above-normal risk-adjusted returns.

Defensive company vs. defensive stock. A *defensive company* has earnings that are relatively insensitive to downturns in the economy. Utility companies and retail grocery chains are good examples of defensive companies. These types of firms typically have low business risk and moderate financial risk. A *defensive stock* is a stock that will not decline as much as the market when the overall market declines. The returns of defensive stocks have a low correlation with the returns of the market. Recalling our review of portfolio theory, defensive stocks are characterized by low betas.

Professor's Note: This terminology is specific to Reilly and Brown[1] as far as I know. In the rest of the known universe, a growth stock is one with rapidly growing earnings. See "growth stock versus value stock" below.

Cyclical company vs. cyclical stock. A *cyclical company* has earnings that tend to follow the business cycle. Steel, automobile, and heavy equipment producers are good examples of cyclical companies. Cyclical companies often have high levels of fixed costs (business risk) or leverage (financial risk). A *cyclical stock* is a stock with rates of return that will change more than the return on the overall market. These are stocks with betas greater than one, indicating more than a one-to-one reaction to changes in the return on the market.

Speculative company vs. speculative stock. A *speculative company* has assets that are very risky, but the assets have the potential to generate very large earnings. Companies that are involved with diamond mining, oil exploration, or some types of real estate are good examples of speculative companies. A *speculative stock* is a stock that is highly likely to have very low or negative returns because it is almost always overpriced. These stocks have a low probability of a return near that of the market but a slight probability of an enormous return.

Growth stock vs. value stock. Often the term "growth stock" is used to mean something different than the definition we used in contrasting growth stocks with growth companies. In the context of growth versus value, "growth" refers to the earnings growth rate. The S&P 500/Barra Growth Index® and S&P 500/Barra Value Index® separate the stocks in the S&P 500 index into growth stock and value stock portfolios. Operationally, this is done based on price-book ratios, but separating index stocks based on their price-earnings ratios would also be a good approximation for this purpose.

The shares of firms with high earnings growth rates tend to have both higher price-book and higher price-earnings ratios than slower-growing firms. The term *value stock* is used to describe stocks that are priced low in relation to their current earnings (rather than expected growth in their earnings) or in relation to the value of their fixed assets, real estate, or cash. Value stocks are characterized by low price-book ratios, low price-earnings ratios, and often, high dividends.

LOS 62.b: Describe and estimate the expected earnings per share (EPS) and earnings multiplier for a company.

Estimated EPS. A firm's earnings per share (EPS) can be estimated using the following equation:

Expected EPS = [(sales)(EBITDA%) – depreciation – interest](1 – tax rate)

Note that sales, depreciation, and interest are estimated per-share values.

Estimated P/E. A firm's expected earnings multiplier (P/E) can be calculated using either of two methods:

Macroanalysis of the Earnings Multiplier. This approach estimates the company's P/E ratio by comparing it to industry and market P/E ratios.

Microanalysis of the Earnings Multiplier. Calculate a point estimate of the firm's expected P/E ratio.

- Estimate the firm's projected dividend payout ratio, D_1/E_1. This is done with comparative analysis of the firm's payout history, stated goals, and industry.
- Estimate the firm's required rate of return on equity: $k = RFR + \beta (R_{mkt} - RFR)$
- Estimate the firm's expected growth rate: $g = $ (retention rate)(ROE)
- Compute the firm's future earnings multiplier: $(P/E)_1 = (D_1/E_1) / (k - g)$

---

1. Frank K. Reilly and Keith C. Brown, *Investment Analysis and Portfolio Management*, 8th ed. (Dryden Press, 2005).

LOS 62.c: Calculate and compare the expected rate of return (based on the estimate of intrinsic value) to the required rate of return.

One way to evaluate the purchase of a stock is to compare the intrinsic value (based on the present value of expected dividends or cash flows) to the current market price. An alternative is to assume that the market price will move to the intrinsic value over some period and then compare the expected total return over the period to the investor's required rate of return. The following example illustrates this method.

Example: Expected return based on intrinsic value

Apton Corp. shares are currently trading at $32.00/share and are expected to pay a dividend of $0.96 over the coming year. Based on an expected growth rate of 12%, an analyst calculates the intrinsic value of Apton shares at $36. Should an investor with a required rate of return of 14.5% purchase Apton shares based on this analysis?

Answer:

If the price of Apton shares is $36 at year end, the total return will be:

$$\frac{36 - 32 + 0.96}{32} = 15.5\%$$

The investor should purchase the shares since the return of 15.5% is greater than the required return of 14.5%.

KEY CONCEPTS

1. We must distinguish between *companies* with earnings that grow, are cyclical, are defensive, or are speculative, and *stocks* with values that grow, are cyclical, are defensive, or are speculative.

2. If a company with rapidly growing earnings is priced to reflect its earnings growth rate, it is not likely a growth stock—it won't provide returns above its required rate of return.

3. In common usage, a *growth stock* has high expected earnings growth, a high P/E ratio, and a high price-book ratio. In contrast, a *value stock* is characterized by slower growth, a lower P/E ratio, a lower price-book ratio, and often a relatively high dividend yield.

4. To estimate a firm's expected earnings per share, an analyst needs to determine the company's sales forecast and profit margin and use the following equation: EPS = [(sales per share)(EBITDA%) – D – I](1 – t).

5. The two methods for estimating a firm's earnings multiplier $(P/E)_1$ are:

   • Estimate the firm's P/E ratio by comparing it to the market and industry P/E ratios.

   • Calculate point estimates for projected payout ratio, required rate of return, and growth rate in dividends, and use this equation: $(P/E)_1 = \dfrac{D_1/E_1}{k-g}$.

6. An analyst can compare his estimate of intrinsic value to the current share price to make the purchase decision, or calculate the expected holding period return assuming the stock price moves to intrinsic value over the period and compare that to the required rate of return on the stock.

CONCEPT CHECKERS: COMPANY ANALYSIS AND STOCK VALUATION

1. Which of the following could be a growth stock?
    A. Expected return = required return.
    B. Expected return < required return.
    C. Required return = market return.
    D. Required return < expected return.

2. Which of the following statements about company and stock analysis is **FALSE**? A:
    A. growth stock always indicates a growth company.
    B. growth company's stock can have below-average risk-adjusted returns.
    C. weak firm can experience temporary above-average risk-adjusted returns.
    D. growth stock earns higher returns than stock of equivalent risk.

3. Which of the following statements is **FALSE**? A growth:
    A. company can be over- or undervalued.
    B. stock is overvalued relative to its risk.
    C. company has above-average investment opportunities.
    D. stock has a higher rate of return than comparable firms.

4. An analyst gathered the following financial information about a firm:
    *   Estimated sales per share $200
    *   An EBITDA profit margin estimate   20%
    *   Estimated depreciation per share $15
    *   Interest per share $5

    If the firm's tax rate is 30%, calculate the firm's estimated earnings per share (EPS).
    A. $6.
    B. $14.
    C. $22.
    D. $28.

5. An analyst gathered the following financial information about a firm:
    *   Estimated EPS $10 per share
    *   Dividend payout ratio   40%
    *   Required rate of return   12%
    *   Expected long-term growth rate of dividends   5%

    What would the analyst's estimate of the future value of this company's stock be?
    A. $33.
    B. $57.
    C. $80.
    D. $86.

6. Which of the following statements about stock valuation is **FALSE**?
    A. If estimated value < the market price, sell the stock; it's overpriced.
    B. If estimated value < the market price, buy the stock; it's underpriced.
    C. If the expected rate of return > the required rate, buy the stock; it's underpriced.
    D. If the expected rate of return < the required rate, don't buy the stock; it's overpriced.

7. Which of the following statements is **FALSE**? A speculative:
   A. stock is usually underpriced.
   B. company has highly risky assets.
   C. company can be over- or undervalued.
   D. stock has a low probability of earning a market rate of return.

8. An analyst has made the following estimates for a stock:
   - Dividends over the next year $0.60
   - Long-term growth rate   13%
   - Intrinsic value $24

   The shares are currently priced at $22.

   Assuming the stock price moves to intrinsic value over the next year, what is the expected return on the stock?
   A. 9.1%.
   B. 11.8%.
   C. 13.0%.
   D. 15.7%.

ANSWERS – CONCEPT CHECKERS: COMPANY ANALYSIS AND STOCK VALUATION

1. **D** If the required return is less than the expected return, the stock is underpriced and should temporarily earn above-normal risk-adjusted returns.

2. **A** Classifying a stock as a growth stock means it is expected to earn above-average risk-adjusted returns, regardless of whether it is issued by a strong or weak firm.

3. **B** It is true that a growth company can be overvalued or undervalued; a growth company is characterized by above-average investment opportunities and typically has a higher rate of return than comparable firms. A growth stock is not necessarily overvalued—it can be over- or undervalued.

4. **B** Expected EPS = [(sales)(EBITDA%) – depreciation – interest] (1 –t)

$$= [(200)(0.20) - 15 - 5](1 - 0.3) = \$14$$

5. **B** $(P/E)_1 = (D_1/E_1)/ (k - g) = (0.4)/(0.12 - 0.05) = 5.7$

$P_1 = \$10(5.7) = \$57$

6. **B** Buy (sell) a stock when the estimated value is more (less) than the market price.

7. **A** Speculative stocks are almost always overpriced.

8. **B** $\dfrac{24 - 22 + 0.60}{22} = 11.8\%$

TECHNICAL ANALYSIS

EXAM FOCUS

This topic review introduces the "story" that underlies technical analysis, and you should understand how this differs from the fundamental analysis view. You should learn what the technical indicator names mean. Confusion regarding which indicators are contrarian indicators and which are smart money indicators is normal. I suggest you try to remember which are the smart money indicators because there are only four of them; then you will know that the others are contrarian indicators. The real distinction here is whose actions are driving the indicator. For smart money indicators, the "smart" people driving the indicator values are bond traders (confidence index and TED spread), exchange specialists (specialist short sale ratio), and investors buying on margin (margin debt).

LOS 63.a: Explain the underlying assumptions of technical analysis and explain how technical analysis differs from fundamental analysis.

Underlying all of technical analysis are the following assumptions:

- Values, and thus prices, are determined by supply and demand.
- Supply and demand are driven by both rational and irrational behavior.
- Security prices move in trends that persist for long periods.
- While the causes of changes in supply and demand are difficult to determine, the actual shifts in supply and demand can be observed in market price behavior.

The major challenge to technical analysis is the efficient markets hypothesis (EMH). Followers of the EMH believe that all available information associated with both fundamental and technical analysis is impounded in current security prices. EMH followers argue that technical trading rules require too much subjective interpretation and that decision variables change over time.

Fundamental analysts believe that a security's price is determined by the supply and demand for the underlying security based on its economic fundamentals, such as expected return and risk. Fundamentalists believe they can forecast value changes by analyzing earnings and other publicly available data.

The difference between fundamental analysis and technical analysis is the assumption about the speed at which new information is impounded into prices. Technicians believe the reaction is slow, while fundamentalists believe prices adjust quickly. In addition, efficient market hypothesis analysts feel the price adjustment happens almost instantaneously.

Fundamentalists, through their research, look for changes in the basis of value, which eventually leads to changes in the supply and demand for the stock. Technicians look for evidence of changes in supply and demand through market signals and indicators. Efficient market followers say all this looking is a hopeless and profitless exercise, since prices will change very rapidly in response to new information.

The difference in the three views is illustrated in Figure 1, where the following interpretations can be made:

- Fundamentalists look for reasons why the valuation band will shift upward. The shift will happen when they find it. Price changes will occur over a period of days or weeks as analysts determine the situation. The fundamentalists' price-adjustment process is described by the path from Point 1 to Point 2.
- Technicians look for signs that the valuation band has moved. Technicians base their strategies on the premise that price changes will occur over a long period, as indicated by the path from Point 1 to Point 3.
- EMH advocates hold that when the value band shift happens, the price will shift rapidly. This adjustment process is described by the path from Point 1 to Point 4.

Figure 1: Technical, Fundamental, and EMH Price Adjustment Process

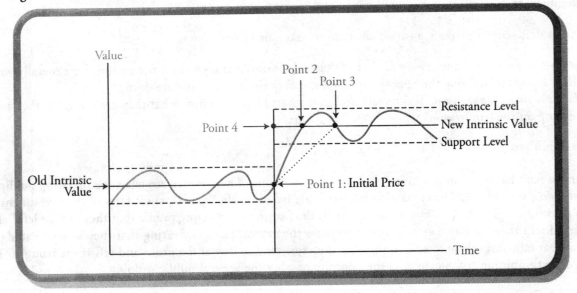

LOS 63.b: Discuss the advantages and challenges of technical analysis.

Technical analysis offers the following advantages:

- It is quick and easy.
- It does not involve accounting data and analytical adjustments for differences in accounting methods.
- It incorporates psychological as well as economic reasons behind price changes.
- It tells *when* to buy (not *why* investors are buying).

The **major challenge to technical analysis** is the *efficient market hypothesis*. Efficient market analysts feel all available information is impounded in the current security price. They argue that technical relationships may not be repeated. Technical analysis is also challenged by the argument that technical rules require too much subjective interpretation and that technical decision variables change over time.

Technical analysis often involves some sort of trading rule. Some of the challenges to technical trading rules are:

- Almost without exception, EMH studies using autocorrelation and runs tests have found no evidence that prices move in trends (i.e., past price patterns may not be repeated in the future). EMH followers say that the market appears to react quickly and completely to the release of new information.
- If technical trading rules worked, the price movements would become a self-fulfilling prophecy. That is, if enough people believe the price is going to rise $5 per share once a specific breakout price is reached, the buying pressure at the breakout price will cause the $5 price increase, although it will likely be temporary.
- If technical trading proved to be successful, others would copy it. As more traders implemented the strategy, its value would be neutralized.
- Interpreting the rules is too subjective, and the decision variables change over time.

LOS 63.c: Identify examples of each of the major categories of technical indicators.

Professor's Note: The wording of this LOS does not ask you to calculate these measures, only to identify them. Focus your attention on what high and low values of the indicators suggest to an analyst, not on the actual numeric values that are identified as bullish or bearish values.

Technical trading rules fall into two broad classes:

- General market movement indicators.
- Individual stock selection indicators (graphs and moving averages).

When analyzing general markets, technicians tend to take one of two views:

- The *contrarian* view. Contrary-opinion technicians (contrarians) argue that the majority is generally wrong, so they recommend doing the opposite of what the majority of investors are doing.
- *Follow the smart money* view. Technicians feel that smart investors know what they are doing, so they suggest "jumping on the bandwagon" while there is still time.

Contrarian View

Contrarians feel that the majority of investors are always wrong. They wait to see what the investing public is doing and do the opposite. The contrarian strategies are based on the "greed/panic" view of the investment process shown in Figure 2. A market advance instills the fear in the investing public that they will be left behind. Their greed tells them to buy. Later, investors panic as the market plunges, fearing that they won't be able to get out. This fear motivates them to sell. In the end, investors tend to buy at the peaks and sell at the troughs. Thus, a wise contrary-opinion technician does the opposite of what the general public is doing.

Figure 2: Contrarian View of the Business Cycle

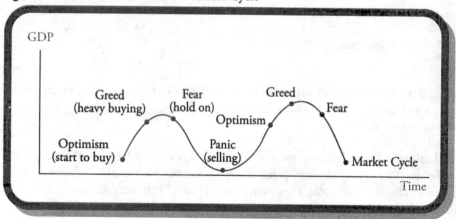

Contrary-opinion technicians use the following six technical indicators:

1. **Cash position of mutual funds.** The mutual fund cash position is a function of investor expectations and the institution's view of market expectations. Contrary-opinion technicians feel that mutual fund cash positions are a good indicator of institutional investors' expectations and that they are usually wrong at picking the peaks and troughs of the market cycle.

$$\text{Mutual fund ratio} = \frac{\text{mutual fund cash}}{\text{total fund assets}}$$

©2007 Schweser

- If the mutual fund ratio (MFR) is greater than 13%, it implies funds are holding cash and are therefore bearish on the market. In this case, contrary-opinion technicians are bullish.
- If the MFR is less than 5%, it implies funds are investing cash and are therefore bullish on the market. Contrary-opinion technicians are therefore bearish.

Professor's Note: Another way to look at this is that when the mutual fund cash ratio is high, contrarians are bullish because these cash holdings indicate potential future buying power in the market.

2. **Investor credit balances in brokerage accounts.** The following is the contrarian view:
   - Falling credit balances mean "normal" investors are bullish, so contrarians will be bearish and sell.
   - Rising credit balances mean "normal" investors are bearish, so contrarians will be bullish and buy.
   - Note that a technical view of a build-up in credit balances would be that there is an increase in potential future buying power in the market, which is considered to be bullish.

3. **Opinions of investment advisory services.** The bearish sentiments index is used to indicate the level of bearish sentiment among investment advisors. It is expressed as the investment advisor ratio (IAR), or:

$$IAR = \frac{\text{bearish opinions}}{\text{total opinions}}$$

   - If the IAR is greater than or equal to 60%, it implies the market is bearish. Therefore, contrarians are bullish.
   - If the IAR is less than or equal to 20%, it implies advisors are bullish. Therefore, contrarians are bearish and sell.

4. **Over-the-counter vs. NYSE volume.** Over-the-counter (OTC) issues are more speculative than NYSE issues, and speculative trading increases at market peaks. The level of speculative trading is measured using the volume ratio:

$$\text{volume ratio} = \frac{\text{OTC volume}}{\text{NYSE volume}}$$

   - If the volume ratio (VR) is equal to or greater than 112%, speculation is high. Therefore, contrarians are bearish, since they feel that the market has peaked.
   - If the VR is equal to or less than 87%, investors are bearish. Therefore, contrarians are bullish and buying.
   - You should note that the VR limits (112% and 87%) vary significantly over time. Currently, the direction of the VR is used as a guide for the degree of speculative trading.

5. **CBOE put/call ratio.** Contrarians use the put/call ratio (PCR) as an indicator of investors' bearishness. As such, contrary-opinion technicians become bullish as the PCR ratio increases.

$$\text{put call ratio} = \frac{\text{puts}}{\text{calls}}$$

   - If the PCR is equal to or greater than 0.50, the market is bearish, so contrarians are bullish.
   - If the PCR is less than or equal to 0.35, the market is bullish, so contrarians are bearish.

6. **Stock index futures.** Some contrarians track the relative number of futures traders who are bullish. These contrarians believe that:
   - When 75% or more of speculators are bullish, contrarians become bearish.
   - When 25% or less of speculators are bullish, contrarians become bullish.

Smart Money Technicians

Smart money technicians use the following four indicators to help them determine what the smart investors are doing.

1. **Confidence index.**

$$CI = \frac{\text{Barron's average yield on 10 top grade corporate bonds}}{\text{Dow Jones Average 40 bonds}} \quad \text{or } CI = \frac{\text{quality bond yields}}{\text{average bond yields}}$$

   Note: this ratio is always less than one.

   In periods of confidence, investors sell high-quality bonds and buy lower-quality bonds to increase yields. Quality bond prices will fall and their yields rise. Lower-grade bond prices rise and their yields fall. Thus, the confidence index (CI) ratio will increase during periods of confidence (e.g., from 0.07 / 0.10 = 0.7 to 0.08 / 0.09 = 0.89). Note that the CI moves in the opposite direction of yield spreads. In periods of confidence, yield spreads narrow and the CI gets bigger. In periods of pessimism, spreads widen and the CI falls.

2. **T-bill—eurodollar yield spread.** Some technicians believe that spreads will often widen during times of international crisis as money flows to a safe haven in U.S. T-bills. An increasing "TED" spread is a bearish indicator.

3. **Short sales by specialists.** Smart money technicians use short sales by specialists as an indicator of future market behavior as follows:

$$\text{specialist short sale ratio} = \frac{\text{specialists' short sales}}{\text{total short sales on the NYSE}}$$

   - If this ratio falls below 30%, it's a bullish sign. Specialists are buying.
   - If this ratio goes above 50%, it's a bearish sign. Specialists are selling.

4. **Debit balances in brokerage accounts (margin debt).** Debit balances in brokerage accounts represent the level of margin trading, which is usually only done by knowledgeable investors and traders.
   - An increase in debit balances would indicate an increase in purchasing by astute buyers. This is a bullish sign for smart money technicians.
   - A decline in debit balances would indicate astute traders are selling stocks. This is a bearish sign for smart money technicians.

Other Indicators of Market Direction

Breadth of market. The technician's story in this case is that:

- The indices represent a few large companies, not the whole market.
- The market has many medium and small companies.
- Frequently the index goes one way while smaller issues go the other. Broad market moves include both large and small companies. How do you gauge the strength of market support, i.e., the breadth of the market? Compare the advance-decline line with the market index.

The advance-decline line is a running total of the daily advances less the declines on the NYSE. If the advance-decline line and the index move together, the movement is broadly based across the market. A divergence between the trend in the index and the advance-decline line would signal that the market has hit a peak or trough.

An alternative to the advance-decline line is the diffusion index. The diffusion index is a 5-week moving average of all of the stocks that advanced during a day plus 50% of the number that remained unchanged, divided by the number of issues traded during the day.

Short interest ratio. Short interest is the cumulative number of shares that have been sold short and not covered by a subsequent purchase. The short interest ratio (SIR) is used to measure the extent of short interest:

$$SIR = \frac{outstanding\ short\ interest}{average\ daily\ volume\ on\ exchange}$$

The SIR is calculated by the NYSE and NASD.

- If the SIR is high (6.0 or above), there is potential demand, a bullish sign.
- If the SIR is low (4.0 or below), there is potential for short selling, a bearish sign.

Stocks above their 200-day moving average. The market is believed to be overbought—a bearish indicator—when over 80% of the stocks are selling above their 200-day moving averages. Similarly, the market is considered to be oversold—a bullish indicator—if less than 20% of the stocks are selling above their 200-day-moving averages.

Block uptick-downtick ratio. Recall that upticks refers to a stock selling at a price above its most recent trade. When blocks of stocks are trading at an uptick price, the market is considered to be a buyer's market. Blocks trading on downticks (prices below the previous price), are an indication of a seller's market.

$$uptick\text{-}downtick\ ratio = \frac{number\ of\ block\ uptick\ transactions}{number\ of\ block\ downtick\ transactions}$$

- This indicator is a measure of institutional investor sentiment.
- If the ratio is close to 0.70, it is bullish; if the ratio is close to 1.10, it is bearish.

Stock Price and Volume Techniques

Dow Theory. The Dow Theory states that stock prices move in trends. There are three types of trends: major trends, intermediate trends, and short-run movements. Technicians look for reversals and recoveries in major market trends.

Importance of volume. Price alone does not tell the story. Technicians attempt to gauge market sentiment as well as direction to determine changes in supply and demand. Thus, they look at the volume that accompanies price movements. Price changes on low volume tell us little. Price changes on high volume tell us whether suppliers or demanders are driving the change.

$$upside\text{-}downside\ volume\ ratio = \frac{volume\ of\ stocks\ that\ increased}{volume\ of\ stocks\ that\ declined}$$

- If the upside-downside (U-D) ratio is 1.50 or more, it indicates that the market is overbought. This is a bearish signal.
- If the U-D ratio is 0.75 or lower, it reflects that the market is oversold. This is a bullish signal.

Support and resistance levels. Most stock prices remain relatively stable and fluctuate up and down from their true value. The lower limit to these fluctuations is called a support level—the price where a stock appears cheap and attracts buyers. The upper limit is called a resistance level—the price where a stock appears expensive and initiates selling.

Moving averages lines. Technicians believe stock prices move in trends. However, random fluctuations in prices mask these trends. By using moving averages (10 to 200 days), technicians can eliminate the minor blips from graphs but retain the overall long-run trend in prices.

Relative strength. When prices of an individual stock or industry change, it is difficult to tell if the change is stock-specific or caused by market movements. If the stock price and the market index value are changing at the same rate, the ratio created by dividing one by the other will remain constant. This ratio is called the relative strength ratio:

$$\text{relative strength} = \frac{\text{stock price}}{\text{market index value}}$$

- If the ratio increases over time, the stock is outperforming the market, a positive trend.
- If the ratio declines over time, the stock is underperforming the market, a negative trend.

Graphs. Some technical analysts are called chartists due to their extensive reliance on charts and graphs to indicate market directions.

- *Bar charts.* Price is plotted against time.
- *Point-and-figure charts.* Price is plotted on the y-axis, but movement along the x-axis is only plotted if a preset price reversal occurs.

Technicians read charts looking for patterns. Why? Technicians feel that history repeats itself, so by looking at past trends, they will be able to identify the beginning of new trends.

KEY CONCEPTS

1. The following are the underlying assumptions of technical analysis:
   - The market price of securities is determined solely by supply and demand.
   - Supply and demand are influenced by rational and irrational factors.
   - Security prices move in trends that persist for appreciable lengths of time.
   - Shifts in supply and demand can be determined by the actions of the market itself.
2. Fundamentalists believe that prices react quickly to changing stock values, while technicians believe that the reaction is slow. Technicians look for changes in supply and demand, while fundamentalists look for changes in value.
3. The advantages of technical analysis are:
   - It is quick and easy.
   - It is not heavily dependent on financial accounting statements.
   - It incorporates psychological as well as economic reasons behind price changes.
4. Challenges to technical trading rules include:
   - The efficient market hypothesis says price adjustments happen too quickly to trade on.
   - The behavior of past prices and market variables may not be repeated in the future.
   - Interpreting technical data requires too much subjective judgment to be usable.
   - The standard values that signal investment decisions can change over time.

5. Contrarian indicators, based on a belief that the majority opinion at a point in time is generally wrong, are:
   - Mutual fund cash position.
   - Investor credit balances in brokerage accounts.
   - Investment advisory opinions.
   - OTC vs. NYSE volume.
   - CBOE put/call ratio.
   - Futures traders bullish on stock index futures.

6. Smart money indicators include:
   - Barron's confidence index.
   - T-bill to Eurodollar yield spread.
   - Short sales by specialists.
   - Debit balances in brokerage accounts.

CONCEPT CHECKERS: TECHNICAL ANALYSIS

1. Which of the following statements is **NOT** an advantage of technical analysis?
   A. It's quick and easy.
   B. It tells the analyst when to buy.
   C. It tells the analyst why investors are buying.
   D. It incorporates psychological as well as economic reasons for price changes.

2. Which one of the following statements about technical analysis is **TRUE**? Technical analysis:
   A. requires very little subjective judgment.
   B. has been shown to outperform fundamental analysis.
   C. is not heavily dependent on financial accounting statements.
   D. only works if technicians can obtain new information before other investors and process it correctly and quickly.

3. When the Investment Advisory "Sentiment" Index exceeds a 60% negative opinion rating, contrary-opinion technicians will do which of the following?
   A. Sell.
   B. Buy.
   C. Hold.
   D. Investment advisory "sentiment" is not a contrary-opinion signal.

4. When the relative over-the-counter (OTC) to NYSE volume ratio is high—that is, the OTC volume exceeds 112% of NYSE volume—contrary-opinion technicians would do which of the following?
   A. Hold.
   B. Be bearish and sell.
   C. Be bullish and buy.
   D. This is not a signal to contrary-opinion technicians.

5. If the Barron's confidence index (CI) increases (and the implied yield spread narrows), investors are doing which of the following?
   A. Selling quality bonds.
   B. Buying quality bonds.
   C. Selling common stocks.
   D. Buying common stocks.

6. When investors are pessimistic, the CI will do which of the following?
   A. Increase.
   B. Decrease.
   C. Remain constant.
   D. Increase sharply then decrease sharply.

7. When debit balances (i.e., margin debt) in brokerage accounts increase, which of the following statements is **TRUE**?
   A. Smart money technicians interpret this as a bearish sign.
   B. Smart money technicians interpret this as a bullish sign.
   C. Contrary-opinion technicians interpret this as a bullish sign.
   D. No information content is contained in the debit balances in brokerage accounts.

8.　Technicians feel that which of the following statements is **TRUE**?
　　A.　Stock prices move in trends.
　　B.　History tends to not repeat itself.
　　C.　Trends continue over short periods.
　　D.　Prices adjust quickly to new information.

9.　Which of the following would be a bullish sign to a smart money technician?
　　A.　The Barron's confidence index increases.
　　B.　The T-bill Eurodollar yield spread widens.
　　C.　The specialist short sale ratio goes above 50%.
　　D.　Debit balances in brokerage accounts decline.

10.　If the relative strength ratio (stock price over market price) increases, which of the following statements is **TRUE**? The market index:
　　A.　is outperforming the stock.
　　B.　price increase equals the stock price increase.
　　C.　price percentage increase is less than the stock price percentage increase.
　　D.　price percentage increase is greater than the stock price percentage increase.

11.　Which one of the following is a bearish signal to a smart money technical analyst?
　　A.　The T-bill Eurodollar yield spread narrows.
　　B.　The Barron's confidence index increases.
　　C.　The specialist short sale ratio falls below 30%.
　　D.　Debit balances in brokerage accounts fall.

12.　Which of the following is considered a bullish indicator to a contrarian?
　　A.　Low/falling credit balances in brokerage accounts.
　　B.　High OTC volume ratio.
　　C.　High put/call ratio.
　　D.　Low mutual fund cash ratio.

ANSWERS – CONCEPT CHECKERS: TECHNICAL ANALYSIS

1. **C** Technical analysis is quick and easy. It gives signals when to buy, and incorporates psychological and economic reasons for price changes. Technical analysis does not have any explanatory power—it does not give a reason why investors are buying or selling.

2. **C** Technical analysis does require subjective judgment to interpret its rules; it has not been shown to outperform fundamental analysis, and it works based on what other investors are doing. Technical analysis relies on price patterns and does not incorporate accounting data.

3. **B** When the majority of people are negative, as the sentiment index indicates, contrary-opinion technicians take the opposite opinion and will be bullish and buy.

4. **B** The OTC market is more speculative than the NYSE market. When people are buying more speculative issues, the majority of people are bullish. Contrary-opinion technicians will take the opposite stance—they will be bearish and sell.

5. **A** In periods of confidence, investors sell higher-quality bonds and buy lower-quality bonds looking for yield. This happens when the confidence index rises or when spreads narrow.

6. **B** When investors are pessimistic, the confidence index falls.

7. **B** When margin debt in brokerage account balances increase, smart money technicians will see this as a bullish sign that investors are buying. Contrary-opinion technicians will take the opposite stance and will be bearish.

8. **A** Technicians believe that stock prices move in trends, that history does tend to repeat itself, and that the trends continue over long periods.

9. **A** A smart money technician will follow the behavior of other investors. Bullish signs would be increases in the confidence index, a narrowing of the T-bill Eurodollar spread, the specialist short sale ratio below 30%, and increases in brokerage account debit balances.

10. **C** If the relative strength ratio (stock price/market index value) increases, the percentage increase in the stock price must be greater than the percentage increase in the market index value.

11. **D** A smart money technician will follow the behavior of other smart investors. Bearish signals would be a wider T-bill Eurodollar spread, a falling Barron's confidence index, a specialist short sale ratio above 50%, and falling debit balances (margin debt) in brokerage accounts.

12. **C** A high put/call ratio indicates investors are bearish, which would be a bullish indicator to a contrarian.

INTRODUCTION TO PRICE MULTIPLES

EXAM FOCUS

This review covers the estimation of several market-based price multiples. Specifically, this review addresses the pros and cons of using the price to earnings ratio, price to book value ratio, price to sales ratio, and the price to cash flow ratio. You should be familiar with the advantages and drawbacks of each of these price multiples. You should also know how to compute each of these multiples, given the relevant market and firm financial information. As you read the material, remember that an analyst doesn't have to pick a ratio but can use the information in all of them. Just understand their strengths and weaknesses.

LOS 64.a: Discuss the rationales for the use of price to earnings (P/E), price to book value (P/BV), price to sales (P/S), and price to cash flow (P/CF) in equity valuation and discuss the possible drawbacks to the use of each price multiple.

LOS 64.b: Calculate and interpret P/E, P/BV, P/S, and P/CF.

Professor's Note: This review is organized according to the types of price multiples. The LOSs are addressed within each category.

Rationales for using price-to-earnings (P/E) ratios in valuation:

- Earnings power, as measured by earnings per share (EPS), is the primary determinant of investment value.
- The P/E ratio is popular in the investment community.
- Empirical research shows that P/E differences are significantly related to long-run average stock returns.

The drawbacks of using the P/E ratio are:

- Earnings can be negative, which produces a useless P/E ratio.
- The volatile, transitory portion of earnings makes the interpretation of P/E difficult for analysts.
- Management discretion within allowed accounting practices can distort reported earnings and thereby lessen the comparability of P/E ratios across firms.

We can **define two versions of the P/E ratio**: trailing and leading P/E. The difference between the two is how earnings (the denominator) are calculated. *Trailing P/E ratios* use earnings over the most recent 12 months in the denominator. The *leading P/E ratio* (also known as forward or prospective P/E) uses "next year's expected earnings," which is defined as either expected EPS for the next four quarters or expected EPS for the next fiscal year.

$$\text{trailing P/E} = \frac{\text{market price per share}}{\text{EPS over previous 12 months}}$$

$$\text{leading P/E} = \frac{\text{market price per share}}{\text{forecast EPS over next 12 months}}$$

Professor's Note: The trailing P/E is what we see published in much of the popular financial press. The leading P/E, P_0/E_1, is the one we calculated from the dividend discount model (DDM).

Example: Calculating a P/E ratio

Byron Investments, Inc., reported €32 million in earnings during fiscal year 2006. An analyst forecasts an EPS over the next 12 months of €1.00. Byron has 40 million shares outstanding at a market price of €18.00 per share. Calculate Byron's trailing and leading P/E ratios.

Answer:

$$2006 \text{ EPS} = \frac{€32,000,000}{40,000,000} = €0.80$$

$$\text{trailing P/E} = \frac{€18.00}{€0.80} = 22.5$$

$$\text{leading P/E} = \frac{€18.00}{€1.00} = 18.0$$

There are several issues to consider when calculating P/Es in practice. While price is observable, we can come up with several different numbers which are all arguably EPS.

When calculating trailing EPS an analyst should focus on that portion of earnings that are expected to be recurring. The footnotes to the financial statements must be used to exclude gains, and possibly losses, on asset sales, foreign currency gains and losses included in net income, and any other items with an effect on earnings better described as transitory than permanent (likely to recur).

Firms may have cyclical earnings. P/Es will be high when earnings are at the bottom of a cycle and low when earnings are cyclically high. One method to adjust for earnings cyclicality is to use "normalized earnings" based on a full cycle or, equivalently, a normalized P/E averaged over a full business cycle. Alternatively, an analyst can estimate normal earnings by using the firm's average ROE over a cycle times the current value of shareholders' equity as an estimate of normalized earnings.

Analysts must also adjust earnings for differences in accounting methods among firms in order to be able to judge their relative valuations based on P/Es. A firm that is capitalizing expenses or using FIFO inventory accounting during a period of rising prices will report higher earnings than a firm that does not, and its trailing P/Es will be lower as a result. Finally, significant differences can exist between P/Es calculated with basic EPS and those calculated using fully diluted EPS.

Advantages of using the price-to-book value ratio (P/BV) include:

- Book value is a cumulative amount that is usually positive, even when the firm reports a loss and EPS is negative. Thus, P/BV can typically be used when P/E cannot.
- Book value is more stable than EPS, so it may be more useful than P/E when EPS is particularly high, low, or volatile.
- Book value is an appropriate measure of net asset value for firms that primarily hold liquid assets. Examples include finance, investment, insurance, and banking firms.
- P/BV can be useful in valuing companies that are expected to go out of business.
- Empirical research shows that P/BV ratios help explain differences in long-run average returns.

Disadvantages of using P/BV include:

- P/BV ratios do not recognize the value of nonphysical assets such as human capital.
- P/BV ratios can be misleading when there are significant differences in the asset intensity of production methods among the firms under consideration.
- Different accounting conventions can obscure the true investment in the firm made by shareholders, which reduces the comparability of P/BV ratios across firms and countries. For example, research and development costs (R&D) are expensed in the U.S., which can understate investment and overstate income over time.
- Inflation and technological change can cause the book and market value of assets to differ significantly, so book value is not an accurate measure of the value of the shareholders' investment. This makes it more difficult to compare P/BV ratios across firms.

The P/BV ratio is defined as:

$$P/BV = \frac{\text{market value of equity}}{\text{book value of equity}} = \frac{\text{market price per share}}{\text{book value per share}}$$

where:

book value of equity = common shareholders' equity

$$= (\text{total assets} - \text{total liabilities}) - \text{preferred stock}$$

We often make adjustments to book value that allow the P/BV ratio to more accurately measure the value of the shareholders' investment and to create more useful comparisons across different stocks.

A common adjustment is to use *tangible book value*, which is equal to book value of equity less intangible assets. Examples of intangible assets include goodwill from acquisitions (which makes sense because it is not really an asset) and a patent (which is more questionable since the asset and patent are separable). Furthermore, balance sheets should be adjusted for significant off-balance-sheet assets and liabilities and for differences between the fair and recorded value of assets and liabilities. Finally, book values often need to be adjusted to ensure comparability. For example, companies using the first in, first out (FIFO) inventory accounting method cannot be accurately compared with peers using the last in, first out (LIFO) method. Thus, book values should be restated on a consistent basis.

Example: Calculating a P/BV ratio

Based on the information in the table, calculate the current P/BV for Alpha Corp. and Beta Corp.

Figure 1: Data for Alpha Corp. and Beta Corp.

Company	Book Value of Equity 2006 (USD millions)	Sales 2006 (USD millions)	Shares Outstanding 2006 (millions)	Price 08/14/06
Alpha Corp.	28,039	18,878	7,001	$17.83
Beta Corp.	6,320	9,475	5,233	$12.15

Answer:

Alpha Corp.:

$$\text{book value per share} = \frac{\text{book value of equity}}{\text{number of shares outstanding}} = \frac{\$28,039}{7,001} = \$4.00$$

$$P/BV = \frac{\text{market price per share}}{\text{book value per share}} = \frac{\$17.83}{\$4.00} = 4.46$$

Beta Corp.:

$$\text{book value per share} = \frac{\text{book value of equity}}{\text{number of shares outstanding}} = \frac{\$6,320}{5,233} = \$1.21$$

$$P/BV = \frac{\text{market price per share}}{\text{book value per share}} = \frac{\$12.15}{\$1.21} = 10.04$$

The rationales for using the price to sales (P/S) ratio include:

- P/S is meaningful even for distressed firms, since sales revenue is always positive. This is not the case for P/E and P/BV ratios, which can be negative.
- Sales revenue is not as easy to manipulate or distort as EPS and book value, which are significantly affected by accounting conventions.
- P/S ratios are not as volatile as P/E multiples. This may make P/S ratios more reliable in valuation analysis.
- P/S ratios are particularly appropriate for valuing stocks in mature or cyclical industries and for start-up companies with no record of earnings.
- Like P/E and P/BV ratios, empirical research finds that differences in P/S are significantly related to differences in long-term average stock returns.

The disadvantages of using P/S ratios are:

- High growth in sales does not necessarily indicate operating profits as measured by earnings and cash flow.
- P/S ratios do not capture differences in cost structures across companies.
- While less subject to distortion than earnings or cash flows, revenue recognition practices can still distort sales forecasts. For example, analysts should look for company practices that speed up revenue recognition. An example is sales on a bill-and-hold basis, which involves selling products and delivering them at a later date. This practice accelerates sales into an earlier reporting period and distorts the P/S ratio.

Calculating a P/S ratio. P/S multiples are computed by dividing a stock's price per share by sales or revenue per share, or by dividing the market value of the firm's equity by its total sales:

$$P/S \text{ ratio} = \frac{\text{market value of equity}}{\text{total sales}} = \frac{\text{market price per share}}{\text{sales per share}}$$

Example: Calculating a P/S ratio

Based on the information in the table, calculate the current P/S ratio for Alpha Corp. and Beta Corp.

Figure 2: Data for Alpha Corp. and Beta Corp.

Company	Book Value of Equity 2006 (USD millions)	Sales 2006 (USD millions)	Shares Outstanding 2006 (millions)	Intraday Price 08/14/06
Alpha Corp.	28,039	18,878	7,001	$17.83
Beta Corp.	6,320	9,475	5,233	$12.15

Answer:

Alpha Corp.:

$$\text{sales per share} = \frac{\text{sales}}{\text{number of shares outstanding}} = \frac{\$18,878}{7,001} = \$2.70$$

$$\text{P/S} = \frac{\text{market price per share}}{\text{sales per share}} = \frac{\$17.83}{\$2.70} = 6.60$$

Beta Corp.:

$$\text{sales per share} = \frac{\text{sales}}{\text{number of shares outstanding}} = \frac{\$9,475}{5,233} = \$1.81$$

$$\text{P/S} = \frac{\text{market price per share}}{\text{sales per share}} = \frac{\$12.15}{\$1.81} = 6.71$$

Rationales for using the price to cash flow (P/CF) ratio include:

- Cash flow is harder for managers to manipulate than earnings.
- Price to cash flow is more stable than price to earnings.
- Reliance on cash flow rather than earnings addresses the problem of differences in the quality of reported earnings, (a problem when using P/Es).
- Empirical evidence indicates that differences in P/CF ratios are significantly related to differences in long-run average stock returns.

There are two **drawbacks to the P/CF ratio**, both of which are related to the definition of cash flow used. We discuss the specific cash flow definitions next.

- Some items affecting actual cash flow from operations are ignored when the *EPS plus noncash charges estimate* is used. For example, noncash revenue and net changes in working capital are ignored.
- From a theoretical perspective, *free cash flow to equity* (FCFE) is probably preferable to cash flow. However, FCFE is more volatile than straight cash flow.

Professor's Note: FCFE is the cash flow available to common stockholders after all operating expenses, interest and principal payments, investment in working capital, and investments in fixed assets.

Calculating P/CF Ratios. There are at least **four definitions of cash flow** available for use in calculating the P/CF ratio: earnings-plus-noncash charges (CF), adjusted cash flow (adjusted CFO), free cash flow to equity (FCFE), and earnings before interest, taxes, depreciation, and amortization (EBITDA). Expect to see any one of them on the exam.

One commonly used proxy for cash flow is *earnings-plus-noncash charges* (CF):

$$\text{CF} = \text{net income} + \text{depreciation} + \text{amortization}$$

The limitation of this definition, as we mentioned previously, is that it ignores some items that affect cash flow, such as noncash revenue and changes in net working capital.

Another proxy for cash flow is *cash flow from operations* (CFO) from the cash flow statement. The limitation of CFO, however, is that it includes items related to financing and investing activities. Therefore, analysts often adjust CFO by adding back the after-tax interest cost:

$$\text{adjusted CFO} = \text{CFO} + \left[\left(\text{net cash interest outflow}\right) \times \left(1 - \text{tax rate}\right)\right]$$

In addition, analysts sometimes further adjust CFO for items that are not expected to persist in the future.

Analysts also often use FCFE and EBITDA as proxies for cash flow. As we mentioned above, theory suggests that FCFE is the preferred way to define cash flow, but it is more volatile than straight cash flow. EBITDA is a pretax, pre-interest measure that represents a flow to both equity and debt. Thus it is better suited as an indicator of total company value than just equity value. Analysts typically use trailing price to cash, which relies on the most recent four quarters of cash flow per share.

Given one of the four definitions of cash flow, the P/CF ratio is calculated as:

$$\text{P/CF ratio} = \frac{\text{market value of equity}}{\text{cash flow}} = \frac{\text{market price per share}}{\text{cash flow per share}}$$

where:
cash flow = CF, adjusted CFO, FCFE, or EBITDA

Example: Calculating P/CF

Data Management Systems, Inc. (DMS) reported net income of $32 million, depreciation and amortization of $41 million, net interest expense of $12 million, and cash flow from operations of $44 million. The tax rate is 30%. Calculate the P/CF ratio using CF and adjusted CFO as proxies for cash flow. DMS has 25 million shares of common stock outstanding, trading at $47 per share.

Answer:

CF = $32 million + $41 million = $73 million

adjusted CFO = $44 million + $\left[\left(\$12 \text{ million}\right)\left(1 - 0.30\right)\right]$ = $52.4 million

market value of equity = $\left(25 \text{ million shares}\right)\left(\$47 \text{ per share}\right)$ = $1,175 million

$$\text{P/CF} = \frac{\$1,175 \text{ million}}{\$73 \text{ million}} = 16.1$$

$$\text{P/adjusted CFO} = \frac{\$1,175 \text{ million}}{\$52.4 \text{ million}} = 22.4$$

KEY CONCEPTS

1. Advantages of using P/E ratios in valuation are:
    *   Earnings power is the primary determinant of investment value.
    *   The P/E ratio is popular in the investment community.
    *   Empirical research shows that P/E differences are significantly related to long-run average stock returns.
2. Disadvantages of using P/E ratios in valuation are:
    *   Earnings can be negative, which produces a useless P/E ratio.
    *   The volatile, transitory portion of earnings makes the interpretation of P/E ratios difficult for analysts.
    *   Management discretion within allowed accounting practices can distort reported earnings.
3. The following are advantages of using P/BV:
    *   Book value is a cumulative amount that is usually positive even when EPS is negative.
    *   Book value is more stable than EPS, so it may be more useful than P/E when EPS is particularly high, low, or volatile.
    *   Book value is an appropriate measure of net asset value for firms that primarily hold liquid assets, including finance, investment, insurance, and banking firms.
    *   P/BV can be useful in valuing companies that are expected to go out of business.
    *   Empirical research shows that P/BV ratios help explain differences in long-run average returns.
4. The following are disadvantages of using P/BV:
    *   P/BV ratios do not recognize the value of nonphysical assets such as human capital.
    *   P/BV ratios can mislead when there are significant differences in the amount (i.e., size) of the assets used by the firms being compared.
    *   Different accounting conventions can obscure the true investment in the firm made by shareholders.
    *   Inflation and technological change can cause the book and market value of assets to differ significantly.
5. The following are advantages of using P/S ratios:
    *   The ratio is meaningful even for distressed firms.
    *   Sales figures are not as easy to manipulate or distort as EPS and book value.
    *   P/S ratios are not as volatile as P/E multiples.
    *   P/S ratios are particularly appropriate for valuing stocks in mature or cyclical industries, as well as start-up companies with no record of earnings.
    *   Empirical research finds that differences in P/S are significantly related to differences in long-term average stock returns.
6. The following are disadvantages of using P/S ratios:
    *   High sales do not necessarily indicate operating profits as measured by earnings and cash flow.
    *   P/S ratios do not capture differences in cost structures across companies.
    *   While less subject to distortion, revenue recognition practices can distort sales forecasts.
7. Advantages of using P/CF include:
    *   Cash flow is harder for managers to manipulate than earnings.
    *   Price to cash flow is more stable than price to earnings.
    *   Using cash flow addresses the problem of differences in quality of earnings that arises when using P/Es.
    *   Differences in price to cash flow are significantly related to differences in long-run average stock returns.
8. Disadvantages of using P/CF include:
    *   Some items affecting actual cash flow from operations are ignored when the EPS plus noncash charges estimate is used. For example, noncash revenue and net changes in working capital are ignored.
    *   FCFE rather than cash flow should be used. However, FCFE is more volatile than straight cash flow.
9. For the P/CF ratio, cash flow can be earnings plus noncash charges, adjusted CFO, FCFE, or EBITDA.

CONCEPT CHECKERS: INTRODUCTION TO PRICE MULTIPLES

1. Which of the following *least accurately* describes the advantages and disadvantages of valuation with the P/E multiple?
   A. Advantage: P/E ratio is popular in the investment community.
   Disadvantage: P/E ratios may not facilitate comparisons across firms.
   B. Advantage: P/E differences are significantly related to long-run average stock returns.
   Disadvantage: The volatile, transitory portion of earnings makes the interpretation of P/Es difficult for analysts.
   C. Advantage: Earnings power is the primary determinant of investment value.
   Disadvantage: Management discretion within allowed accounting practices can distort reported earnings.
   D. Advantage: P/E valuation can accommodate negative earnings.
   Disadvantage: P/E valuation is difficult to use for firms with relatively few fixed assets (e.g., service firms).

2. Which of the following *least accurately* describes the advantages and disadvantages of valuation with the P/S multiple?
   A. Advantage: P/S is meaningful, even for firms in financial distress.
   Disadvantage: P/S ratios are not as volatile as P/E multiples. This may make P/S ratios more reliable in valuation analysis.
   B. Advantage: Sales forecasts are not susceptible to distortion from revenue recognition practices.
   Disadvantage: Reported sales figures are easier to manipulate than earnings or book values.
   C. Advantage: P/S ratios are particularly appropriate for valuing stocks in mature or cyclical industries, as well as start-up companies with no record of earnings.
   Disadvantage: P/S ratios do not capture differences in cost structures across companies.
   D. Advantage: Like P/E and P/BV ratios, empirical research finds that differences in P/S are significantly related to differences in long-term average stock returns.
   Disadvantage: High growth in sales does not necessarily indicate operating profits as measured by earnings and cash flow.

3. Valuation using discounted cash flow techniques is preferred to the P/E multiples approach when:
   A. earnings per share are negative.
   B. the dividend payout is low.
   C. the expected growth rate is very high.
   D. the target firm has a normal capital structure.

4. The Larson Corp. had revenue per share of $400 in 2002, earnings per share of $5.00, and paid out 50% of its earnings as dividends. If the return on equity (ROE) and required rate of return of Larson are 15% and 11%, respectively, what is the appropriate P/S multiple for Larson?
   A. 0.12.
   B. 0.18.
   C. 0.19.
   D. 0.90.

5. Which of the following regarding the use of P/BV measures is **FALSE**?
   A. Book value provides a relatively stable, intuitive measure of value.
   B. Book values are not very meaningful for firms in service industries.
   C. P/BV ratios can be compared across similar firms if accounting methods differ.
   D. Book value is often positive, even when earnings are negative.

6. P/BV ratio analysis is *most suitable* for a firm:
   A. with accounting standards consistent with those of other firms.
   B. with a negative book value.
   C. in the service industry without significant fixed assets.
   D. with accounting standards different from other firms.

7. Which of the following statements regarding the use of P/S multiples in stock valuation is **FALSE**?
   A. P/S multiples are positive, even when earnings and book value are negative.
   B. Revenue is relatively easy to manipulate compared to earnings.
   C. The use of P/S multiples facilitates analysis of the effects of changes in pricing policy and other corporate strategic decisions.
   D. P/S multiples are not as volatile as P/E ratios.

8. An analyst gathered the following financial data about Argott, Inc.
   - Market value $500
   - Sales $2,000
   - Earnings   –$50
   - Book value $250
   - Cash flow $50

   What is the price to book value ratio for Argott, Inc.?
   A. –0.10.
   B. 0.10.
   C. 0.25.
   D. 2.00.

9. Which of the following statements about price multiples is **FALSE**?
   A. Cash flow figures are typically more stable than earnings figures.
   B. P/BV and P/CF ratios should be used in conjunction P/E ratios in fundamental analysis.
   C. Firms with low P/BV ratios tend to outperform high P/BV ratio firms on a risk-adjusted basis.
   D. Firms with low P/BV ratios tend to underperform high P/BV ratio firms on a risk-adjusted basis.

10. Which of the following accounting variables is *least subject* to manipulation?
    A. Sales.
    B. Earnings.
    C. Inventory.
    D. Cash flows.

Use the following data to answer Questions 11 through 13.

An analyst gathered the following information for JoJo Enterprises, Inc.

- Share price $25.00
- Stockholders' equity $100 million
- Retention rate   60%
- Return on equity (ROE)   10%
- Shares outstanding   10 million
- Expected sales $36 million
- Total operating expenses $17 million
- Operating expenses include $1,400,000 in depreciation and amortization

11.   JoJo's P/BV ratio is *closest* to:
      A. 1.22.
      B. 1.77.
      C. 2.50.
      D. 3.15.

12.   JoJo's P/S ratio is *closest* to:
      A. 4.18.
      B. 5.31.
      C. 6.27.
      D. 6.94.

13.   JoJo's P/CF ratio (using EBITDA for cash flow) is *closest* to:
      A. 12.25.
      B. 13.16.
      C. 15.71.
      D. 17.33.

ANSWERS – CONCEPT CHECKERS: INTRODUCTION TO PRICE MULTIPLES

1. **D** P/E is useless when earnings are negative. P/E may be effectively used to value firms in the services industry.

2. **B** It is an advantage of the P/S ratio that sales figures are not as easy to manipulate or distort as EPS and book value. A disadvantage of the P/S ratio is that revenue recognition practices can distort sales forecasts, although less so than P/E or P/BV.

3. **A** When the earnings per share are negative, the P/E ratio is not meaningful. This problem can be offset somewhat by using normalized or average EPS values.

4. **C** First, use the DDM to get the current price:

$$P_0 = \frac{D_1}{k-g} = \frac{D_0(1+g)}{k-g} = \frac{\$2.50(1.075)}{0.11-0.075} = \$76.79$$

where:

$$D_0 = E_0(\text{payout ratio}) = \$5.00(0.50) = \$2.50$$

$$g = \text{ROE}(\text{retention rate}) = 0.15(0.50) = 0.075$$

Then compute price-to-sales as: $\dfrac{P_0}{S_0} = \dfrac{\$76.79}{\$400.00} = 0.19$.

5. **C** Differences in accounting methods make comparisons based on P/BV problematic.

6. **A** P/BV ratios can uncover signs of misvaluation across firms that have consistently applied accounting standards.

7. **B** Relative to earnings, revenue is difficult to manipulate.

8. **D** Market value / book value = $500 / $250 = 2.

9. **D** On a risk-adjusted basis, firms with low P/BV ratios tend to outperform high P/BV ratio firms.

10. **A** Sales figures are not as easy to manipulate or distort as EPS and book value, which are significantly affected by accounting conventions.

11. **C** BV = $100,000,000; BV/share = 10; P/BV = 25 / 10 = 2.50

12. **D** sales per share = 36,000,000 / 10,000,000 = 3.60; P/S = 25 / 3.60 = 6.94

13. **A** EBITDA/share = (36,000,000 − 17,000,000 + 1,400,000) / 10,000,000 = $2.04; P/CF = 25 / 2.04 = 12.25

FORMULAS

$$\text{IRR: } 0 = CF_0 + \frac{CF_1}{(1+IRR)^1} + \frac{CF_2}{(1+IRR)^2} + \cdots + \frac{CF_n}{(1+IRR)^n} = \sum_{t=0}^{n} \frac{CF_t}{(1+IRR)^t}$$

$$\text{NPV} = CF_0 + \frac{CF_1}{(1+k)^1} + \frac{CF_2}{(1+k)^2} + \ldots + \frac{CF_n}{(1+k)^n} = \sum_{t=0}^{n} \frac{CF_t}{(1+k)^t}$$

$$\text{payback period} = \text{full years until recovery} + \frac{\text{unrecovered cost at the beginning of the last year}}{\text{cash flow during the last year}}$$

$$\text{AAR} = \frac{\text{average net income}}{\text{average book value}}$$

$$\text{PI} = \frac{\text{PV of future cash flows}}{CF_O}$$

$$\text{WACC} = (w_d)[k_d(1-t)] + (w_{ps})(k_{ps}) + (w_{ce})(k_{ce})$$

cost of common equity:

$$k_{ce} = \frac{D_1}{P_0} + g$$

$$k_{ce} = RFR + \beta[E(R_m) - RFR]$$

$$k_{ce} = \text{bond yield} + \text{risk premium}$$

after-tax cost of debt = $k_d(1-t)$

cost of preferred stock = $k_{ps} = D_{ps} / P$

$$\text{DOL} = \frac{\%\Delta EBIT}{\%\Delta sales}$$

$$\text{DOL} = \frac{Q(P-V)}{Q(P-V)-F} = \frac{S-TVC}{S-TVC-F}$$

$$DFL = \frac{\%\Delta EPS}{\%\Delta EBIT}$$

$$DFL = \frac{EBIT}{EBIT - interest}$$

$$DTL = DOL \times DFL = \frac{Q(P-V)}{Q(P-V)-F-I} = \frac{S-VC}{S-VC-F-I} = \frac{\%\Delta EPS}{\%\Delta sales}$$

breakeven point: $Q_{BE} = \dfrac{F}{P-V}$

EPS after buyback $= \dfrac{\text{total earnings} - \text{after-tax cost of funds}}{\text{shares outstanding after buyback}}$

effective tax rate on dividends $= $ corporate tax rate $+ (1-$ corporate tax rate$)($individual tax rate$)$

expected rate of return from expectational data: $E(R) = \sum\limits_{i=1}^{n} P_i R_i$

expected rate of return from historical data: $\bar{R} = \dfrac{\sum\limits_{t=1}^{n} R_t}{n}$

variance of returns from expectational data: $variance = \sigma^2 = \sum\limits_{i=1}^{n} P_i \big[R_i - E(R) \big]^2$

variance of returns from historical data: $variance = \sigma^2 = \dfrac{\sum\limits_{t=1}^{N}(R_t - \bar{R})^2}{n}$

covariance from expectational data: $cov_{1,2} = \sum\limits_{i=1}^{n} \Big\{ P_i \big[R_{i,1} - E(R_1) \big] \big[R_{i,2} - E(R_2) \big] \Big\}$

covariance from historical data: $cov_{1,2} = \dfrac{\sum\limits_{t=1}^{n} \Big\{ \big[R_{t,1} - \bar{R}_1 \big] \big[R_{t,2} - \bar{R}_2 \big] \Big\}}{n}$

$$\rho_{1,2} = \frac{Cov_{1,2}}{\sigma_1 \times \sigma_2}$$

$$\sigma_p = \sqrt{w_1^2 \sigma_1^2 + w_2^2 \sigma_2^2 + 2w_1 w_2 \sigma_1 \sigma_2 \rho_{1,2}} \text{ or } \sqrt{w_1^2 \sigma_1^2 + w_2^2 \sigma_2^2 + 2w_1 w_2 Cov_{1,2}}$$

equation of the CML: $E(R_P) = RFR + \sigma_P \left\{ \dfrac{\left[E(R_M) - RFR \right]}{\sigma_M} \right\}$

total risk = systematic risk + unsystematic risk

$\beta_i = \dfrac{Cov_{i,mkt}}{\sigma^2_{mkt}}$

capital asset pricing model (CAPM): $E(R_i) = RFR + \beta_i [E(R_{mkt}) - RFR]$

zero-beta CAPM: $E(R_{stock}) = E(R_{zero\ beta\ portfolio}) + \beta_{stock} [E(R_{market}) - E(R_{zero\ beta\ portfolio})]$

margin call trigger prices:

for margin purchases $= P_o \left(\dfrac{1 - \text{initial margin}}{1 - \text{maintenance margin}} \right)$

for short sales $= P_o \left(\dfrac{1 + \text{initial margin}}{1 + \text{maintenance margin}} \right)$

price-weighted index $= \dfrac{\text{sum of stock prices}}{\text{number of stocks}}$

market value-weighted index $= \dfrac{\sum \left[(\text{price}_{today})(\text{number of shares outstanding}) \right]}{\sum \left[(\text{price}_{base\ year})(\text{number of shares outstanding}) \right]} \times \text{base year index value}$

preferred stock valuation model: $P_0 = \dfrac{D_p}{k_p}$

one-period stock valuation model: $P_0 = \dfrac{D_1}{1 + k_e} + \dfrac{P_1}{1 + k_e}$

infinite period model: $P_0 = \dfrac{D_0 \times (1 + g)}{k_e - g} = \dfrac{D_1}{k_e - g}$

multistage model: $P_0 = \dfrac{D_1}{(1 + k_e)} + \dfrac{P_2}{(1 + k_e)^2} + ... + \dfrac{D_n}{(1 + k_e)^n} + \dfrac{P_n}{(1 + k_e)^n}$

where :

$P_n = \dfrac{D_{n+1}}{k_e - g_c}$

$E(R) = (1 + RFR_{real})(1 + IP)(1 + RP) - 1$

$$RFR_{nominal} = (1 + RFR_{real})(1 + IP) - 1$$

expected growth rate: g = (retention rate)(ROE)

earnings multiplier: $\dfrac{P_0}{E_1} = \dfrac{\dfrac{D_1}{E_1}}{k - g}$

expected EPS = [(sales)(EBITDA%) − depreciation − interest](1 − tax rate)

directional technical indicators:

$$\text{short interest ratio} = \frac{\text{outstanding short interest}}{\text{average daily volume on exchange}}$$

$$\text{uptick-downtick ratio} = \frac{\text{number of block uptick transactions}}{\text{number of block downtick transactions}}$$

"smart money" technical indicators:

$$\text{confidence index} = \frac{\text{quality bond yields}}{\text{average bond yields}}$$

$$\text{specialist short sale ratio} = \frac{\text{specialist's short sales}}{\text{total short sales on the NYSE}}$$

contrarian technical indicators:

$$\text{mutual fund ratio} = \frac{\text{mutual fund cash}}{\text{total fund assets}}$$

$$\text{investment advisor ratio} = \frac{\text{bearish opinions}}{\text{total opinions}}$$

$$\text{volume ratio} = \frac{\text{OTC volume}}{\text{NYSE volume}}$$

stock price and volume techniques:

$$\text{upside-downside volume ratio} = \frac{\text{volume of stocks that increased}}{\text{volume of stocks that declined}}$$

$$\text{relative strength} = \frac{\text{stock price}}{\text{market index value}}$$

Corporate Finance, Portfolio Management, and Analysis of Equity Investments
Formulas

$$\text{trailing P/E} = \frac{\text{market price per share}}{\text{EPS over previous 12 months}}$$

$$\text{leading P/E} = \frac{\text{market price per share}}{\text{forecast EPS over next 12 months}}$$

$$\text{P/V ratio} = \frac{\text{market value of equity}}{\text{book value of equity}} = \frac{\text{market price per share}}{\text{book value per share}}$$

where :
book value of equity = common shareholders' equity
= (total assets − total liabilities) − preferred stock

$$\text{P/CF ratio} = \frac{\text{market value of equity}}{\text{cash flow}} = \frac{\text{market price per share}}{\text{cash flow per share}}$$

$$\text{P/S ratio} = \frac{\text{market value of equity}}{\text{total sales}} = \frac{\text{market price per share}}{\text{sales per share}}$$

CF = net income + depreciation + amortization

$$\text{adjusted CFO} = \text{CFO} + \left[(\text{net cash interest outflow}) \times (1 - \text{tax rate})\right]$$

INDEX

Notes